CONVOY PQ13 -
UNLUCKY FOR SOME

Morris O. Mills

CONVOY PQ13 -
UNLUCKY FOR SOME

First published by Bernard Durnford Publishing
The Old Museum, Bramber, West Sussex BN44 3WE
England.
2000

A catalogue record of this book
is available from the British Library

ISBN   0 9535670 2 8

Format, design and cover by StewART

Printed and bound by Antony Rowe Ltd
Bumper's Farm, Chippenham, Wiltshire.

CONVOY PQ13 -
UNLUCKY FOR SOME

Morris O. Mills

Published by

Bernard Durnford Publishing

CONTENTS

DEDICATION

In loving memory
of my wives (deceased)
Anne & Georgina
&
To our daughters
Avril & Aileen

FOREWORD

I wrote this book with the
burning desire that others could
understand what we suffered.

Morris O. Mills
Goonhavern,
Cornwall
July 2000

CHAPTER 1
EARLY DAYS

This was the last time I saw my Grandfather, then well into his nineties, and dying. Bending over I took his hand, so thin and frail I was afraid to exert any pressure. "Hello, Granddad, it's Morris here." Eyes, already clouding with the shadow of death flickered uncomprehending over my face. Quietly, in a low whisper, he was rambling. His mind somewhere back in his Navy days. He was in a world of ships and rolling Oceans, strange ports and mystic smells. I was filled with sorrow and yet, somehow comforted by the thought of this grand old man slipping away on the ebb tide of life wrapped in the dreams of his youth.

I had last visited him in August 1941, when my ship was berthed in Surrey Commercial Dock, London, inward bound with a cargo of pit props from Archangel, North Russia. I had been on leave with my parents in East Anglia. My father, and I, had gone rabbit shooting in nearby fields to augment the meagre weekly meat ration of three, or four ounces. I had bagged a plump hare and decided to take it to my Grandparents on rejoining my ship. They were overjoyed at the sight of so much fresh meat but my Grandmother, being a townie, kept repeating, "Oh, Dear, oh, dear, what on earth am I going to do with it?" "Don't worry, Grandma, I'll sort it for you," and so the envious neighbours were treated to the spectacle of me, in full uniform, wearing a piny, skinning and cleaning the animal. Knowing my Grandmother, I'm sure some of the neighbours got a portion.

My Grandparents lived just outside Lewisham, South East London, on a hill from where one got a grandstand view of the Blitz then raging over London. Every night my Grandmother would fill a flask with tea, prepared sandwiches, and spent the night in the tiny Anderson shelter at the bottom of the garden. On the night I stayed my Grandfather, and I, stayed up all night playing cards, drinking beer, and yarning about our sea experiences - mostly his. Occasionally, the house would rock with a bomb blast and we would go outside to see how near, and what damage the bomb had caused. From our elevated position it was as though we were looking into Dante's Inferno. The sky lit up by probing searchlights, Ack Ack Guns belching angry balls of fire into the sky, great eruptions on the ground as thousands of bombs and incendiaries descended. The East- End of London appeared to be totally on fire and the glow of fires rolled under, and lit up, low laying clouds.

It was a horrendous sight, and I began to worry about Grandmother in her lonely shelter at the bottom of the garden. "Do you think we should go and see if Grandma is all right?" "No, no, lad, she'll be fast asleep. Don't want to wake her. Come on, let's have another hand of cards." God! I thought, they go through this night after night.

That was two years ago. In the interval I had made further voyages and finally back to Russia with Convoy PQ13. My ship had been bombed and sunk resulting in my left foot being blown off. I had been involved in a sea battle on HMS Edinburgh while attempting to return to the UK as a survivor. When that warship had been sunk I was returned to North Russia where I spent many terrible months, being bombed out of one hospital, and in time travelling across the vast expanse of North Russia.

Despite my ordeal I was determined to return to seafaring and fitted with an artificial leg, and re-kitted with uniform, I was paying my last respects to my Grandfather before joining my ship. I was deeply saddened at the thought of never seeing him again. Never again to hear those vivid and fascinating stories of his life in the Royal Navy. If only he had written a book what a story he would have had to tell.

Now, over fifty years on, with the end in sight, I have an overwhelming urge to tell my story. To endeavour to capture that period in my life that transcended, and encapsulated, every emotion - World War11.

I shall begin at the beginning. I was born on the 25th of May 1924 at 20 Nelldale Road, Bermondsey, London, to Royal Artillery Gunner Thomas Oliver Mills and Ethel nee-Townsend. The little terraced house was one of many in endless drab Streets on the South Bank of the River Thames, long since demolished and replaced with skyscraper blocks of flats. It was my Grandparents home and I guess we stayed there partly because my parents had no money, and partly because my father was stationed at Woolwich Barracks. Certainly, I can remember it very well, especially the little garden with a ram shackled shed at the bottom where my Grandfather taught me my ABC, and twelve times tables, by the most efficacious method I know, that of a smart smack around the ears when I forgot.

This somewhat harsh treatment in no way diminished my love for my Grandfather. He was my hero. A stocky built man of medium height, with brick red complexion and a shock of red hair. He had joined the Royal Navy as a boy rating about the time the Navy was turning from sail to steam. He had served in every naval station around the world, seen service in the China Boxer uprising, the Boer War and World War 1. He rose to the rank of Chief Petty Officer and was a 1st Class Diver. A large photograph of him in full diving gear sitting on a stool on the deck of a warship, hung in the front parlour. I was constantly drawn to it and gazed in wonder and admiration. The front room was a temple to his sea service and was festooned with memorabilia of his travels around the world. There were Ostrich eggs from Africa, stuffed snakes from India, delicate porcelains and tapestries from China, and lots more. A dry, stuffy, museum like atmosphere pervaded the room, and I was strictly forbidden to enter unless accompanied.

When Grandfather completed his time in the Royal Navy he joined the Metropolitan River Police. Many were the fascinating stories he would spin of his exploits on the river. Chasing suspect craft indulging in smuggling, or transporting stolen goods. Spine tingling tales of the many bodies recovered from the dark waters of the Thames. It was a time of dreadful degradation and privation for the working classes striving to scratch a living on the waterfront. Many gave up the struggle and committed suicide. The accident rate amongst river men and seamen was high, a dark night, a slippery deck or, as was usually the case, too much drink and over the side they would go, lost in the murky depths of the Thames.

12

Grandfather used to tell me with some amusement that the river police used to receive a small payment for recovering bodies. This varied between the North Bank and South Bank, and between the various boroughs. When a body was recovered they would endeavour to secure it from prying eyes, and then manoeuvre it in the direction of the most profitable Borough. This macabre act might reward them with a few extra pence, which went a long way in those days.

Apart from teaching me the alphabet and times tables, Grandfather broadened my education by taking me to all the wonderful and historical places in London. The Tower of London, Museums, Greenwich Royal Naval College, Tower Bridge, and not just to look at it going up and down but to go into the very bowels of the machinery. He never paid admission, all doors were opened to him. Many years later I realised that all the important people; ticket collectors, doormen, caretakers, were either retired Royal Navy or River Police. They were a band of brothers bound by their collective experiences. Wherever we went, Grandfather would be sure to end up in some cubby-hole drinking tea with the custodian, yarning away about the good old days. I would sit wide eyed silently drinking in all this sea lore.

I must have been about four years old when father left the Army and we moved from London to Peterborough. Dad got a job with the London Brick Company, and for a short time we lived on a dilapidated houseboat on the River Nene. To my childish mind this craft was nothing less than a ship on the high seas. Our life afloat soon came to an end when Dad joined the Huntingdonshire Constabulary and we moved into a police house. This was far from salubrious, there was no electricity or gas, the only means of light being paraffin lamps. There was no indoor toilet and we made use of a dry closet at the bottom of the garden that was emptied weekly. On collection day, Mother would rush around the house making sure all the windows were shut to avoid the awful stench of the horse drawn soil cart. Toilet paper was unheard of, we would cut old newspapers into squares and thread then with string to hang on a nail in the dry closet. Using the toilet at night was an ordeal, one had to don shoes and top coat and make one's way down a pitch black garden ignoring spiders, mice, and rats that scurried around this malodorous spot. Small wonder we rarely felt the urge to go at night-time.

We children, for I now had a brother and sister, not only had a large garden to play in but also an adjoining field with a stream at the bottom where we could paddle and fish for newts and stickle-backs. The farmer who owned the field never objected to our playing in his hay barns. It was a wonderful environment for young children to grow up in.

I was fast growing into a wild, excitable boy, whose head was filled with all sorts of wild adventures. I had no conception of time, frequently staying out late and missing meals. Mother was in poor health and driven to distraction by my antics. Dad frequently gave me a good hiding but it did no good. The long summer holidays were too much for mum, and I was packed off to my Grandparents in London. At first, Grandfather would meet me off the train at Kings Cross Station, but later I would make my own way across London. I could have only have been ten years of age. I have to smile today when I see the little darlings being escorted right up to the school gates.

Grandfather dealt with me as though I was a boy seaman, barking orders from the quarter deck, his vocabulary peppered with nautical terms. If I stepped out of line I was ordered to pipe down, or, do you want a touch of the rope's end boy? Lights out was bedtime and rise and shine time to get up. I loved it and already at that tender age I was absorbing the mystic of the sea and seamen.

My father was a strict disciplinarian who believed every one should pull their weight and as I was the eldest that meant me. I was given regular jobs to do about the house. Every morning before going to school I had to clean and polish all the shoes - including my father's police boots. Every Saturday I had to blacklead the old fashioned grate and run errands for my mother. I felt no resentment, it was just a natural way of life. I also got a part time job assisting the milkman who drove a horse drawn cart with a large milk churn. My job was to run around the houses collecting jugs from the elderly, filling and returning them. I might add this was done in the morn-ings before going to school, and I thought it was fun.

For this I received the princely sum of two shillings and six pence that I gave to my mother. In return she gave me six pence pocket money, one shilling was put aside for my holidays, and the

14

remainder considered my keep. I was proud to be making a contribution to the household and looking back those strict moral standards served me well in later life when times were hard and difficult.

When I was eleven, Dad was transferred to St Neots. In those day's policemen were transferred on a regular basis to prevent the local bobby becoming too friendly with the locals. Something I could never imagine my father doing - he would have run his Granny in if necessary!

St. Neots was a charming, old fashioned country town standing on the banks of the River Ouse, spanned by a Norman Bridge. At one time barges plied the river delivering grain to the warehouses that supplied the local brewery and bakeries. The focal point of the town was a very large market square, here were held weekly markets selling all manner of goods. At night-time the scene was lit up with flaring gas lamps creating a medieval ambience. The highlight of the year was a visit from a circus, with swings and roundabouts, side shows and fortune tellers. What excitement it engendered in the young - and not so young. I still retain a memory of a side show where a rather elderly gentleman, or so he seemed to my young eyes, dressed in an old fashioned bathing costume, climbed a tall ladder and dived into a small canvas tank. Leaping out, spraying water all around, he would dash amongst the spectators shaking a cloth cap. That was worth a penny of my money any day.

There was always a dancing bear performing tricks in response to the vicious tugs on the ring in its nose. No one appreciated the cruelty involved. The handler would make the animal advance on the young girls who would scatter, screaming with excitement and fear, while the manly young men would jeer at their feminine weakness - but noticeably keeping their own distance. In those days I never dreamt the sight of wild bears roaming the forests would become commonplace to me.

We lived in St Neots for three years, a period when I grew out of childhood into adolescence. Like all young animals, I became aware of strange sexual emotions. We boys started chasing girls, although we never knew what to do when we caught them. Some of the girls were very easily caught and must have been disappointed at our response. This problem had to be solved and my first encounter

15

was with a girl called Doris, the school flirt. We were both in the last year of school and lived in the same small street. Meeting her one dark night we were larking around at the rear of a garage when, before I realised what I was doing, my hand slid under her jumper and I was playing with her plump breasts, rolling her erect nipples between my fingers. Totally aroused my free hand was desperately trying to get into her knickers, Doris was laughing and giggling, and twisting her body to assist me in my endeavours. I was on the point of succeeding when a crashing blow to the side of my head sent me reeling. When the stars flashing before my eyes had cleared I saw my father standing there, dark as the night in his police uniform. "Just you get yourself home right away, boy. I'll speak to you later." He never did, but then I guess that as an ex Army man he knew I would have to sow my wild oats sooner - or later!

Shortly after this it was harvest time, and the corn stood high in the fields. Several of us lads on the outskirts noticed Doris, and the elder brother of one of our gang, making their way to the centre of the field where they vanished. Curiosity aroused we began tracking Indian fashion, and arrived at the scene undetected. To our astonishment we saw Doris on her back, legs wide apart, and Jack laying between her plump thighs. Doris was grunting and groaning in ecstasy, when they climaxed we all rose with a cheer and after shouting a few obscenities ran for our lives in case Jack caught us and gave us a good hiding. Ah! Those ancient country pursuits.

Of course I came into contact with Doris every day, impossible not to do so, we were in the same class and lived in the same street. She was not in the least embarrassed at being caught 'In flagrante delicto' Quite the reverse, her attitude being if you've got it flaunt it. She continued to proposition me with invitation to meet in secluded spots. Fortunately, a mixture of fear of the consequences, and a modicum of common sense kept me out of the hands of this nymphomaniac, but, boy! That girl could have taught me a thing or two.

Life was not all fun and games. Mother's health took a turn for the worst, my young sister had suspected poliomyelitis, and Dad had to go away on a two month Detective course. So, at the age of thirteen I had two sick members of the family to look after, and a house to run with no assistance whatsoever. It was a black, black, period in my young life, but it did prepare me for the many hardships I was to meet on life's rocky road.

By the time my father returned from the Detective course, Mum's health had improved and my sister no-longer suspected of having Polio. Feeling free as a bird, I escaped from the house and got a part time job in a grocer's shop as an errand boy. There was another lad there and we were a couple of devils! Our job was to deliver groceries in the town. Loading the carriers in the shop was a proper pantomime. The grocer would line up the groceries on the counter and we would load the carriers according to our rounds. At this stage, the grocer's wife would come stomping down from the flat above shouting and swearing, "Just you stop those buggers, Fred, until I've had a look in those carriers. I know you're pinching sweets. Think you can fool me - do you? As for you..." Pointing at me, "You're worse than the rest...a bloody copper's son." We would vehemently protest at this vile accusation, our faces shinning with innocence. Outside, we would mount our bikes, ride round the corner before producing all manner of goodies from the strangest places. Laughing, we would ride off munching our spoils.

With only a few months to go before I left school, an idea that had been germinating in my brain for a long time, went off like a rocket. I had to run away to sea. All the exciting stories of sea life fed me by Grandfather, and Uncle Joe, could no longer be denied. I had to go and find out for myself. I packed a small case and told my parents I was going to visit my Grandfather. They thought nothing of it - I had done it before. Arriving in London I made straight for St. Katherine's Dock in the Pool of London, which I knew well from many visits with my Grandfather. In those days access to the docks was relatively easy, one simply walked in. Seeing a small, British flagged ship, I boarded her and asked if there were any jobs for a deck boy. A kindly seaman took me into the messroom. Giving me a mug of tea he asked the usual questions, name, age and address. I lied about my age but foolishly gave my home address. "Well, now son, Captain's ashore, when he returns I'll see about getting you a berth. Just you stay here until he returns." If I had been older, and wiser, I would have smelt a rat!

I was so carried away with the shipboard atmosphere, the salty, tarry smells, the noise of cargo being worked, that time flew.

Looking out of the porthole I could see ships lining the dockside and tugs bustling about their business. I was in another world when a policeman entered saying, "I understand your only thirteen and a half, and still at school." And in the time old fashion, "You'd better come along with me, lad." In other words, I was nicked! I was taken to Wapping Police Station, which again I knew well as Granddad had been stationed there. We had visited it in my younger days.

A severe looking sergeant told me my father had been sent for, and I'd better sit down and behave myself unless I wanted to go into a cell. Some hours later my father entered the station and, without a word, or glance at me, spoke to the officer at the counter who raised a flap and ushered him into a small office. Obviously the sergeant's domain. I could faintly hear the murmur of voices punctuated by burst of laughter. Mugs of tea kept passing in. By now I was a nervous wreck Eventually, my father emerged. "Well, cheerio sergeant, nice meeting you." "You too, Tom. Keep in touch." For the first time, Dad acknowledged my presence. "Right, boy, lets be going." His tone had a strong hint of menace. The journey home was grim, and silent. Leaving me in the care of my mother, he said, "Right, boy, I've got some things to do in the station, when I come home I'll speak to you." Mother shook her head in a helpless manner, "That was a very silly thing to do, Morris. You've made your father very angry."

Later that evening we settled down for our talk. I sensed Dad had conquered his earlier rising temper. He was a strict disciplinarian, a hard case, but above all a fair man. He listened to my lame excuse without comment, then explained that while he understood my feelings, and desires, no son of his was going to go to sea as a common deck boy. There had to be a better way and he would help if I promised not to be so stupid in the future. Feeling fully ashamed I promised not to do it again. "Right, tomorrow I'm taking you to see a retired sea captain to see what advice he can give."

Captain King was an amiable old sea dog in his late seventies, living on his own in a bungalow on the banks of the River Ouse. A sprightly figure, above average height with a mop of snowy white hair that he had let get out of control. Ruddy complexion with startling blue eyes that pierced through one, as if demanding an answer. He greeted my father like an old friend. "Hello, Tom, so this is your boy who thinks he can run off to sea." Turning to me, "I hear the police dragged you off a ship and clapped you in irons." He gave a chuckle, "Shows the boy's got spirit, Tom, but not much sense I fear." Then in a serious vein he outlined the appalling conditions of going to sea in the lower deck of a merchant ship. Living in a cramped hovel of a forecastle, terrible food, being a scivvy to the sailors, doing every imaginable dirty job. "Not very glamorous, eh, lad?" Those blue eyes bored into me. "I wouldn't send my dog to sea in those conditions." So saying he patted his dog's head as though to reassure it. "No, lad, the only way to go to sea is as a trainee deck officer - and that's not easy either." Captain King explained that shipping companies accepted bound apprentices from the age of sixteen years, with good academic background. Some superior companies were looking for degree standards. My heart sank into my boots when I heard this. What possible chance had I?

Frankly, I admitted my academic standards were virtually nil. The old sea dog shook his head sadly, "Well, son, I think you are going to have great difficulty in finding a company to accept you. You've got two years to go before your sixteen. I suggest you study like hell paying particular attention to Maths, Algebra and Trigonometry. If you can master those subjects I suggest you write to companies who operate cargo ships, and set their own standards." Seeing my downcast features, he said, "Listen, boy, if you want something desperately badly, you can do it. Good luck."

Back home, Dad and I had another serious talk Dad was already studying through a correspondence course with Bennet's College for future police exams. "Look, Morris, I will enrol you in a General Education Course with Bennet's College providing you don't waste your time, or my money." This was a generous offer and I was most grateful. Such was my burning desire to get to sea that I buckled down to my studies for the next two years. How I bitterly regretted those wasted years at school as I battled with Algebra, Equations, Logarithms and Trigonometry in the quiet of my bedroom.

Shortly after my interview with Captain King, I left school at the age of fourteen, in the early summer of 1938, and immediately got a job in the local brewery. It was a mundane, fill in, type of job, but it did bring me into contact with a life long love affair - beer! It was a glorious summer that year. I was working and had money in my pocket. I was playing cricket for the town's second team. We had a battered old punt and spent hours fishing and swimming. I had taken a fancy to a girl called Edith Allen, who was completely indifferent to my advances. Life was very sweet, and then Dad was promoted to Detective Sergeant and transferred to Huntingdon. I was sorry to leave St Neots, I would miss all my mates, the boxing club, cricket, fishing, etc. It had been a period in my life when I had grown into a confident - if somewhat cocky - young man.

CHAPTER 2
PREPARING FOR SEA

Huntingdon was the county town of Huntingdonshire, now absorbed into Cambridgeshire. The old town consisting of Georgian houses and shops, spreads from the High Street out to a sprawl of council houses. A brisk half hour walk in either direction will take one into the country. The town is, of course, is renown as the birthplace of Oliver Cromwell, Lord Protector.

My father was stationed at Police Headquarters, a large rambling house with offices, cells, and garages to the rear. There were also a number of police houses for inspectors and sergeants stationed there. I was delighted to find my old school chum, Don Mash. We had lived in Stanground when our fathers had been stationed there. His father was now an inspector. We became inseparable. Because Don was an only child, we decided to become blood brothers by the simple act of cutting our wrists, and mingling blood. I know it sounds perfectly childish, but in a strange way it bonded us.

We had barely moved in when, Dad, never one to let the grass grow underfoot said, "Right boy, I've got you a job with Murket Bro.'s, Motor Engineers. You start Monday morning." There were no 'Ifs' or 'Buts!' The matter was settled.

Murket Bro.'s extended from the High Street for some distance to the rear, ending at a quiet one way street, separated by a brook. The premises were entered by an arched drive way between two show rooms. Above were the firm's offices. Through the arch was a small courtyard with an antiquated cinema called the Grand. Running round the cinema was a road leading to the mechanical works and paint shop. The workshop was a large hangar type building with huge sliding doors at either end, which were kept open for the passage of vehicles. This was fine in summer time, but hellish in winter, when one was laying under a lorry. The paint shop ran parallel with the one way street, and a running brook. There was a large area of scrap that bordered on a wall dividing it from houses and a pub.

The Murket Bro.'s were an odd bunch. Alfred was the dynamo, always dressed in stripped trousers and black half cut jacket. He was a small, wry man with sharp features. He never seemed to walk normally, his pace somewhere between a trot and running. One would be working on a job and he would rush up gabbling away in a high staccato voice, then rush off before you had time to decipher the message. Harry was a shadowy figure in the office and has faded from my memory. William, or Billy as we called him, was a larger than life character. Fat and jolly, his responsibility was the cinema. He was crazy on Westerns and the patrons were fed a regular diet of Cowboys and Indians. As employees, we could go to the Grand anytime free, but preferred to go to Hippodrome and see a decent film.

George Harris was the general foreman, and quite a character he was. Always dressed in sports jacket and tweeds, with never a speck of oil on his apparel. He was small in stature with ruddy complexion, clipped, bristled, ginger moustache, and he held himself like a ramrod. I always thought of him as a miniature sergeant major. He, and Billy, were in constant state of war over Billy's attempt to poach us young lads away from our mechanical duties to carry out odd jobs in the cinema - painting or repairing seats. I'm convinced they both enjoyed these battles, and were invigorated by them. In any case Billy usually won - after all, he was the boss.

After I had been working there for some time, I began to notice George, and the mechanics, slipping over the wall into the pub at lunch. Nothing daunted, I followed. George looked up in astonishment. "What the bloody hell are you doing here, young Mills?" Looking suitably chastened, I lied, Well, George, someone said you were looking for me, so I thought I'd better come over." George nearly exploded. "Do you hear that? He demanded of the others.

"You lying bastard, I'm a good mind to put my boot up your arse." Then shaking his head, more in sorrow than anger, he said to the publican, "Allright, Harry, give the cheeky bugger half of shandy." "I only drink bitter, George." "Christ almighty!" Exploded George. "You're under age and you're old man's a copper. Don't you know we could all get done for this?" In mock despair he said. "Allright, Harry, make that a bitter."

Many years later I learnt that George, Harry, and the Murket Bro.'s were all Freemasons, and members of my father's lodge. They must have had many a good laugh at my expense!

The paint shop was a low wooden building that could take two lorries. Fred Saunders, the foreman, was a tall gangly man in his early forties. Dressed in paint stained overalls with a battered cloth cap pulled over one eye, cigarette permanently dangling from the corner of his mouth, blue smoke swirling around his head, he would be in deep concentration as he inscribed lettering on the side of lorries. Joe Bloggs, Coalman, would become a thing of beauty. Apart from his artistic talent he had a wicked sense of humour. He never referred to me by name, always Bexton Slake in allusion to that fictional detective Sexton Blake. In time he became the Mayor of Huntingdon.

On warm, sunny days, we lads used to eat our sandwiches sitting on the rail by the brook. The fact that the girls from the Hosiery Mill, just across the river, passed this way on their lunch break was an added attraction. Many of them lived in Cowly Road that led off the bottom road. Naturally, we lads use to whistle, and call over as they passed. One in particular was the target of our attention. Younger than the rest she sparkled with vivaciousness, laughing, teasing, and dancing among her companions. I whistled over and shouted, "Want to come out with me tonight, darling." To my surprise she ran across the road and put her tongue out at me. Not at the others - but at me. Standing there in a simple summer dress that outlined her curvaceous figure, a mass of shimmering auburn hair that tumbled about her shoulders, I felt a frisson of excitement run through me. I made a sudden movement as though to catch that delicious pink tongue protruding from full red lips. She jerked back with a laugh, for a split second our eyes locked and I was lost in their dancing, brown depths. I knew then I had to have this girl.

Suddenly my bravado evaporated, and I said sheepishly, "Well, would you like to come out with me tonight?" She wrinkled her nose like a pixy as she thought it over. "You'd better watch that one." Shouted an older woman. "His old man's a copper." She laughed, "Well, if your father is a policeman I think I should be safe. Yes, I'll meet you at seven thirty outside the Grand." She was about to go, but turned round, "By the way, what's your name?" I told her, and asked hers. "Alice Robson." She laughingy replied as she ran off to join her companions.

I was totally infatuated with this enchanting girl. Medium build with a well-rounded figure, lovely legs, and an attractive oval shaped face that shone with impishness. I spent every possible minute with her. Was it any wonder my mother began to worry. "You're never home these days Morris, are you seeing a girl?" Embarrassed, I admitted I was. "Well, you must bring her home for tea, we'd love to meet her." This was the moment I had been dreading.

I had, of course been to Alice's home many times. The last council house in Cowly Road, bordering on a lane, and meadow, deep in wild grasses and flowers. We would wander through the waist high foliage before sinking from sight, loosing ourselves in love making.

I had been to Alice's home many times, and was accepted as one of the family. Mr Robson was an ex soldier who lost a leg in the 1st war. He was a charming countryman, and could usually be found resting in an old stuffed chair with his leg off. Mrs Robson was a motherly soul who would always give me a hug, and kiss, when I visited. Obviously, money was short and the furnishing basic, but it was a loving home and I always felt relaxed. I have happy memories of suppers on warm summer evenings in the kitchen. The back door open to a vista of fields and trees, Mr Robson tucking into cold potatoes and meat, Mrs Robson trying to get me to eat more, and Alice teasing me unmercifully. All the while laughter and talk - so unlike my own home. Mr Robson would put down his jug of 4X Ale and say, "Your Pa caught any murderer's lately?" Chuckling at his little joke. On other evenings he would say, "Youm caint take my gal out tonight, Misses and I be going to the Legion." Alice would say, "That's all right Dad, Morris, and I, will stay in and look after the kids." Eyeing the ample sofa.

24

Come the dreaded day to bring Alice home for tea. I was not relishing the prospect knowing it was bound to be an ordeal for Alice. Our living room contained good solid oak furniture which mother polished every day. There were a handsome, combined bookcase and writing desk, and through the glass one could see the titles of Legal Books, and Police Journals, as befitted my father's promotion to Detective Inspector. Mother had laid the table with a brilliantly white starched table cloth. There were piles of tastefully cut sandwiches, a multicoloured jelly, newly turned out of a fancy mould, quivering in the centre. Finally, my mother's pride and joy, a silver plated cake stand with delicious cream cakes. My heart sank at the sight. Putting my arm round Mum, I said, "You shouldn't have gone to all this trouble, Mum." "Well, Morris, we don't want this young lady of yours thinking we don't know how to behave - do we?" What could I say?

Calling to collect Alice, I found the usual chaos. Dad reclining in his chair, Mum dashing after the children who, as usual, were running wild. Alice was ready and quite took my breath away. Dressed in a cream dress with black piping down the centre to just above the knee. Raised collar with a hint of cleavage, and raised platform shoes. Normally she did not wear makeup, but I detected a faint colouring of the cheeks and a trace of lipstick. Her glorious hair was caught at the nape of the neck with a coloured ribbon. At that moment I would willingly have died for her. I took her hands, "You look wonderful, Darling." Pulling her towards me I kissed her, to the squeals of delight from the children. Mrs Robson was beaming in the background, and Pa Robson said, in mock tones, "Now, just you mind your manners, I don't want to come along to the cop shop and bail you out."

The evening was much as I expected - dreadful! Dad, in his best Inspector's voice tried to keep the conversation going. "How are your family keeping?" "Very well, thank you Mr Mills." Pause. "Is your father's leg bothering him?" "No, I don't think so, Mr Mills." Still longer pause. "What's your brother doing these days?" - It sounded like what's your brother up to! Mother was lost for words, and Alice, poor thing, was tongue tied. How my heart bled for her. Had it not been for my younger brother, a born comedian, it would have been total disaster. Adopting a theatrically posh voice he said, "Do have another sandwich, pater." Proffering a plate. Alice choked on a mouthful. Then, raising his cup to Alice, with little finger outrageously extended he said, "Cheers, old girl." Alice's hand frantically sort mine under the table cloth, and from the pressure, I knew she was having difficulty controlling herself. Thankfully, that evening was never repeated.

That summer was idyllic, long hot days, warm languorous evenings that melted into velvet dusks. We would roam through the meadows smothered in wild flowers. May Thorn bushes laden with white flowers like snow drifts, gave off their sweet perfume. We would sink into the tall grasses and be lost in a world of our own. We spent a lot of time punting on the river. Leaving the old town we would soon be in the isolation of lush meadows sweeping down to the river. Willows spread a green canopy over the banks. All around, nothing but cattle feeding in the meadows, water fowl scuttling among the bulrushes, and fish darting through the clear water. At one point the river in taking a bend had scoured out a little bank, some three feet deep with a sandy bottom. A knarled old tree with roots partly exposed by the river wash threw a green canopy overhead, as though to hide us from the inquisitive gaze of feeding cattle. This was our little secret harbour, and never have I known a sweeter place.

It was extremely hot, and the waters looked deliciously cool and inviting. "Shall we go in for a swim?" I suggested. We had no costumes. Discreetly, back to back, we slipped out of our light summer clothes and slipped into the water. At first we swam in a self conscious manner, almost furtive, as if ashamed to look at each other. This was beyond the bounds of human nature. We stopped feigning indifference to our nakedness and devoured each other with our eyes. I was entranced by the perfection of her body softly undulating in the clear water, glistening white like marble. The seductive movement of her firm breasts, and hair streaming behind in golden strands like some water nymph. We playfully swam around each other, and then we were together embracing, the heat of her belly searing me through the cool water. We kissed long and lingering as we sank below the water, to rise spluttering, and laughing. Returning to the bank I held her as though I never wanted to let her go, the sensuous pressure of our bodies driving me wild. Like the crashing seas on the shore, torrents of passion flooded over us, and then we were one.

26

Later, all passion spent, we slowly made our way back. We were both very quiet, deep in thought. I was thinking, "Oh, God! Now you've really complicated your life," when Alice, in a husky voice, said. "Morris, do you really and truly love me?" I let the punt drift midstream and sat beside her. Over and over, I told her how much I loved her, but it was not enough. " Why must you leave me soon? Why must you go to sea? Why now when we have just..." Lost for words her voice trailed away. I cupped her face in my hands. "Alice my love, are you sorry we have made love?" She gripped my wrists savagely, and with eyes blazing, said fiercely. "No! No!. You're mine now - mine."

How could I explain, or even make her understand the demonic forces that had driven me from childhood to be a seaman. We had been going steady for two years, she knew, and had lived with, my burning desire to go to sea. Perhaps, in her heart, she always knew she would take second place.

For several weeks I had been writing to shipping companies for an apprenticeship. It was a torturous process. I started alphabetically and it was not until I reached the letter S that I received a reply. Sir William Reardon Smith Ltd. Invited me to an interview at their Cardiff Head Office. The interview was one of the most daunting experiences of my life. The Boardroom was a large, impressive room with a massive polished table running its length. Silver inkstands and trays with cut glasses, leather bound blotting paper and writing material. The walls decorated with oil paintings of company ships, and at the top a large painting of the founder, Sir William Reardon Smith, looking severely down on the proceedings. The present, Sir William, sat some distance from me at the head, and various Directors sat around the table The whole atmosphere permeated wealth and power.

Sir William opened the interview by asking me why I wanted to go to sea. This was easy and I was able to overcome my nervousness, and spoke for some time. The Directors fired various questions at me. I remember one was "What is your ambition?" "Oh, to be a Captain, Sir." I answered without hesitation. This produced a few smiles. Another asked why I had chosen this company. "Well, Sir, I know this is one of the largest shipping companies in the world and prospects for a keen, ambitious person must be good." This seemed to go down well. In all truth, I had never heard of them until I plucked their name from a shipping list.

Sir William then got down to harsh facts. "I see from your application you have no academic qualifications to offer us." This was the moment I had been dreading. I explained how, on the advice of a retired sea captain, I had studied intensively during the past two years through a correspondence course with Bennets College. Sir William asked if I felt qualified to take their examination today. "Yes, Sir." I replied confidently. Sir William quietly conferred with his Directors. "Well, that seems satisfactory, our decision will, of course, depend on the results of your examination. Thank you for attending." I thanked Sir William, and the Directors for granting me an interview.

Mr Low, the clerk who had been taking notes, rose and escorted me from the Boardroom. Outside, my legs felt decidedly wobbly as the tension eased out of my body. I was taken to small room, plainly furnished with a table and chairs. An old fashioned clock on the wall ominously marked the passage of time, the small hand clanking the seconds away. Placing a set of papers before me I was advised to read them carefully, and tackle the easier one's first. "You have precisely two hours." The examination was quite comprehensive comprising English, Maths, Geography and a written precise on why I wanted to go to sea. With a sinking heart I got down to the task. It seemed no time before Mr. Low came back to collected my work, informing me it would be a week, or so, before I would be notified of the results.

Two weeks passed in an agony of suspense then, arriving home from work, my mother handed me a large envelope heavily embossed with the company seal. I held it in trembling hands, examining it from every angle, afraid to open it. Finally, Mother in a burst of exasperation said. "For God's sake open it!" With drawing the contents, I found a letter from Mr Low. "I am directed by the Board of Directors to inform you they are pleased to offer you an Apprenticeship as a trainee Deck Officer with said Company, etc., etc." How can I describe my feelings? I know I was nearly physically sick with joy - I had made it.

Also enclosed was a set of Indentures for signatures in appropriate places. It was a handsome, antiquated document, full of legalised clauses and phrases that would not have been out of date in Nelson's times. I still treasure it. I was also required to sign a document agreeing to undertake a course of studies with the Cardiff Nautical College. Finally, there was a long list of seagoing gear that I had to provide at my own expense. I was instructed to let the Company know when all these formalities were completed, when they would appoint me to a ship.

Several weeks elapsed before being appointed to a ship, and in the meantime I continued working at Murkets, and to court Alice. Now that my going was imminent our relationship was strained. Naturally, she was very downcast at my going, while I was in a euphoria of excitement at the prospect. There was no middle ground here and I thought the quicker I go the better.

War clouds were rapidly gathering. Hitler attacked Poland, and on the 3rd of September 1940, Chamberlain declared war on Germany. My family, and I, were sitting in the living room when his sombre tones droned out of the wireless. "And consequently we are war with Germany." We sat stunned as the import of his words sank in. Mother, turning to me said firmly, "You're not going to war, Morris," then to my father, "He won't have to go will he, Tom? He's too young." Dad, fully aware I was waiting instruction to join a ship, said. "Don't worry, Ethel, Morris is joining the Merchant Navy, they don't fight Germans."

Famous last words. The first casualties of the war were merchant seamen when the SS Athenia was torpedoed, and sunk with heavy loss of life on the first day of the war. On a per capita basis the Merchant Navy lost more men than the Armed Forces. One in five merchant seamen were killed. Thirty-five thousand in all. The first year of the war was referred to as the 'Phoney War' due to lack of action on the fronts. There was nothing phoney about the Battle of the Atlantic that raged from day one. So horrendous were the losses of ships and lives that Churchill forbade publication of tonnage losses, fearing public morale would be affected. At one stage the fate of this country hanged on the tenuous thread of convoys battling across the Atlantic to bring food, and war supplies, to this country.

During this period I came home from work to be handed a letter. Mother said in a sad voice, "This is for you, Morris." We both new its contents before I opened it. "You are instructed to join the SS New Westminster City, at Erwell Park Wharf, Manchester." I had a few days grace to obtain seaman's documents.

It was a warm, sultry evening, when I called on Alice to say goodbye. Her parents were sad to see me go, after all, I had been a regular visitor to their home for two years, and was accepted as one of the family - perhaps a future son-in-law?

Alice, and I, sadly wandered through the meadow to our favourite spot. I had been dreading this moment and was determined to adopt a light, nonchalant attitude, but soon succumbed to the poignancy of our farewell. I loved this girl passionately, she was mine, body and soul, and I began to doubt my sanity leaving all this love for an uncertain future. We lingered long until the sun gave way to a deep purple night, and we could no longer prolong our separation.

My mind was in a turmoil as I walked home. Of course I was emotionally upset at leaving her, but overriding all other feelings was this driving desire to go to sea. The past two years had been a struggle striving to improve my education, applying to shipping companies, the strain of interview, examinations, and the anxiety of awaiting results. Yes, it had been a hard slog but I was proud to think I had achieved my goal.

CHAPTER 3
JOINING SHIP

My departure from home was quiet, and restrained. Mother shed a few tears and admonished me to take care of myself. Dad walked me to the station, a firm hand shake and I was on my way to the adventure of my life.

Arriving at Manchester railway station, I stood on the concourse wondering what my next move was. A passing taxi spotted me for a 'greenhorn' in my new uniform and shiny case. "Joining your ship, Jack? Hop in and I'll soon get you there." He must have taken me half way round Manchester, and then no doubt overcharged me. I was even stupid enough to give him a tip. I later learnt I could have got a bus for a few shillings.

Erwel Park Wharf was lined with ships in various stages of discharging or loading cargo. Ships' derricks and shore cranes were swinging bales and packages overhead, while dockers were dashing about with wheelbarrow and trolleys, shunting the cargo here and there. It was not easy picking out my ship as all names were painted out during war time, and a painted name board on the bridge substituted. Eventually, arriving at the foot of the gangway to the New Westminster City, I found she had just discharged a cargo of grain, and was riding high in the water. At 5000 tons she looked enormous and the bridge towered above me. Feeling overawed, I mounted the gangway and was met by a young man dressed in a tattered uniform who introduced himself as the Chief Officer. "Bring your case lad, and I'll show you to your cabin." When I say my cabin I am of course joking, it was barely 10 ft by 10 ft. Here four apprentices lived; slept, ate, and tried to pursue their studies.

31

"Right, lad, get out those fancy clothes and get your dungarees on. I hope you remembered to bring some?" "Yes, Sir." "Good, I'll get the Senior Apprentice to sort you out." When he had gone I took in my dismal surroundings. Home from home it certainly wasn't! There were six bunks, a wooden table screwed to the floor, a bench seat fixed to the bulkhead and one small loose bench seat. A small cupboard to hang clothes in one corner and a tiny food locker in the other. Apart from the door there was one porthole. The practice of carrying six apprentices had ceased some years ago, and the mind simply boggled at the thought of six strapping young men occupying this minuscule space. The two spare bunks were put to good use, the top one as storage space for spare gear, the lower acted as a settee, not that one could ever sit on it being totally filled with suit cases and such like. Each bunk had its own drawer where our underclothes and working gear were stowed.

Snr. Apprentice Vernon Edmunds entered the cabin. He was nineteen, tall and fair. I soon learnt he was not a very communicative person, and difficult to get along with. He had only another year's sea time to complete before sitting the second officer's certificate. "Hello, so you're our first tripper." We shook hands. Pointing to the top foremost bunk "That's your bunk." I soon learnt this bunk was reserved for first trippers. The mechanism for steering the ship was by rods and chains from the wheelhouse to the stern quadrant, and a section passed inches away from my head. Every movement of the wheel was accompanied by a loud clanking as the rod revolved, and this was constant at sea. In time I came not to notice it.

Changed into working gear, Edmunds took me to the top of number 3 hold from which a fog of grain dust was rising. "Here, take this cloth and tie it round your face, stop you choking." We climbed over the hatch combing and descended into the depths by means of a narrow iron ladder, to be enveloped in a dense yellow cloud of grain dust. Our job was to sweep down the stringers and strakes, and prepare the hold for the next cargo. So began my first working day as a trainee deck officer.

The next few days were spent doing various dirty jobs. We were normally on deck by 7 am. My first task was to take a two gallon galvanised bucket down to the engineroom, fill it with fresh water and return to the bridge, climb three bridge ladders to the top of the

Monkey Island and replenish the tank that served the Captains quarters. This had to be done several times - especially if the Captain took a bath - and that bucket began to weigh a ton. I became the 'Goffer' to all and sundry. It was all part of the learning process. I was the 'butt' for the usual standard sailor jokes. "Oi, mate, go down to the storeroom and get some red oil for the port lamp and some green for the starboard one." Or, I was ordered down into the hold and find the golden rivet that every ship was, mythically, alleged to have, and give it a polish. Of course, I was not that naive but played along with the game.

When the crew began preparing the ship for sailing, I worked with the deckhands closing the hatches. A scary job for a sixteen year old, walking along narrow beams settling in hatch boards. One slip and there was a hell of a way to fall. Derrick's wires were reaved in and made fast, and the derrick lowered into their goosenecks. This was real sailor work and I loved every minute of it.

Ships invariably sail at the most inconvenient time, and this was no exception, we left at midnight. It was pitch black, raining, and cold. Typical Mancunian weather. War time blackout prevented us from showing any lights. My station was on the stern for letting go. The deckhands were in a foul mood having been dragged out of their warm bunks, and a steady stream of swearing filled the air. Viciously I was pushed about as I impeded them. No one told me what to do, or where to lay a hand. Above all, I could hear the Bosun cursing them for a set of landlubbers. The Bosun (Taffy, I called him for I never learnt his true name) was one of the hardest men I ever met. A Welshman of about sixty, a little over five and a half foot tall, and nearly as rotund. He was enormously strong and had a vocabulary that would strip paint off metal. I have seen him lift heavy shackles one handed and toss them into the store locker. He was a nasty, vicious man, who always wanted to fight anyone. I believed he had no living relatives, and certainly no friends. He was a dangerous, rocky island in the sea of life, and well worth steering clear of.

My first encounter with him was on that dark, rain sodden night. "What are you doing you stupid, fucking bastard?" It appears I had upset him. "Nothing." I said miserably. I could just make out his leathery features as he peered up at my six foot two inches. "Christ!

You're a big bugger, do you want a fight?" "No, Sir." This caused an explosion of rage. "If you ever call me' Sir' again I'll put you on your back you cheeky bugger. I'm the Bosun, and don't you ever forget it." As if I would!

The journey down the Manchester ship canal took seven days, with many locks to pass through. Partinton Lock, Runcorn, Eastham Lock, and finally Ellesmere Port. It was a perfect opportunity for me to learn how to handle mooring ropes, and I soon became a proficient member of the team. The journey down the canal also provided the opportunity for several crew members to desert, among them one of our apprentices. I cannot remember him but his desertion proved a bonus in that we had more living space during the voyage.

We arrived at Port Sunlight, Ellesmere Port on 7th August 1940. The berth opened into a large factory that manufactured soap. Older folk may remember adverts for Sunlight soap, even buying a cake and cutting off slices for the weekly wash. I have no idea why we tied up there for we didn't load soap. To go ashore we had to pass through the factory, wherein hundreds of Northern lassies worked. They were a fearsome breed and we poor sailors had to run a barrage of crudity. Pointless to pause and exchange banter for they would have your pants off before you could say 'knife'. Once clear of the factory there was an endless vista of drab, dreary, back to back houses. I found it utterly depressing, so unlike the lush, green county I had so recently left.

Leaving Port Sunlight we proceeded to Liverpool where we loaded tanks and shells in the lower holds, and crated aircraft on the main deck, sailing on 12th August 1940. The two main areas of land warfare were North Africa, where the Eighth Army was fighting Rommel, and the Russian front, where the Russians were fighting a desperate battle of survival. It was obvious we were destined either for the Mediterranean or Russia. Our fate was sealed when we took a northerly course through the Western Isles and headed for Iceland. It did not make much difference to me where we went, It was all one great adventure. The voyage to Iceland was just long enough to settle me into shipboard routine, at least I knew the sharp end from the blunt end! We dropped anchor in Hvalfjord on 20th August and sailed the following day in a small convoy of seven ships bound for Archangel, North Russia. It was noticeable that all the ships carried crated aircraft. The largest ship, the Llanstephen Castle, also had a contingency of RAF personnel who would assemble the aircraft in Russia, and teach them how to fly them.

The voyage was quite pleasant with sunny days and a moderate sea. Nearing the Arctic ice fields the temperature did plunge at night time, as I found out to my cost. There was a magnificent display of Aurora Borealis one night, and Captain Harris decided to give us a lecture. We were mustered on the afterdeck and foolishly I turned out with only a seaman's jersey. Within minutes I was chilled to the bone. The Northern Lights were spectacular, shafting the Arctic skies with a dazzling array of magnificent rainbow colours, flashing and darting through the heavens, reflecting on the seas like sparkling jewels. Dull, grey ships would momentarily be transformed into glittering gems as the myriad splendour darted over their fat, ugly forms.

This was my first encounter with Captain Harris, a stockily built man with weather beaten face. His gold braided cap barely concealed a shock of red hair. Standing on the stern with hands thrust into his uniform jacket pockets, a backdrop of silvery sea lit by the Northern Lights, rising and falling, he looked every inch a sea captain. He came from Appledore, Devon, and spoke with a rich Devonshire burr.

The lecture over, I fully expected him to ask how I was settling down, instead he curtly dismissed us and returned to his quarters. I need not have worried at not being spoken to - in time I would positively appreciate it! As time progressed I appeared to become his 'Bête noire' and came to dread the peremptory command "Mills, the Captain wants to see you at the double." Of course I was wild and young, and deserved all I got.

At an early stage of the voyage the Chief Officer sent for me. No longer the scruffy individual who welcomed me aboard at Manchester, now a smartly dressed officer with three gold bands on either sleeve. "Right, young man, I think it's about time we taught you how to be a seaman. Go aft to the Carpenter's store and he will teach you how to splice ropes and wires." A short companionway took me into the storeroom, a tomb like space dimly lit by a single light. All around were coils of ropes and wires. Towards one side was a work bench piled with tools, and a vice. The smell of ropes, tar, and oil was all pervasive. As I entered a figure bending over the vice straightened, his head brushing the deck-head. From the wrinkled face that peered at me he could have been sixty, seventy, or even eighty - who knows - he just looked so incredibly old. Somewhere in the depths of his chest came a rumbling sound. "Vas oo vant." No one had told me our carpenter was Swedish and had very little English. Even worse, no one had warned me he was mad - quite mad! His manner was completely bizarre, one moment childlike, laughing and giggling in Swedish, the next, ranting and raving, throwing objects around and wildly waving a marlin spike in his huge hands. To me, it was incomprehensible such a man could be engaged as a Petty Officer on a British ship, but to see him at work with ropes and wires was to see an artist at work. I spent several scary days learning this art with one eye on the marlin spike in his whirling hand. He may have been Swedish, and mad, but he certainly taught me how to splice, parcel and serve ropes, for which I was grateful.

Long before we sighted land we began to smell Mother Russia. The salty tang of the sea gradually gave way to that indefinable aroma of Russia, somehow old and earthy. Then there was the tang of timber and pine as the forests came into view. Large logs that had escaped from the numerous saw mills, restlessly, ebbed and flowed with the tides, occasionally striking the ship's hull with a reverberating thud, that made us, momentarily, catch our breath.

Although Archangel is within the Arctic Circle, this was August and it was very hot and dusty. It was that brief time of the year when the Arctic sun never sets. The dock area was stacked with sawn timber, the main export of Archangel. The air swarmed with vicious, biting mosquitoes that descended from the surrounding forests. For two days they devoured me then, as though they had had enough of me, left me in peace. The town didn't look very exciting from the ship, its stark, unrelenting drabness only relieved by the golden cupola domes of the churches shining in the sun.

Ever optimistic, Jolly Jack Tar would soon ferret out the hot spots, and find some pretty girls to spend his money on. Boy were we in for a shock. One by one, we trooped up to the Old Man's cabin for an advance on wages. "How much do you want, Mills?" "Could I have five pounds, please Sir?" "Five pounds!" He exploded. "You don't have that much in wages. You can have two." Inflation was then rampart in Russia. I cannot recall the rate of exchange but it was several hundred Roubles to the Pound, and I received a large wad of notes making me feel like a millionaire. The machinations of inflation were quickly brought to my attention. Entering a State GUM store, I made for the jewellery counter intent on getting a present for Mother. The display looked cheap and tawdry, but I saw a gilt chain with a green stone - no doubt glass - but it looked pretty, and I indicated I would have it. The assistant was a stony faced woman, with Mongolian features. Neither of us spoke a word of each other's language, and she appeared indifferent - even hostile - to my attempts to find out the price. Finally, in exasperation, I held out my large wad of notes and was shocked when she removed most of them. I had no means of protesting, or refusing to buy it, she had my money and that was that. My intention to get Alice a present was no longer possible. I had almost blown my entire advance of two pounds - a lot of money in those days - on a cheap piece of jewellery I could probably have bought for five shillings in England. It was a very chastened young man that left that store.

To console myself, I decided to have a beer, but was frustrated not being able to find anything resembling a pub, or bar. I did see in a square, a kiosk selling drinks, and ordered what I took to be a beer, parting with most of what was left of my roubles. If it was beer, then I can only say it was the most horrible beer I have ever tasted! So ended my first day on Russian soil. I returned to the ship greatly disillusioned and fed up

So, there I was, with the prospect of two to three weeks in Archangel and no roubles. Tough - eh! I was bemoaning this fact in general whilst working with the sailors, when an old salt said, "Yer know what you want to do mate, get some old clothes, put them under your arm and walk about the market square. The Ruskies will fight each other to buy them. I know, I've been there many times." I thanked him for the advice pointing out I was a first tripper - I had no old clothes. The sailor scratched his head. "Tell you what mate, I'm not going ashore in this poxy place, I've got some old clothes and a pair of old shoes that are just about done, and old Sam here, my 'oppo'....Oi Sam, yer not going ashore ar ee?" Sam nodded agreement. "You can get a bit of old clobber for the lad, carn't ee?"

Sam nodded again. I thanked my benefactors, then, carefully, so as not to offend, "What's in for you?" "Ah, now mate, I'll tell yer what you do, you nip along to the Chief Steward and get two cartons - no, make that three cartons of ciggies - one each for me and Sam, and the other you can flog in the market - you'll get a good price. The Chief will give them on tick and by the time you get back you'll have enough overtime to pay for them." It sounded simple, but I was worried.. "What do I do in the market?" "Do! - You don't do anyfing, just amble around taking yer time. The bloody Ruskies will be mobbing you, gabbling like turkeys, waving wads of roubles, when you see the biggest wad take it and go." It worked like a dream, and I was quickly in funds. I was shocked later to discover I had broken several Soviet laws, principally, black-marketing and profiteering. It was only by the Grace of God there were no policemen around or I would surely have been arrested, and imprisoned, for the Russians don't mess about.

With my ill-begotten gains, Mac, my fellow apprentice, and I, decided to go into Archangel and enjoy ourselves. Wandering through the more salubrious parts of the town we came upon a grand looking building, with fluted columns either side of the foyer. There was an extremely long column queuing for entrance, automatically assuming it was a cinema, we tagged on. Mac. and I, were arguing on the merit of going in, "Bound to be in Russian - we won't understand it." I countered with, "Well, we haven't anything else to do." When a passing Russian Naval Officer paused. "Angliske Matros?" We confirmed it with a "Da", without more ado he took our arms and marched us to the head of the queue. Not one voice was raised at this blatant queue jumping. The Russian officer spoke authoritarily to the cashier, who gave us tickets and refused our money. We thanked him, and with a salute he went on his way.

Inside we gasped at the ornate splendour of the theatre; seats in deep plush velvet, gilded boxes with curtains around the hall. There was a large orchestra pit that we thought unusual for a cinema, even more so when the players filed in. The conductor tapped his baton. The curtain rose and the opening bars of Tchaikosky's Swan Lake flowed forth. Mac. and I, looked at each other in amazement. "Bloody Ballet, come on, I'm getting out," said Mac. "No, you're not." I hissed. "This bloody lot will lynch us." Already we were getting dirty looks for whispering.

This, for the Russians, was a magical experience, they were being transported out of the hellish life they led into the uplands of beauty, and ravishing music. Of course, we didn't appreciate it at that time, and on the way back to the ship Mac said in all seriousness, "Morris, promise me you won't say a word of this to anyone on the ship - they might think I'm queer." Already he was worrying over his reputation as a lady killer. I laughed, "You don't think I want any one to know we have been to a poncy ballet, do you? Let's say we picked up a couple of smashing girls and had a ball." We both laughed, Yet, deep down in my subconscious a cord had been struck, and a love of the classics had been born.

The ship now loaded with timber; the holds being full, the timber pit props were stacked horizontally on the main deck and we resembled a floating haystack. One could literally walk across the timber to the forecastle. Our cabin, and others, on the main deck could only be accessed by a series of steps down. What little light our porthole gave was now blocked out and we lived in semi-darkness. The chat was that if we were torpedoed we would be virtually unsinkable. This was reassuring until some Jonah pointed out that the shock of an explosion was bound to shift the timber imprisoning us in our cabins - not a cheerful thought!

We sailed 28th August 1941 in convoy QP1 comprising fourteen ships, half of them Russian. They particularly took our attention when we observed women working around their ships. As the port of Archangel receded I fervently hoped I would not see it again. A forlorn hope for I was destined to become more intimately acquainted with Archangel in a year's time.

It was a quiet voyage home with no enemy action. Jerry had not yet woken up to what was going on in his own back yard. The weather was kind until we ran into heavy seas off Iceland, and the timber on the foredeck worked loose. This required the Bosun, and some sailors, to go on top of the timber and tighten the holding wires by means of bottle screws. There was the usual cursing as they struggled to carry out this task on the slippery timber, with the added danger of a foot becoming trapped, and crushed, in the working timber. The Bosun, in his usual maniacal manner, thought an AB was not pulling his weight and threatened to knock his block off. The AB, who was a big fellow, was stung into action and went for the Bosun. It was a crazy situation as they fought, and rolled about the timber that had no safety rails. Of course, our tough, little Bosun, settled the matter. What amused me was that Captain Harris, who witnessed the start of the fracas from the bridge, retreated into the wheelhouse. Obviously, he had no desire to have his Bosun up on a disciplinary charge.

Convoy QP1 arrived in the Orkneys on 10th October, where we formed into a small coastal convoy and sailed for Surrey Commercial Docks London, arriving at the height of the Blitz. As we approached the upper reaches of the Thames we were filled with foreboding. A heavy pall of smoke hung over the City, and our nostrils were filled with stench of burning. On entering the dock we found the dockside lined with ships discharging timber. Vessels were secured to buoys in the centre of the dock, and with assistance from tugs we were secured to such a buoy. Hardly had we secured than a flotilla of tugs and lighters surrounded us greedy for our cargo. With the exception of the officers and apprentices, the crew were immediately paid off. Later in the day the Captain called me up to his cabin, where I found an elderly gentleman in civvies sitting in an easy chair. Captain Harris, looking up said, "Ah, Mills. I'm letting Edmunds and MacGowan away first for leave, they have been on the ship longest. You will standby until they return and then it will be your turn. Understood?" "Yes, Sir." Turning to the elderly gentleman, he said. "This is Captain Ward, he will be relief Master while I'm on leave. Turning to Captain Ward, almost apologetically, "This is the first time I've taken leave in a year. The other nodded sympathetically. Turning to me, "You will report to Captain Ward 0700 hrs for orders. That's all," I was dismissed.

I was somewhat chagrined at not getting away on leave straight away, and returning to my cabin indulged in some swearing. The others, of course, were smirking at my discomfort. Having relieved my feelings I settled down to read a large pile of mail that had come aboard. Mail could never be delivered to ships but was addressed to the Ministry of Transport, where it piled up during the voyage. Alice didn't appreciate this and had been writing every week, so a dozen - or more - pink envelopes endorsed with S.W.A.L.K awaited my attention. I think the colour of the envelopes must have matched my cheeks. Edmunds and MacGowan, busily packing their cases, indulged in crude remarks as to my sexual prowess, and begged me to read one of them before they left. Needless to say, they got a short answer!

Reading these letters so full of passion, and love, was a sobering experience. For months she had been thinking of me, and yearning for my return, while I, happily engaged in my duties as a seaman had barely spared her a thought. I felt almost ashamed.

The following morning I reported to Captain Ward for orders. He was an affable gentleman. "Now, sonny, all I require is a pot of tea in the morning at 0700 hrs, and a jug of hot water for shaving." The following morning I felt a gentle shake and Captain Ward said. Come on lad, you've slept in." Apologising profusely I rushed to do his bidding. The next morning was a repeat performance. On the third morning the Captain admitted defeat and got the watchman to take over. The problem was that at sea one always got a shake from the man going off watch, and as I had no alarm clock I found it impossible to wake. As I said before, Captain Ward was a very amiable man and only wanted a quiet life. Had he been a crusty old sea Captain, he would have had my guts for garters!

London was being savagely attacked by massed German bombers, particularly the East End and the docks. How ironic I thought having been to Russia, a country fighting for its very existence, never hearing a gun fired in anger, and now I was caught in the very epicentre of a blitz. The previous night had been horrendous with bombs, and incendiaries, falling in, and around the docks. Buildings, and wharves were on fire, the conflagration made worse by the huge amount of stored timber. Searchlights probed the clouds, weaving, and meshing in a web of light. Batteries of guns poured boxes of red hot steel into the heavens, and above all the thunderous explosion of bombs. It was possibly the worst night of the blitz. We, on the ship, had a nerve racking time rushing around with fire hoses, and buckets of sand, but mercifully we were not hit.

The following night it was thought the Luftwaffe would pause to regroup, so I nipped ashore for a pint. I was only a short distance from the dock when the sirens began to wail, almost simultaneously the Ack Ack guns opened up, and ugly shards of red hot metal rained down from the skies. Gouts of flame rose as bombs exploded with a shattering roar, and buildings burst into flames.

"Bloody Hell!" I thought, this is no place to be and dived into the nearest building that just happened to be the Red Lion. I found myself in a narrow corridor with a heavy curtain at the end, pushing through I found myself in fantasy land. The bar was packed solid, a piano bashing out Knees up Mother Brown, or such like, every one was singing, shouting, or laughing. Mugs of beer passing overhead to customers in remote corners. The noise was tremendous. By now the bombs were falling very close and the bottles behind the bar were playing a merry tune.

"Make way for the Navy." Someone shouted as I struggled to the bar. "What yer drinking, Jack." Shouted someone. "Cor blimey, mate, put yer money away - on me." By the time I fell out of the pub I was half-seas-over. The East End was a calamitous sight, a sea of fire. Looking towards Surrey Commercial Dock I could see flames belching into the night. "Oh my God!" I thought, what if the ship's been hit. Hurrying back I was relieved to see her undamaged in the centre of the dock. Getting back was a hazardous job, all the lighters having been disturbed by bomb blast and my familiar route altered. I just had to take a chance and leap from lighter to lighter, hoping I was going in the right direction. The devil must have been with me that night for, apart from the chaos around me, my head was spinning like a top!

The seven days my fellow apprentices had been away passed in a flash, and then it was my turn. The joys of that first leave are but a distant memory. Alice was overjoyed at my return and her passion re-lit all the tender feelings I felt for her, and for a time I forgot about the sea, and ships. It was a difficult time, for she had to work during the day, it was late October, cold, blacked out nights, no lush meadows to stroll, no secret harbour to visit, but we still managed to be wrapped up in each other. During the day I visited my local where I was received as a celebrity, and pressed for my war stories. I could hardly tell them my most dangerous experience had been in London last week!

My pleasure was rudely shattered on the fifth day of my leave when I received a telegram instructing me to return to the ship immediately. I was annoyed, they'd kept me waiting for leave and now they were cutting my leave from seven days to five. To hell with it, I'd say I was away from home and never received the telegram. I knew my Mother had signed for it. I would go back on Monday which was the official day to return, which is what I did. Arriving at Surrey Commercial Dock I was horrified to find no ship, and wandered round the dock like a little boy who had lost his mummy. Eventually, I pulled myself together and went to the Dock Master's office. "Excuse me, Sir, can you tell me where the New Westminster City is?" He consulted a ledger. "Sailed Sunday, now at anchor off Gravesend waiting to sail." I explained my predicament. "Best get your self down to Tilbury quick as you can and see if you can get a boatman to take you out - that is she's not already gone." With a leaden heart, I raced across London and caught a train to Tilbury from Fenchurch Street Station. On Tilbury Landing stage I could see the ship still at anchor but, how was I to get out to her. Seeing a boatman about to cast off I hailed him. "Are you going out to the New Westminster City." "No, mate, and named another ship" Could you do me a great favour and put me onboard my ship?" He looked doubtful. "Depends whether they've got a Jacob's ladder over the side. Can't wait for them to rig one. If they haven't you'll just have to come back with me." The boatman circled the New Westminster City and there to my immense relief was a Jacob's ladder. I thanked my saviour, and hastened on board. Amazingly, neither my absence on Sunday, nor the mysterious manner of my joining was noticed. I swore then never to deviate from the strict letter of the law.

We sailed from Tilbury 30th October 1941 and arrived in the Tyne three days later to fill our bunkers with coal, before sailing north about Scotland to Loch Ewe. This vast sea loch was the regular assembly point for convoys, and after spending several cold, wet, miserable days swinging round the hook we embarked for New York.

CHAPTER 4
NEW YORK ADVENTURE

The voyage across the Atlantic was uneventful, which was pleasantly surprising considering the U-boat war was raging with savage intensity. We were not so lucky on our return. The weather was typical Western Ocean stuff - severe to gales - which had every one either climbing a mountain or running down the other side, as the heavily laden ship rose and sank into huge wave troughs. On those rare occasions when the weather moderated, the Chief Officer would employ the sailors topside on maintenance jobs, such as chipping and scraping the deck. A vile job at the best of times, but in winter, with strong winds whipping the crests of waves and sending the spray flying over the deck it was hellish. The Mate had no mercy and unless there was a danger of a man being swept overboard, the job had to be done. This practice ceased many years ago with the introduction of special paints that are sprayed on in dockyards. Another filthy job, now passed into history, was oiling the mast stays and running gear. One was hauled to the masthead with a bucket containing an evil concoction of fish oil, and a cotton swab, and as one descended the oil was rubbed into the wires. With the erratic motion of the ship, and strong winds, we rapidly became smothered in the stuff. Despite repeated washings the stink hung about one for days.

I took it all in my stride. I was young, strong, and cockily considered myself a seaman with one voyage under my belt.

Off duty, there was little to do except sleeping or reading. There was a radio in the officer's wardroom, and while we apprentice officers were not forbidden to use it, it was generally frowned upon. On this occasion, around ten in the evening, I smartened myself up and went into the wardroom, which, as expected, I found empty. Switching on the radio I tuned into the American stations, we were now nearing their coast. I soon picked up the popular American bands; Jimmy Dorsey, Harry James, Duke Ellington and Glen Miller. The wardroom was dimly lit, throwing a soft glow on the leather back seating on which I was curled. The dining table gleamed with a polished oak hue. In the corner the bottles and glasses glittered in the small bar.

Glen Miller's band was playing 'Why do Robins sing in December' this was Alice's, and my, favourite tune. We had danced to it, played it on the gramophone, and made love to it. I was transported as she materialised in my mind. I could feel the warmth of her body as I held her, her perfume flooded my senses, her low, husky voice spoke endearments. Then a terrible apparition shattered my dream. It was Captain Harris in a towering rage. Bridge coat thrown over night attire, shock of red hair unruly and spiked like flaming daggers. "What in God's name do you think you are bloody well doing?" He snarled. I was dumbfounded, unable to think what terrible crime I had committed. "Listening to the radio, Sir." I mumbled. Listening to the radio - listening to the radio!" He almost screamed. "Don't you bloody well realise my cabin is above?" His finger savagely stabbed at the deckhead. "Here I am trying to get some sleep and you're playing that bloody jungle music." He appeared to choke on his words. "If I hear another bloody sound from you you'll regret the day you joined this ship!"

Back in my cabin I ruefully reflected on why, oh why, do I always seem to cross the Captain. Even on my first voyage I managed to upset him. How was I to know one never went to the bridge by the starboard ladder? This was holy ground, reserved only for the Old Man. The first time I made this mistake the Captain emerged from his cabin, and demanded to know where I thought I was going. "To the bridge, Sir." I answered, thinking I was showing some intelligence. I then received a lecture on ship etiquette, with a warning I was not to sully his deck again, unless sent for. Reaching the coast, the convoy split up and went their independent ways. The coast was ablaze with lights, and after blacked out Britain, seemed a blasphemy. I felt a strong urge to shout, "Put that light out!" The Nantucket Light beckoned us into the River Hudson and soon New

York came into sight. I was a little disappointed, the perspective dwarfed the Statue of Liberty and famous skyline, but as we got nearer I could only stand and gape at the panorama before me.

We berthed in Brooklyn, in what appeared to be a vast marshalling yard. To get ashore one had to take a long walk to a bridge that spanned the rail tracks, then an equally long walk to the dock gate. Alternatively, and unauthorised, one could cross straight across the tracks. This was dangerous as wagons were constantly being shunted along the lines. Nevertheless, being lazy young devils this was the route we preferred. I can still hear the mournful wail so peculiar to American trains as they worked through the night.

I had many exciting experiences in New York, but the two that stick in my memory are a coffee pot, and meeting Mr and Mrs Smith. First, the coffee pot. On the day of arrival Dockers descended on the ship to start unloading. Hatches were opened, derricks rigged, and coils of ropes and wires snaked across the deck. I was returning from the galley with a pot of steaming coffee when I tripped, in falling I splashed the contents into my face. Apart from the pain I could feel my skin blistering, so I went to see the Chief Steward, the nearest one can get to a doctor on a merchant ship. After calling me a silly bugger, he painted my face with Gentian of Violets that left me looking like an Indian on the war path. At first I was shy of going ashore with a bluey, blotchy, red face, but soon realised my face was my fortune. Every where I went, bars, restaurants, cinema - even the skating rink in Central Park - no one would allow me to pay. I was treated as a Limey Hero. "People would say, "Gee, buddy, you must have been torpedoed?" When I replied, "Well, no, I actually spilt a coffee pot in my face." They would stare in total disbelief and say, "You Britisher's are sure some modest son's of bitches."

I went to a cinema one evening in Brooklyn, and as I bent forward to buy a ticket the bright lights of the cashier's box illuminated my blotched face, and the young lady recoiled in horror. Recovering, she said in a broad Brooklyn drawl, "Say, Pal, youse a British sailor, ain't yaa. Whatya get sunk? Brother youse guys are sure going through hell." Pointing to my face. "Say, was the ship on fire?" I shook my head. "Sorry, can't say too much - the war you know." "Gees, you poor guys." Calling an usherette over, "Got a wounded British sailor here Madge, see he gets a good seat." The first film over, the newsreels came on and included shots of the war in Europe, and a convoy battle. The news reels over, much to every one's surprise the lights went up, and the Manager walked onto the stage. "Ladies and gentlemen, you have just seen some real live action shots of a convoy battle, and I'm honoured to say we have here, tonight, a wounded British sailor from that very battle..." At this point a spot light hit me direct It had been very well staged. Spontaneous applause broke out. I was acutely embarrassed and wished the ground would swallow me up. I had an insane urge to get up and shout, "IT WAS ONLY A COFFEE POT!"

Fortunately, my face quickly healed and I returned to being a mere mortal. Frankly, I was getting fed up with this hero lark. Shortly after, I had a summons to report to the Captain. "Oh Gawd! What have I done now?" I knocked and entered his cabin, looking up, he gave me a long searching look, it was the kind of look that had me frantically searching my brain trying to remember what I had recently 'cocked up.' "Ah, Mills, It's the practice of New Yorkers to send invitation cards on board ships to a social evening. Makes them feel they are doing their bit - so to speak (America was not yet in the war) I have here a card from a Mr and Mrs Smith asking me to nominate one of my young officers.." At this point he had difficulty equating me with the expression 'young officer' "And I have decided you will represent the ship." I groaned inwardly. All I wanted to do was go ashore with Mac. Beer and girls, that's what I was after, not sipping tea with some elderly American couple. Captain Harris looked hard at me. "Is that all right?" "Yes, Sir." I said meekly. "Right, Mr and Mrs Smith will pick you up 1700 hrs tomorrow. Smarten yourself up, don't keep them waiting, and for God's sake look as though you are enjoying yourself."

When I got back to my cabin and told the others of my fate they fell apart laughing. "You silly sod." Said Mac.
"Why didn't you make some excuse?"
"What the bloody hell could I have said?" I demanded indignantly
"Well." Said Mac, off handidly. "I'm lucky, I've got an Aunt in New York" I looked at Mac. in surprise.
"I didn't know you had an Aunt in New York, Mac."
"Of course I haven't you silly bugger, but the Old Man can't prove it - can he?" I made a mental note to acquire an Aunt next time in New York.

Sharp at 1700 hrs I stood at the foot of the gangway dressed in newly pressed uniform, crisp white shirt, polished shoes, and peak cap squarely on my head. I was nobody's fool! I knew the Captain would be inspecting me from the bridge. A large limousine pulled up and, at first, I paid it little attention. I was expecting a more modest car with an elderly couple inside. Mr and Mrs Smith stepped from the car and introduced themselves. They must have been in their early forties, expensively dressed, suave, and very friendly. Mrs Smith obviously spent a lot of time on her make up, and coiffure. I could not fail to notice the expensive rings on her fingers. On top of that she was a damned attractive woman. To say I was over awed would be putting it mildly. I almost wished it had been a beat up Chevvy with an elderly couple that was picking me up.

However, on the drive to Manhattan - where they lived - they completely put me at my ease with small talk. "By the way Morris, we have invited some friends over to meet you. Hope you don't mind?" "No, Sir, not at all." I replied. Mr Smith laughed, "Listen Morris, you're not on your ship now, so cut out this Sir business. My name is John and this is Margaret." Of course I found it impossible to be so familiar, and stuck to Mr and Mrs where necessary.

The car whispered through the canyons of Manhattan, and slipped into an underground car park. A plush elevator whisked us up their apartment in this skyscraper building. It was an enormous apartment with large rooms leading one to the other through archways - no doors There were a dozen guests already waiting to greet me, including their daughter, Susan. She was about two years older than I. Attractive, but rather distant as we chatted over cocktails - my first experience of this drink - before going into the dining room. It was a sumptuous meal with various courses and wines to match. I noticed Mrs Smith smiling in a motherly way as I wolfed my way through the courses. The meal over, we retired to a large, comfortable lounge, with a wall to wall window overlooking the dazzling lights of Manhattan. I remember thinking they'll never believe me back home when I tell them about it.

Drinks were served and the guests got down to the serious business of plying me with questions on the conditions in war time Britain. I have never thought of myself as a talker, but I waxed eloquent on the subject. I told them about the severe food rationing, how commodities were measured out in ounces. Clothes rationed by coupons. The means of heating and lighting severely restricted. Then, I really captured their complete attention when I described the blitz in London, and how my Grandmother who was in her late seventies, would nightly fill a Thermos flask, make some sandwiches, and then spend the night in the Anderson shelter.

"What's an Anderson, Morris?" Enquired an elderly lady. "Well," I explained. "You dig a six foot by four foot hole at the bottom of the garden and you cover it with sheets of concave metal, you then spread as much earth as possible over it. There are two wooden benches to either sit, or lay on, and there is usually a duck board to keep one off the damp earth."

There was a shocked silence before another guest spoke. "Dear God! You did say your Grandmother was in her seventies? Does she have any heating?" I shook my head. "No. Just a hole in the ground."

To change the mood, another guest enquired what my father did. "He's a Detective." Again I had their attention. "Scotland Yard?" Someone asked. It seemed too involved to go into an explanation - and perhaps I was bragging a little - so I said,"Yes." "Gee, a real Scotland Yard Detective." It was said with genuine awe.

Fortunately, I was rescued by Susan from over stretching myself. Taking me by the arm, she lead me into another room, "That's enough gabbing, I'll show you the television." I had previously admitted I'd never seen TV, and was looking forward to the experience. After several minutes of twiddling with the knobs, and seeing a series of banal pictures flash before my eyes, she switched the set off with an air of finality, sat back, and studied me closely. I felt embarrassed under this scrutiny, and, in defence, stared boldly back. She was an attractive girl, tall, fair hair; cut short, nice legs encased in silk elegantly crossed before me. After what seemed aeons - but could only have been seconds - she spoke. "Tell me Morris, do you have a girl in every port?"

"Of course I do - doesn't every sailor?" We both laughed, and chatted freely about ever day things that interest young folk. I found her intelligent, bright, and amusing, and was quite enjoying her company when her father came in. "Sorry to have to break this up Sue, but I must get Morris back to his ship."

She pulled a face. "Oh dear! Just as we were getting to know each other. Say Pop, could Morris come over on Saturday? I'll get some of the gang over and we could have a party." Mr Smith looked enquiringly at me. "Depends on whether Morris wants to come?" I thanked them both, saying," I would be very pleased to come, but it rather depends on whether my Captain would give permission.""Don't worry about that Morris," said Mr Smith with a smile, "I'll speak to Captain Harris." Which made me think Mr Smith must be someone important in shipping. When it came to saying goodnight, I held my hand out to Susan, but was surprised to be given a full, warm kiss on the mouth, which took me completely by surprise, and had me blushing.

I arrived back on board in the early hours of the morning. The ship was floodlit and dockers working round the clock. My cabin mates were fast asleep, from the grunts and snores it sounded as though they had a boozy night. I was too uptight to sleep and lay on my bunk smoking, contrasting the affluent life style I had just left with my present situation, an iron box 10ft x10ft. I thought of the girl I had recently met. Attractive, only daughter of rich parents. Just finished college and apparently with no plans, or ambitions for the future. I was puzzled by her manner towards me. Half the evening she had practically ignored me, as though I was of no consequence. I'm not immune to pretty girls, but I thought 'Right Miss Snooty Pants if that's your attitude I'll ignore you too!' Then a complete metamorphose, she became a warm, gushing girl, free with her kisses. Now she's doing her damnedest to embarrass me. When she insisted I come over on Saturday for a party I thought her motive was to show me off to her friends. 'Look what I've got, a British sailor - perhaps have some fun at my expense.' Well. I was bound to get a good meal and a few drinks - I could live with that!

Come Saturday, and I made my way from Brooklyn to Manhattan by rail. I announced my presence into the intercom, the door swished open into the foyer and I took the elevator to their apartment. Susan met me at the door, putting her arms around my neck she gave me a long kiss. I was completely taken aback Was she trying to make a fool of me or was this accepted American social greeting? Linking arms, she said. "So glad you managed to come Morris, come and meet the gang." There were a dozen, or so, young people around twenty years old. The boys all shook hands and the girls did, indeed, kiss me politely. Perhaps I was being hyper sensitive over Susan? They were a friendly group and made me feel at ease, pressing soft drinks and titbits on me during conversation. Of course, the boys wanted to know all about life at sea in war time, and any battles I had been involved in. At that point in my sea career I had seen very little enemy action, but I had a vivid imagination, and feeling a fraud, I regaled them with accounts of U-boat attacks, ships sinking, and being dive bombed by enemy planes. It must have been good for it had them sitting on the edges of their chairs, and the girls opened mouthed. One chap had the temerity to ask me what I would do when Britain was occupied by the Germans. At that stage, Great Britain stood alone with it's back to the wall, and invasion a real prospect. Like my countrymen, I was intensely patriotic and would willingly die to prevent our country being occupied. The suggestion was a slur on Britain, and I was very angry. "Listen." I said coldly. " The last time Britain was occupied was 1066 by the Normans. Many have tried since - including Napoleon - and we are still a free, independent country. Britain will never be defeated!"

Looking rather crushed, the chap who posed the question apologised. They were all upper class New Yorkers from wealthy families, and while they were obviously intelligent people, they did not strike me as being very worldly wise, and appeared to have a strange idea of the British. I think they must have seen some old British films. You know the type, Gordon Harker the perennial Cockney, and Jack Buchanan the upper class twit. Ergo, Britain consisted of two classes - Cockneys and Upper Class Twits. No way was I going to be thought of as a Cockney (although I think they are the salt of the earth) and so I gradually adopted a posh accent. Susan, who had previously heard my normal, well modulated, accent-less voice, was quickly onto my subterfuge, and smiling broadly egged me on.

At some stage in the evening the furniture was pushed back and couples danced to music from a gramophone. Dancing not being one of my skills, I hung back. A bright young thing said. "Come on Morris, lets dance." Taking her hand I said, "I say, that's frightfully decent of you." The poor thing nearly collapsed with laughter. Later, Susan took me aside, "You go easy, big boy, or they'll all be wetting their pants." Her arms encircled my neck as she pulled me down to be kissed. Again I was embarrassed, and blushed like a country bumpkin - which I suppose I was! I was trying hard to be correct, and polite, to my hostess but realised I was not in control.

When the party broke up, Susan took me to another room to say goodbye to her Mother, who was quietly reading. Again Susan sprung a surprise on me saying, "Morris is leaving now, Mom. Is it OK if he comes for Sunday lunch?" I felt compelled to say, "Hang on, Susan, I'm a working man, I can't go ashore when I fancy, I have to ask permission." "Don't be so silly." Tossing her head. "Do you want Daddy to speak to your Captain, or do you want me to come down to your boat..." "Ship." I corrected. "All right, silly old ship then, and see your nasty old Captain?" My mind boggled at the thought!

During the next few weeks I was a constant visitor to the Smiths. One evening he took us to Radio City to see a vaudeville show featuring Sophie Tucker and Georgi Jessel, well-known American vaudeville artistes. It was very funny and smutty. After the show Mr Smith took us backstage and introduced me to the artistes. Another indication he was an influential man. Other evenings Susan, and I, did the town. We would wander round Times Square going to Joes Oyster bar tucked away in a corner. We went to Jack Dempsey's Bar hoping to see the great man, who just happened to be away that night. We would stroll arm in arm down Broadway taking in the lights. Right from the beginning I made it clear I just didn't have the money for this rich living, but any mention of money was silenced. So I allowed myself to be swept along in this fantastic dream world. I was conscious, however, that it was always Susan who wanted to hold hands, link arms, slip an arm round my waist when walking, and take every opportunity to kiss, and I felt uneasy. This was a pleasant interlude, but there was only one love in my life.

My stay in New York was drawing to its inevitable close when Mr Smith suggested we visit their parents in Yonkers. We drove through the New York Tolls onto the Highway, passing through the Bear Mountains. Mrs Smith was having a friendly argument with her husband. "Slow down John, there might be some bears for Morris to see." "I can't dear, I'm in the fifty mile lane and if I change the cops might jump me." The broad highway was divided into different speed lanes, and it was an offence to change lane until the next Toll was reached.

It was a pleasant journey with Sue, and I, indulging in a little flirtation whenever her parent's attention was distracted. The Grandparents lived in a large, typically American bungalow, with a veranda fronting onto a broad street. We were made very welcome, and a sumptuous meal laid on for us, followed by drinks. Neighbours passing by were called in and I was introduced as the young British officer our Susan's going out with.

Driving back we were all quiet and subdued. We had eaten well, and drunk more than a little wine. Mr and Mrs Smith were conversing quietly up front, while Sue, and I, sat intimately in the dimness of the rear seat. Leaning close, she whispered. "Morris, I think I've fallen in love with you." Oh, hell! I thought. This I can do without. "I like you too." I said glibly. She sat up sharply. "Only like!" I saw Mr Smith's eyes switch to the rear mirror. "No! No! of course not, I'm very fond of you. I think you are a wonderful girl, but you know I'm sailing tomorrow. Could be anywhere in the world - might never get back to the States. We both knew this was inevitable - didn't we?" A long silence followed, then. "So, this is goodbye?" "I'm sorry Susan, but it has to be."

CHAPTER 5
HOMEWARD BOUND & LEAVE

The New Westminster City left Sydney mid-December 1941. We had high hopes of being home for Christmas. The ship was loaded with ammunition and tanks for Russia, and crated Carnation Milk for the U.K. The crates were stowed in No.2 hold and the tanks in the tween deck immediately above, shackled to ring bolts.

Clear of land we soon ran into heavy weather that rapidly developed into one of the worst Atlantic gales recorded. The ship was labouring badly, plunging her head into the oncoming seas at the same time rolling onto her beam-ends in a sickening manner. Life lines were rigged and it was a case of one hand for the ship, and one for yourself. The ship's log recorded "9am 14th December 1941, hove to. Violent pitching and roll. Shipping heavy water. 4pm whilst carpenter attending to steering gear, vessel pooped, and heavy seas washed him into the scuppers, fracturing his ribs. He was at once treated as per medical guide and put to bed. 5.20pm, heavy seas stove in No.2 shelter deck, got adrift and caused some damage to crates and adjoining cargo. 11pm weather moderating, proceeding with voyage".

Many were the heroic and unsung deeds of Merchant seamen during the war, but how many I wonder involved swimming in Carnation Milk chasing a runaway Army Tank?

What the ship's log, and ego of Captain Harris, glossed over was, when No.2 hold was stoved in there was an ominous, persistent, dull thudding noise coming from down below, as though something was striking the ship's bottom. Obviously something had

54

broken loose. It was not long before the Mate called us on deck and sheltering in the lee of the bridge, shouted, "Come on lads, we've got to get for'ard into the masthouse and go down into the hold to find out what the bloody hell has broken loose". There was no arguing with the Mate, picking the right moment we dashed across the deck and dived into the masthouse, slamming the door shut before the next wave came crashing onto the deck. We descended by an iron rung ladder to the depth of the hold. Here, the sound of the gale was muted; giving way to the harsh screech and grind of tortured metal as tanks strained at their shackles. In the light of a cluster lamp we saw a gaping hole in the tween deck where a tank had wrenched itself free, smashing its way onto the crated Carnation Milk below, viciously reducing it to a pulp as it gyrated around the hold with the ship's motion. We had to get down into the debris of smashed crates floating in a nauseating stinking pool of Carnation Milk swirling each and every way with the mad motion of the ship. Somehow, we had to lasso this iron monster before it smashed its way through the hull. Picture if you can the nightmarish scenario. The vastness of the hold intermittently lit by the harsh light of a cluster lamp that frantically swung and jerked as the ship rolled in the sea. One moment blinding light, the next darkness. Overhead, tanks straining to break their bonds and come crashing down upon us. Below, the malevolent tank charging back and forth as though intent on crushing our bodies to bloody pulp. Armed with wires, ropes and baulks of timber, we chased this monster, and after many submersions, and desperate leaps to safety we succeeded in capturing it.

Battered, bleeding and covered in this glutinous muck, we retired to the washroom and sluiced our aching bodies with buckets of sea water. The Old Man didn't have the decency to issue a tot of rum. Even worse, any action taken for the safety of the ship did not qualify for overtime payment. The merchant seaman of that day certainly had a tough life.

In view of the damage sustained we were diverted to Sydney, Nova Scotia, for repairs. All cargo in No.2 hold was taken out leaving a disgusting pool of dirty, oily, evil smelling Carnation Milk. We were all standing around the hatch peering down on this mess when we became aware of the Bosun's presence. "well lads", he said in a nice friendly voice, "I suppose you are wondering how we are going to get that shitty mess out, well I'll tell you - first, you get out of those nice, warm, comfy clothes and put your dungarees on, then you can get your lazy arses down there and fucking well bail it out with buckets". He broke out into a cackle of amusement, and screwed his face into what he thought was a smile - it looked more like a grimace of pain! Clearly he was enjoying himself as he had not offered to fight anyone.

"Christ, Bos', we'll bloody well freeze down there", exclaimed an AB. It was mid-winter in the far north of Canada and the temperature was well below freezing.

"Don't worry mate", said the bosun, "You just give me your next-of-kin and I'll see they hear you died a hero"

We descended to the bottom and stepped into a foot, or so, of this obnoxious liquid that clamped its icy tentacles around our feet and ankles, cutting off circulation almost immediately. The topside had been bearable in warm clothing, now, confined to the lower hold and only wearing dungarees, the cold became intense. Our laboured breathing vaporised into a fog that hung over our heads. A large metal bucket was lowered into the hold and we set to with a will scooping the mess with our individual buckets, and throwing the contents into the larger container. Our hands were frozen and we kept slipping on the sticky deck, no wonder our aim was erratic, and we occasionally deluged each other. Tempers began to rage, and perhaps it was this that fired us up to complete the job. My reward for my labours was sixpence an hour overtime. I guess I earned about four shillings for that day's work, by today's standard about perhaps two pounds?

Of course one could not always guarantee to get one's just rewards. Every apprentice was required to keep an overtime book which was presented to the Chief Officer on termination of voyage. Chief Officers were notorious scrooges, their one aim in life to save the company money and thereby further their promotion prospects. The overtime book was a cat and mouse game. "What's this Mills? You never worked nine hours overtime on that clean up job in Sydney".

"Oh, yes I did Sir".

"Rubbish, I'm knocking an hour off". All square at this stage as I did only work eight hours. Further deep inspection of book, followed by a gleam of anticipation. "What's this? Five hours stowing ropes in New York - you must think I came aboard on the anchor chain - that job only took three hours". Looking suitably crestfallen, I apologised. "Sorry Sir, I must have made a mistake". What the Chief Officer failed to realise was that on that particular day I had observed him going ashore smartly dressed, and as I was anxious to see my girlfriend, I quickly changed into my No.1's and followed suit. In fact, I did no work that day, so you win some - and you lose some.

Sydney, Nova Scotia, in those days was a real Wild West Town. Dirt streets wound through ramshackled wooden buildings with wooden side walks, and hitching rails for horses. Red Indians used to come down river with their canoes laden with furs. After they had traded their furs they would hang around the liquor store hoping a white man would sell them some hooch. Of course it was illegal to sell spirits to Indians, but a fair trade ensued. I cannot remember seeing any bars or saloons, and the liquor store was only allowed to open a few hours a day. It was almost a dry town.

Being proverbially 'skint' we usually made for the Seamen's Mission which was roughly a mile from where we were berthed. It was a long walk up hill on a dirt road. Here we could have a meal, play cards, or read in a quiet room. Saturday there was always a dance. On one occasion we must have had a particularly salty meal - perhaps it was salt cod - anyway, on the long walk back we were overcome with a raging thirst, seeing an isolated shack, Mac suggested we knock on the door and ask for a drink of water. A grizzly old timer answered our knock. "Please Sir, could you give us a drink of water?" The old timer stared at us blankly. "Water". He made the word sound positively obscene. "Don't drink water, partners - water's only for fur washing".

Not too often I thought looking at his grimy appearance.

"I got beer partners - want some?" Can fish swim! He led us into a rough and ready room, the furniture looked as though it had been knocked up from old bits of timber. "Just you sit yourselves down boys, and I'll get the beer".

We learnt later, that folk in this wild outpost don't go down to the store for their beer, no 'Siree', they make their own in a shack out back, and it's pure dynamite. He returned with a large stone jar and some enormous mugs.

It was obvious he didn't have many visitors in this isolated spot and he was 'Dang Well' going to enjoy himself, and settled down for a good old yarn. "Where ya from fellows?" When we said Britain he nodded vaguely, as though he had heard of such a place. "Heered tha'rs some sort of 'sheebang' over tha, you guys come for a rest?" We laughed. "Sort of".

Our friend was a trapper and we were fascinated with his tales of hunting wild animals, including bears. As the night grew longer, and wilder he kept filling our mugs with his potent brew until I came quite confused with the number of trappers in that spinning shack! I have no recollection of how I got back to the ship. I only know I woke the following morning fully dressed in my bunk with a shocking hangover!

We sailed from Sydney shortly before Christmas, and so our festivities were spent in mid-Atlantic. The galley staff put in a special effort and we had a good meal. Cook surpassed himself with a splendid trifle, and Chief Steward issued a generous tot of rum. Later, leaning on the rail watching the long parade of grey merchantmen wallowing in the valleys of long Atlantic rollers, I could not but feel nostalgic as I thought of the family, and Alice, back home enjoying their Christmas. No doubt they would be thinking of me, wondering where I was, and if I were safe. Looking out over that vast watery panorama I knew U-boats lurked in those cold depths. Were they enjoying their festivities, perhaps raising their glasses to past and future victories? Was the commander perhaps, at this very moment, lining up his periscope for a shot at our ship? The cold air made me shiver, and for the first time I felt a little homesick.

The severe gale that had afflicted us since leaving Sydney moderated somewhat after Christmas. The mountainous seas continued to advance upon us from the stern. One of my regular jobs was to take readings from the log that was affixed to the taffrail, right astern. The mechanism recording the passage of the ship through the sea by means of a spinner attached to a long rope. The revolutions being recorded on a dial. Gripping the rail, I was mesmerised by the height of the advancing waves that threatened to engulf the ship. The torpedo-like spinner would climb the watery mountain then, as the wave rolled under the stern lifting 10000 tons as though it were a cork, spinner and rope would drop out of sight. It was awesome. Movement was both difficult, and tiring. Either bent forward climbing a hill or running down the other side.

It was late in the afternoon, I had just finished reading the log and was sitting in the cabin chatting to MacGowan, when a dull explosion made our ears pop.

Rushing on deck we observed a ship on the port side slowly falling out of station, a funereal plume of smoke rising from the stricken victim. In the half-light, gouts of flame lit up the scene. Action stations were immediately sounded and we rushed to our stations. Of course, there was nothing we could do but it relaxed nerves to be at one's post and feel the cold steel of a gun. Shortly after, another ship was torpedoed and sank rapidly. We could just see the crew desperately trying to get their lifeboats away.

We were lucky - if that's the right word - all the action was on the port side of the convoy. Out there men were being killed and mutilated, fighting for their lives in that stormy sea. The convoy, like some elderly lady passing a drunk in the street, lifted its skirts and remorsefully steamed on, ignoring the victims. There was nothing we could possibly do. To have stopped would be to invite a torpedo.

In those early days of the war, convoy escorts were almost non existent. We had a vintage World War 1 destroyer on our starboard flank, immediately the action started it steamed round to the port side, leaving us completely exposed. Had there been a U-boat out there he could safely have come to the surface and sunk us. These were the 'Happy Hunting Days' for U-boat commanders.

We safely completed the voyage to the U.K. and in dense fog steamed down the East Coast to Hull. Ships' Masters never enjoyed sailing in convoys, they like the freedom of plenty of sea room.

Sailing in convoy in thick fog was horrendous. All vessels continuously blowing their horns. Lookouts fore and aft, straining ears and eyes, to pierce the fog and catch the possible sight of a grey monster bearing down out of the swirling mist. In these conditions, ships sailed like ghosts in a spectral grey world and successfully entered the River Humber, docking at midnight, 12th January, 1942.

The country was in the grip of a severe winter and snow lay overall. It was a Sunday, and the ship, as though covered with a white shroud, lay silent. The crew had been paid off in the morning. This, of course, didn't apply to the apprentices who were retained as general 'Dog's Bodies.' We had been working flat out since the early hours of the morning coiling down ropes and wires. Attaching rat guards to mooring ropes - we used to joke this was to stop our own rats from deserting! By the afternoon we were exhausted and were relaxing in our dingy cabin, dressed in dirty sea jerseys, dungarees and sea boots, lounging on our unmade bunks, making the air blue with our cigarettes. We were far from happy; the only thing on our minds was leave. The state of the cabin was revolting. The mess table bore the remains of our hurried breakfast and spilt coffee stains. Articles of discarded clothing were scattered around. It was not a pretty sight!

About midday, there was a loud bang on the door and Captain Harris entered accompanied by the Chief Steward. We instantly sensed he was in a towering rage from the angry glances shooting between the accommodation and ourselves. Now, at sea, Sunday is the regular day for Captain's inspection, but Christ Almighty! We had only docked at 0030hrs, the crew had been paid off and we apprentices had been knocking our guts out. Surely to God, he was not going to inspect us? Oh, yes, he was! He literally exploded. "Jesus Christ, what a bloody pig sty! Look at this table," waving his hands over the pile of dirty crockery. Scuffing his shoes on the deck. "What a filthy mess, I could grow potatoes in this muck." True, but overlooking the deck outside was covered in several inches of dirty snow - of which he had brought in a generous portion. Opening our small food cupboard he nearly had a fit. Not I hasten to add because it was empty, its usual state after weeks at sea, it was the green mould with shreds of past repast adhering to it which seemed to upset him.

Having exhausted every complaint he then descended to personal abuse. We were not fit to serve on his ship. He had the strongest doubts about our parentage. He would adversely report us to the company. He would write to our parents. Finally, like a well run dry, he stood and glared at each one of us, then he delivered his 'Coup de grace'. There would be no leave until this filthy mess had been cleared up. With the benefit of hindsight, I now realise the Captain had been up all night navigating the ship in thick fog, the tricky business of entering dock, followed by the business of dealing with port authorities and the discharging of crew. The poor man needed a dog to kick and we just happened to be it!

We were shocked and humiliated by the ferocity of his tongue-lashing. We were stung to anger. Apart from our pride, we realised he might just withhold leave until it suited him, and so we set too with a will. A tin of white paint and varnish were scrounged from the paint locker. Bulkheads and deckhead were scrubbed and painted a brilliant white. Bunk boards draws and locker were sand-papered and varnished. All the brass work, porthole, handles and the brass gimbal holding our oil lamp were buffed up until they shone like golden jewels in the dim wintry light. Mess table and deck scrubbed white and odd pieces of purloined canvas spread over them to keep them pristine.

The following Saturday, having completed the job, and feeling satisfied, we decided to go ashore for a drink. Going down a drab dock-side street we passed a second hand shop, there in its grimy window plastered with anti blast tape, as though guarding the crown jewels, lay a roll of Chinese silk cloth garishly embroidered with dragons, snakes and other Chinese symbols in fantastic colours. It was hideous. It stopped us dead in our tracks. Without a word being spoken we knew we must have it. A diabolical plan was instantly formulated in our minds.

Entering the shop, an old man appeared to materialise from a pile of junk. When he told us the price MacGowan said, "Get stuffed" and made to walk out. The old chap grabbing his arm named a new price. After a great deal of haggling, realising he was not going to get another penny out of us he settled for our offer, grumbling away about being bloody well robbed.

Back on board we soon demonstrated our skills with scissors, needles, cotton and pins. In no time the bolt of cloth was transformed into four bunk curtains. The porthole had two small curtains either side with cute bows. There was sufficient cloth left to drape over the mess table. When we were finished we took in the scene and were lost for words. It was magnificent - just like a whore's boudoir!

Sunday morning we were up early, washed and shaved, and dressed in uniform. Bunks made without a crease and the counterpanes with company logo neatly folded. Not a spare bit of clothing anywhere. Sharp on 1100hrs came a bang on the door and the Captain entered. I simply cannot find adequate words to describe the expression on his face. At first we thought he was going to have a fit. He stood rooted to the spot mesmerised by the dazzling array of dragons and snakes, his eyes seemingly blinded by the lurid colours. His normally florid features flushed into a deep crimson and his eyes threatened to pop out of their sockets. Behind him, the Chief Steward was in mortal danger of exploding as he desperately tried to contain his laughter. There was a long awful silence then, without a word Captain Harris abruptly departed.

His departure left us in a state of helpless hilarity. We literally collapsed with laughter and tears rolled down our cheeks. It was a wonderful, wonderful, moment. When we had recovered we immediately took down the offending drapery and threw it away. It had cost us our spare cash and hard work but, by God! It had been worth it. The following morning the Mate told us we could go on fourteen days leave. Utter bliss. In fact it became intolerably long, made worse by receiving a telegram extending leave by a further seven days. This was no magnanimous gesture on the part of the Captain. It transpired alterations were being made to accommodation, and extra guns being fitted. By the time I received the telegram I was nearly broke and was only saved by a few pounds I had put aside while working at Murket's garage.

My reception at home was, as expected, warm. Mother cried, hugged and kissed me, then started endlessly fussing. Was I getting enough food? Was I keeping warm on the ship? Was the Captain looking after me? That made me smile. Mother was looking tired and strained which I put down to the war, rationing, and of course having a son at sea with constant news of horrendous losses of merchant ships filling the headlines and newsreels. Dad shook me by the hand and asked the usual question, "Have a good trip, Son?" As though I had been away on my holidays. Good old Dad, I thought. As usual preoccupied with his police duties.

"I expect you will be wanting to stay at home tonight and have a rest." Mum looked anxious, as willing me to say yes. I failed to pick up the urgency of her request. "Well, Mum, I think I should go round to Alice, and let her know I'm back. I won't be long." Leaving the house, I thought I'd just pop into the George for a quick one first. The bar was crowded with servicemen and their female companions. As I pushed my way forward I was astonished to see four of my closest mates ensconced in a corner. Algy - yes, that was his name - Thornton, a 2nd Lt. in the Army Air Corps., David Willis wearing the uniform of the Royal Marines, John Williamson a pilot officer in the RAF, and my childhood mate Don Mash, in the Coldstream Guards. What a reunion we had! Much drink flowed as we exchanged experiences.

Strange to relate, I was the only one who had seen enemy action and the others regarded me as a bit of a veteran. Of the five of us, only Algy was to survive the war unscathed. David Willis was killed in action, John Williamson was shot down on his first raid and killed, Don Mash had his leg smashed in Germany, and I lost a foot in Russia. How could we have known on that wild, happy evening, that Thor, the Teutonic god of war, was poised over our heads preparing to strike us down.

At some time during our celebrations, a local chap slapped me on the shoulders, "How do, Morris, glad to see you back. Have a drink." Through bleary eyes I said, "No thanks, I'm doing fine." Raising a full glass. His voice droned on through my befuddled brain. Local knowledge seemed to be his topic and I wished he would go away until he said, "You're Father is doing all right, eh!" The remark could have been referring to his police duties, but it was said with a snide smirk. I sobered immediately, "What the hell are you talking about?" My transformation from a drunk to a six foot three inches tough merchant seaman alarmed him. "Sorry, Morris, thought you knew. Didn't mean any harm." "Thought I knew what." I demanded menacingly." "Well" he whined, "That Mrs

Ellison is a tasty bit of goods." Somehow he escaped my grasp and vanished in the crowd.

Mrs Ellison was indeed an attractive woman; I would be lying if I denied she had not escaped my admiring glances in the past. Her husband, George, owned a furniture shop. He was a plump, jolly man, several years older than his wife, Elsie, who was tall with a shapely figure that went in and out in all the right places. She had shining black hair and a Latin complexion. Somewhere in her genes was foreign blood. Above all she had a free and coquettish manner. It was not difficult to imagine my father, middle forties, and tall, handsome, and exuding authority being attracted to her or she to him.

The following night the gang had a farewell party in the George. They were all rejoining their units. David and John's happy smiling faces we would not see again. Algy, with the luck of the devil would see the war out as a Captain with the DSO. The last I heard of him he was a Potboy in a pub in East Anglia. He was a strange character. Don would eventually return to Huntingdon with his badly damaged leg and lead a painful existence as a Dental Mechanic. My life is recounted in this autobiography.

Needless to say, it was an uproariously drunken evening. The following morning I had a tremendous row with my kid sister who called me a drunken sot, and accused me of upsetting Mum. I knew it was not my behaviour that was upsetting her, and told my sister to mind her own bloody business. I left the house in a tearing temper and went into town where I chanced to pass Ellison's shop. Seeing Mrs Ellison alone in the shop, on impulse, I decided to go in and have it out with her. I was taken aback when she said, "Hello, Morris, nice to see you. Your Dad said," an embarrassed expression flitted over her face, "You were home again." She knew she had said the wrong thing. Suddenly I felt deflated. What was to be gained by having a blazing row with this woman? She would probably dissolve into tears leaving me feeling a proper swine, so I mumbled hello and left the shop.

All that day the thought of my father having an affair nagged away at my brain. I knew I had to confront him. This was not an easy decision for I had never argued with him on any issue, indeed, such was his strong discipline I would have been afraid to do so. But this was too serious a matter to be avoided, so when I got him on his own I blurted out, "Dad, I've been hearing some ugly rumours. They say you are having an affair with Mrs Ellison, It's not true is it?" There was a long pause while he fixed me in a long, cold, steely stare.

"It's none of your business, boy." He had dismissed the matter, and myself. But I would not let it drop. "Listen, Dad, let's get two things straight. I'm not a boy, I'm a man, and I've been around. Secondly, it is my business because I'm talking about my Mother. Have you thought what this is doing to her?" I went on at length throwing caution to the wind, fully expecting the full fury of his temper. He listened to me through out not saying a word then, rising, "I must get round to the station." The subject was closed. I never knew how deeply he was involved with Mrs Ellison, but the affair - if such it was - came to an abrupt ending. I claim no credit whatsoever. I think he had already decided these rumours were detrimental to his police career, not to mention his marriage. Either way, an uneasy atmosphere pervaded the house during my leave.

I had now been home nearly a week. My mates had returned to their various units. I had an embarrassing meeting with my father's alleged paramour, a violent row with my sister, and a confrontation with my father. "God!" I thought, two more weeks to go. The thought of returning to the ship with its freedom, comradeship, and excitement of shipboard life was tantalisingly appealing. At the back of my mind was the nagging guilt I had not contacted Alice. She would know I was back. It was a small town, and I was well known.

It was January, dark, cold, and around five o'clock I stood outside the large gate of the hosiery mill. It was a large building standing on the opposite bank of the River Ouse, and manufactured clothing for the forces, employing a large percentage of the women of Huntingdon. In my heavy blue bridgecoat and gloves, I was barely visible in the gloom. The gate opened sharp on five and the women poured out in a chattering mass. Some recognised me and shouted greetings. Then I saw Alice, muffled up against the cold, her flowing hair captured under a woollen hat, revealing only her laughing, impish face.

My heart skipped a beat. She was linked in arms with two other girls, chattering away. Seeing me she stopped abruptly. I heard her say; "You go on, girls." Slowly she came over. "Hello, Morris, I didn't expect to see you." Her voice was as cold as the night. I felt a tremendous urge to take her in my arms and kiss her, but we were surrounded by a swirling mass of departing women. Instead, I took her arm, "I'll walk you home." I felt her body go taunt at my touch. "I got home on" I began to say. She cut me short, "I know." I was floundering, "You'll never guess whom I ran into the other night, Algy, Don" again she cut me short, "I know." Feeling slightly injured I said, "Well, you know they are special mates of mine and as they are going back to the war we had to have a farewell drink - might never see them again." Alice made no reply, merely shrugged her shoulders. Arriving at her gate I tried to embrace her, tell her I loved her, how sorry I was for upsetting her, but she slipped through the gate closing it between us. "I'll come round later." I said. "Not tonight Morris, I've got things to do."

That night I lay sleepless in my bed. The full moon spread its cold light over the gardens beyond my bedroom window. The siren had sounded; above I could hear the distinctive drone of a Dornier bomber. It was not coming to attack this little county town; its job was to sneak up on Lancaster bombers returning to base at Wyton Air Field from a raid on Germany. I resolved to settle the matter with Alice the following night.

Around 7pm I knocked on the door and was warmly received by Mrs Robson. "Hello, Morris, lovely to see you - come in - come in.". While I was greeting Mr Robson she was busily helping me out of my coat. Pa Robson eased himself more comfortably in his chair. "Hello, boy, you'm have a good trip. See any action?" "Now, Dad," admonished Mrs Robson, "Don't ee go talking war. Morris come home for a bit of peace." Going to the foot of the stair, she shouted, "Alice, Morris is here, come down." I heard a muffled, "In a minute." When she came down she barely glanced at me as she said, "Hello, I'm going to make some tea." and vanished into the kitchen. Her parents exchanged glances of consternation. Mrs Robson rose and went into the kitchen and I could hear sounds of a low argument. Pa turned to me, "You and my gal having a spot of bother?" I told him briefly how I had met some old mates in the George and we had a farewell party. "You're an old soldier, Mr Robson, you know how it is." He nodded sagely, "Mm, women!" was all he said. Alice and her mother returned with tea and Alice pointedly sat opposite me, ignoring the sofa I was occupying. I had brought a present of silk stockings and a blouse for her in New York. It was gift wrapped and emblazoned with the stores name. Macy's of New York. "Coo," said Mrs Robson, "That looks exciting, aren't you going to open it, dear?" Alice appeared indifferent, "Later, Mum." By now my patience was running a little thin. Right girl, I thought, if that's your attitude I'd be better off in the George, enjoying myself, and was trying to think of an excuse to leave without offending her parents. At this juncture, Pa spoke up, "You know what I think, I think you two young uns should go out for a walk."

We walked down the lane flanking their house in sullen silence, snow crunching beneath our feet. The hedges sparkled with hoary frost. The lane opened into a large field transformed into a carpet of silver in the full moonlight. In the far corner a copse of trees stood sentinel, their branches bare and stark pointing to the sky. Was it only a few months ago Alice, and I, on warm sultry evenings had lain under their green canopy swearing eternal love? Our senses pervaded by the sweet smell of wild grasses and flowers. I had been teasing her when she pushed me back, and plucking a buttercup, held it under my chin. I laughed, and asked her what she thought she was doing. Bending over, her face partially hidden by her cascading auburn hair that lightly brushed my own, I could see her deep brown eyes, serious and misting, like two luminous pools. "I'm seeing whether you love me." "That's a silly country tale."

Then, realising this was not a jesting matter, "Well, what do you see?" She shook her head in a puzzled manner, "I don't know - I don't know - you keep leaving me." I felt a wave of love for this girl engulf me. "But Alice, I'm a sailor, its what I do, I can't change it. You always knew that." Cupping her face in my hands I drew her down, "I love you, I always will."

That was six months ago and here we were walking in sullen silence, unable to find the right words to break the spell. I could stand it no longer, roughly I pulled her resisting body close. My attempts to kiss her were evaded by a twisting head until I managed to plant a generous kiss on the tip of her nose. This was quite ridiculous and we both broke out into laughter. The spell was broken. Her parents were much relieved when we returned arm in arm, laughing and talking. The rest of the evening passed pleasurably with Alice snuggling up to me on the sofa, while I regaled them with amusing stories of incidents on the last voyage, the coffee pot, swimming in Carnation Milk, and decorating the cabin. But I made no mention of the death that stalked us in the depths of the oceans.

We spent every possible hour together. Alice suggested we spend a day in Peterborough and stay overnight at her Aunt's. We caught the morning bus and spent an enjoyable day doing what young people did in those days. We went swimming, roller skating, and in the evening saw a film, before catching the last bus to Woodston where her Aunt lived. Auntie was an elderly widowed lady, living on her own. She made us welcome and seemed pleased to have company. After the usual courtesies she showed me to a small bedroom with a single bed. It was freezing cold and, of course, there was no central heating in those days, so I quickly got undressed and got between the sheets. I was just drifting off to sleep when I heard the door quietly open and shut. I thought someone was taking a peek to see if I had settled.

The outline of Alice was just visible in the dim light as she slipped out of her night-dress, and into bed, her warm, soft body blending with mine. It was a delicious shock and I hissed, "Alice, your Aunt's next door - she will hear us!" "Well don't make too much noise." She giggled under the sheets.

The following morning I awoke alone. Had I been dreaming? When I was called down for breakfast I found Alice demurely eating. "Did you sleep well?" enquired Auntie. "Yes, thank you. I had a very good night." Alice's expression was well controlled "I was worried you might have been cold." "Oh, no," I assured her, "It was a lovely warm bed. Best night I have ever had."Alice's flowing locks fell around her face hiding her expression, but her shoulders were visibly shaking, and she appeared to be choking which quite upset Auntie.

We crammed every moment into the remainder of my leave, until the last day. I had arranged to call for her at 7pm, we would have tea and then go for a last walk through the countryside to say our lover's goodbye. I left home early which was a big mistake. It gave me too much time. I swear I had no intentions of going into the George, but fate decreed otherwise. Passing the George I ran into Billy Walker, we had been work-mates in Murket's for two years. Billy was now in the Army. After greeting each other, Billy insisted we have a drink for old time's sake. "No way, Billy. This is my last night and I'm off to see my girl." Forcibly taking my arm, "Come on mate, you've got half an hour to spare, time for a couple." And of course there was if we had kept it to a couple!

Billy, himself, was a likeable rogue and greatly prospered after the war. I recall some years later while temporarily staying with my parents; Dad was called out to investigate a burglary in a large country house, and asked if I would like to come for the ride. It was a large country house set in its own land, with tennis courts and swimming pool. Imagine my astonishment when the owner turned out to be Billy. After pumping my hand he took me aside. "Bloody hell! Morris, but its good to see you again. Remember that night in the George during the war? I told you to pack the sea in and join me running lorries, well you were a mug to turn it down, mate." He waved his hand expansively over his land. "You could have had some of this." Perhaps he was right, and yet, I could not see myself ducking and diving around the law. Sadly, I had a distressing streak of honesty running through my backbone!

So engrossed was I with Billy's plans for the future I completely lost track of time. With a shock I realised it was past nine o'clock and in a panic rushed to Cowly Road. Alice was livid. Emotionally, she had been preparing herself for another parting, and yet again, I had squandered her precious moments drinking with a pal. "I never want to see you again - you can go to hell!" slamming the door in my face. How prophetic those words were.

I walked home in a turmoil of emotions. Disbelief, anger, hurt pride, how could she do this to me over a paltry two hours? Why could she not understand the bonds of friendship between mates, especially when we were all going to an uncertain future? I totally failed to understand her feelings, and shook my head at the complexities of life. Tomorrow, I would be rejoining my ship. I had been home three weeks and frankly it was enough. I was yearning to get back to the excitement and adventure of sea life. There would be little time to mope over a lost love.

The journey from Huntingdon, through East Anglia to Hull and been incredibly long and weary. The train was packed to capacity with servicemen laden with their equipment, rifles, kitbags, gasmasks, tin hats and greatcoats. Every seat was occupied; they sat and lay in the corridors, even the toilet seats were commandeered. The atmosphere was thick with tobacco smoke that hung in a blue cloud obscuring the dim carriage light. The train crept through the blacked out countryside like a thief in the night, with many unexplained stops. Sometimes, in a black empty void of country, occasionally, in a blacked out rail station with Military Police patrolling to prevent any one disembarking to stretch their legs. Through the window blinds we could see distant twinkling lights and faint 'crump'of bombs. "Some poor buggers are getting it tonight." Came a disembowelled voice from the tobacco fug. Frankly, we were too fed up and tired to care.

With a jolt the train came to a halt in Paragon Station, Hull. The troops disentangled themselves from their cramped positions with much cursing and swearing. "Watch your fucking head, mate." As a kitbag was heaved off a rack, "Get out of my sodding way, car'nt you." "Oi, you silly bugger, you've picked up my rifle." and so the soldier's vocabulary rippled up and down the train. Military Police were stationed along the freezing, snow covered platform collecting their respective troops. A Navy shore patrol was checking passes, my Merchant Navy Uniform drew a few suspicious glances as if to say, shall I check that one. Fortunately, they ignored me and I passed out of the station and caught an early morning bus to Alexandra Dock

CHAPTER 6
REJOINING

Walking through the dock gate I caught a quick glimpse of the policeman's face peering out of his small, grimy window. Evidently it was too cold for him to come out and check my pass. A long walk through the dock brought me to the New Westminster City.

Pausing, I let my eye wander over her. She was big, fat, and ugly, but I had grown to love her. Just over 5,000 tons she was a typical steamer of her period. Right for'ard a raised fo'c'sle for the deck and engineroom ratings. Mid-ships, a four deck bridge accommodating the Captain and deck officers, navigating bridge, wheelhouse and wireless shack. Aft, engineers and catering staff, and boatdeck. On the stern, below deck accommodation for twelve military gunners. Total complement being eighty crewmembers. Apart from the military gunners, there were several MN gunners who had completed a DEMS (Defensively Equipped Merchant Ship) gunnery course, of whom I was one.

Prior to going on leave the ship's armament had been a 4.7pdr anti-submarine gun on the stern, a 7pdr anti- aircraft gun and two machine guns. I immediately noticed this had been strengthened by twin Oerlikon 20-mm cannons on the engineroom deck and two more on the Monkey Island immediately above the bridge. In addition, PA Rockets had been fitted either side of the wheelhouse, and concrete slabs bolted around the bridge superstructure. It didn't require an Einstein to figure out this was going to be a very dangerous voyage.

I had little contact with our soldiers apart from occasionally joining them for drills. It was said they joined the Maritime Regiment to

71

escape the 'Bull' of army life. Our lot was not so lucky for their NCO was a retired Marine Corporal, brought out of the Reserves. While it was impractical for him to actually parade them, he certainly kept them on the go with gunnery drills. The drills were dummy runs; we never fired the big gun. Our Marine Corporal was not happy about this, and felt we should experience the real thing. During the last voyage he had approached the Old Man requesting a practice shoot and, much to every one's surprise, the Captain agreed. The Commodore of the convoy was advised and flags flown indicating we were going to fire a practice shot. Action stations were sounded and the gunners rushed to their stations. There was a man either side of the breach, one for elevation the other distance. One opened the breach, another placed the shell and cordite in, a further gunner rammed shell and cordite home. On the shout, "Ready." The Corporal pulled the lanyard.

The effect was stupendous; there was an ear-splitting crack, a sheet of flame leapt from the barrel followed by a belch of choking, black, cordite smoke. Being so close to the explosion we did not appreciate the effect on the ship. It was as though the poor old girl had an almighty kick up the backside that sent shock waves through her iron vitals. Engineers swore the engines leapt out of their beds. Electric lights were broken and odd bits of crockery smashed. A film of dust rose in the accommodations. The Old Man was not best pleased and came storming down from the bridge. "Guns." He roared, "If you ever fire that bloody thing again I'll have it, and you, thrown overboard!" After he had gone our Marine turned to us with a seraphic smile on his old leathery face. "Now, me hearties, if a bloody great U-boat pops up you'll know what to expect." So saying, he gazed wistfully over the Ocean as if willing one to oblige.

I smiled at the memory as I went aboard. From the activity around me there was no room for lingering doubts. There would be no hula-hula girls this trip. It had to be an Arctic convoy. This would be my second voyage to North Russia. The first had been a pleasant trip in August, with no enemy action, and hardly prepared me for the horrors that would come. None of this remotely entered my head, I was seventeen years of age, an Apprentice Navigating Officer, fit, bursting with energy and, above all, doing a job I loved.

Stepping over a mass of ropes and wires, I entered an empty cabin. I was first back from leave. My fellow apprentices were a good bunch of guys, we had been together nearly two years. Vernon Edmunds was the senior with nearly four years sea time, and about to take the examination for 2nd Mate's Certificate. Norman Bartlett came from the Rhonda Valley, and was fervently Welsh, not easy to get along with. Now, the remaining apprentice was my kind of man. James MacGowan was a few months older than I. Tall, dark, and handsome; a lady-killer if ever there was one. It was fatal to go ashore with him!

Returning one evening after a dance in the Paragon Club we just managed to catch the last bus back. The only other passengers were two young ladies of undetermined age. Of course Mac. immediately started chatting them up. When they rose to get off Mac. nudged me," Come on Morris, were getting off here." I should have had more sense, but we all got off and went laughing and chatting down the blacked out street. Arriving at a doorway, they invited us in for a drink. Inside a gas lamp was lit revealing a dingy room. Mac. by this time was getting very intimate with one of the girls who kindly offered to show him her bedroom. Giving a huge wink he vanished up the stairs leaving a very embarrassed me with the other girl. With the absence of Mac. all my bravado vanished. As a distraction, I picked up a photograph of a soldier from the mantelpiece and asked who it was. "Oh, that's my husband. He's in the Eighth Army." "Right." I said, thanks for the drink - I'm off."

It was in the early hours of the morning and I walked for miles through deserted streets, in a strange district, before I found the docks. Later Mac. asked what was wrong last night. "Oh" I said nonchalantly, "I didn't fancy mine." "You're a silly sod, Morris. I lay it on the line for you and you go and bugger off!" Mac. would never have understood. He once took me home to meet his widowed Mother, a charming lady who doted on her only son. In her eyes he could do no wrong. I also saw the other side of Mac., the quiet, devoted son, completely hiding the rascal he really was.

I was first back from leave, and changed into working gear before making my way to the galley to scrounge a mug of coffee, which I was enjoying in the peace of an empty cabin, when there was a knock on the door and the Third Officer entered. Peter Kavanagh was twenty years of age, having just completed his apprenticeship and obtained a 2nd Mate's Certificate, as indicated by the brand new gold braid stripe on his arm. Settling himself comfortably on the settee he helped himself to a cigarette. "Have a good leave, young Mills?" I thought this a touch condescending - he was barely two years older than me - "Not too bad, Third." I replied. I sensed he was in strange territory, adjusting from apprentice to full officer status. After further small talk he stubbed his cigarette out, and rising, said in his best officer's voice, "Right, I've got a job for you. There's some Arctic clothing on the quay, roust out a couple of AB.'s and get it onboard." Springing to attention, I gave him a cracking salute. "Yes, Sir." Peter screwed up his face. "Alright - alright - don't be so bloody cheeky!" I knew we would get on a well.

The crew's accommodation was right forward in the forecastle. Sailors' and firemens' quarters separated by a common alleyway. The Bosun and Carpenter, being petty officers each had a minuscule cabin barely six by four feet, looking onto the open deck. Port side was a toilet and shower to serve twenty-four men. I knocked on the Bosun's door and received an unintelligible grunt, I entered. The Bosun, who I had previously served with, was crammed into a corner eating 'Burgoo'(Porridge) from a bowl. "Bosun, the 3rd Mate wants two AB.'s to get some stores aboard." Barely pausing from shovelling porridge into his mouth, he said in his rich Geordie accent, "Bugger the 3rd Mate." Adopting a cajoling tone, I said, "Awr, come on Bos', its Arctic clothing; warm under clothes, boots, socks, fur hats - the lot." The spoon became suspended in mid-air, a gleam of interest showed in his eyes. "Allreet, lad, tha ' better take Pooly and Lewis."

Entering the crew's quarters was like entering some medieval dungeon. Its dimensions were roughly nine feet at the broad end tapering to a point at the bow. Iron bunks lined the bulkheads and the only furniture was a wooden table and two bench seats. There were no lockers for clothes - assuming they had any - and any cases were pushed under the lower bunks. Loose articles of clothing were either hung on lines across the forecastle, or festooned around their bunks. A coal-burning bogey with a pipe chimney was the only source of heating. In the dim light the ashes crunched under foot as I entered. The stench was appalling, and here twelve men lived, ate, and slept, all for £24 a month.

The two AB.'s I had been sent to contact were strangers to me, having recently been sent by the Merchant Navy Pool. They had the reputation of being tough, degenerate characters. I shouted, "Are Pooly and Lewis here?" which brought forth a torrent of expected abuse. Having isolated my two, I said, "Bosun wants you topside to get some stores on board, ten minutes, pronto." "Bugger the Bosun." Snarled Pooly. Well, well, every one is showing their independence this morning, about time I had a go. "And bugger you too." I snarled back. "Be on deck in ten minutes or you're in deep trouble." And beat a hasty retreat before I came to any physical harm.

Joining the 3rd Mate on the quay, I reported the AB's would be out in ten minutes. "I suppose that means thirty minutes - if we are lucky - time for a smoke." Surprisingly, they both appeared shortly afterwards. Pooly was a big nasty individual, with the blotched face of a drunkard with bruising showing he had recently been in a fight. Every job he was given triggered a stream of obscenities and continual moaning. Mr Pooly, and I, were to cross swords before this voyage was over. Lewis was a little rat of a man who continually egged Pooly on to be insubordinate.

The stores were eventually got on board. We were astonished at the quantity, and quality. Woollen underclothes, leather jackets, kapok coats with helmet type hoods, knee length leather boots, and gloves. Distributing this gear to the crew was quite an experience. Feeling rather like Father Christmas, we entered the sailor's quarters. Were we received with gratitude? Were we hell! Nothing but complaints. "Here, Mate, these boots are too tight." Me, "Well you asked for eight's - what the hell do you expect me to do?" "Why are we only getting one pair of sea-boot socks?" and so on. This from a group of men who invariably drank their pay-off and then pawned their raincoats for a last drink before joining ship. I had watched these men come aboard inadequately dressed for winter in Hull - never mind the Arctic. I had the last laugh when I informed them all gear was to be returned in good order at the end of voyage. Cunning little Lewis, piped up, "What if it gets lost or pinched?" I shrugged my shoulders," Makes no odds to me Lewis, it's deducted from your wages."

Crossing the alleyway we entered the firemen's quarters. This was even more daunting than the sailors. The company always carried

Arab firemen, and although I had served nearly two years on the ship I had never been in there. It was the same proportions, as the sailors' yet somehow seemed darker, and more sinister. The same awful smells with a sickly, pungent aroma which I later came to know as Hashish. When we entered the whites of eyes glowed ghostly out of the dimness as they peered through clothing festooned round their bunks. In a corner I noticed a headless chicken lying on the deck, its blood streaking the deck. No doubt, part of their custom of preparing food.

We explained the purpose of our visit to the Headman. What followed was sheer farce. The first item we gave to the Donkeyman, which caused an uproar, as they demanded to know, "Why he get - I no get?" We tried explaining every one would get his share, to no avail. Item by item we went through this pantomime until the last item was issued. Gratefully, the 3rd Mate, and I, escaped into the clean, fresh air, which we drew deeply into our lungs to expel the noxious odours.

For the next few days I was engaged on normal deck duties, when I received a summons to report to the Captain, at once. "Oh, my God, what have I done now." I thought as I hurriedly made my self-decent. A sharp "Enter." Followed my knock. Captain Wm. Harris, was a small, stocky man, with a shock of red hair, and was commonly called, Ginger, behind his back. No one would ever dare to address him other than Sir, or Captain, for he had a flaming temper to go with his hair. He had spent his entire sea career in the service of Sir Wm. Reardon Smith, and was highly regarded. To me, he was the 'Old Man' and it came as a shock some years later to find he was then, in fact, forty years old.

The Master's day room, come office, was comfortably appointed. It was half panelled in oak, with three highly polished brass port-holes. In one corner a desk, opposite an ornate sideboard and wine cabinet. Easy chintz covered chairs faced an imitation fire-place. A door lead off to a bedroom with a double bed. Master's wives frequently sailed with their husbands in peacetime. Indeed, one of his sons had been born in that bed. Beyond the bedroom were bathroom and toilet. It all sounds grand, but it should be remembered that in peacetime, the Master was the company's representative and, apart from conducting business affairs, entertained prominent businessmen.

I was no stranger to the Captain's salubrious quarters, having been called before him on numerous occasions - too often in my opinion. Usually, to be told I was a useless article and should have joined the Army.

My very first visit to the 'Holy of Holiest' is still vividly burnt in my memory. The ship was in port and I was told the Captain wanted to see me. When I entered his cabin he was seated behind his desk going through some papers. He did not look up, or speak. Seated in an easy chair was his wife, busily knitting. Mrs Harris looked up and smiled a welcome. "I've sent for you young man to see how you are getting on." Taken aback, I replied, "Very well, thank you Mrs Harris." She nodded, "Did you go ashore much in New York?" "Yes, Ma'am." "Now tell me truthfully, did you do anything you shouldn't have done?" I was rapidly getting out of my depth and looked to the Captain for guidance, who studiously ignored me. "Oh, no, Ma'am." Thinking I had not followed her drift, she qualified the question. "You understand what I am saying, don't you? Have you been with any bad women while ashore?" Blushing frantically, I recoiled at the very thought and vehemently assured her I had never done such a thing." She appeared satisfied and I thought my ordeal was over. No such luck! Her next question nearly floored me. "Are you keeping your underwear clean and tidy?" Totally overcome with embarrassment, I could only manage a strangled, "Yes." "Good, now go down and bring it up for me to see." She was a lovely lady, and it gave me great pleasure to meet her again many years later.

Returning to Captain Harris. Again he was seated behind his desk studying some papers. "You sent for me, Sir." He grunted keeping me on tenterhooks as he continued to study the document; finally laying it down he looked up. A shiver of apprehension passed through me when I saw my name and realised it was my service record. "I see from your record you have done a D.E.M.S gunnery course." The tension flowed out of me. "Yes, Sir, I did a course on the 4.7pdr when we were last in Liverpool." Of course he knew that. "Hmm, I don't think we shall have much use for that where we are going. Bombers are more likely to be the problem.

I suppose you did notice we have extra 20-mm cannons fitted?" Up to this point I had been quite overcome at being spoken to as a human being. "Yes, Sir, first thing I noticed returning from leave." "Mm, well, I'm going to need more gunners so I'm sending you on a machine gun course at RAF Beverley. Stand by to be picked up 0700hrs tomorrow." He gave me another long look, then shook his head, as though doubting the wisdom of allowing me near any lethal weapon. "Dismissed." I floated out of his cabin on 'cloud nine.' Instead of getting an expected bollocking I was going on a gunnery course. Life was wonderful.

It was freezing cold at 0700hrs, when the RAF three-ton truck loomed out of the darkness. An aircraftman jumped down and consulted his clipboard. "You, Mills - right hop aboard." The truck was already full of budding gunners from other ships. We drove out of Hull, through the blacked-out countryside and eventually arrived at the RAF Airfield Beverley. We disembarked and were shown into a hanger where various weapons were laid out. An elderly Flight Sergeant who had been called out of the Reserve List, and didn't look too happy about it greeted us. No time was wasted and we soon got down to the mysteries of the Lewis, Hotchkiss, and Oerlikon guns, which we stripped down, reassembled, and then repeated the process. We learnt how to load, aim, and fire. Naturally, our efforts were not always successful and we would hear our Instructor softly ejaculating under his breath, "Oh, my Gawd - God help England - Bloody Hell - Roll on my Pension," and such other homilies whenever we made a mistake, which I have to admit was quite frequent! We had a spell in the Astrodome where we were instructed in aircraft recognition, and took turns in simulated firing at silhouettes flashing across the dome.

On the last day of the course we were taken out onto the airfield for the real thing. I had the impression our dear old sergeant was nervous.

"Now pay attention you men, the thing up front is called an aeroplane - " a cockney voice interrupted him, "I seed one of them fings last trip, Sarge', tried to drop a bloody bomb darn our funnel." "And what did you do?" enquired the sergeant. "I bloody well shit myself." "Ah." Said the sergeant sagely, "Very proper, lad, very proper. Now if we can get back to business. The thing up front is an aeroplane, the thing its towing is a drogue or, to you ignorant matloes, the target. Now if any one shoots the plane down they will bloody well have to pay for it." He got his titter of laughter for his well-worn joke. Of course, neither the plane nor target was in any danger whatsoever. We returned to our respective ships clutching certificates confirming we were qualified machine gunners? I think Hitler would have seen the joke!

Back on board we were preparing the ship for sailing which was fast approaching. It was then that I developed a nasty boil plumb in the centre of my right hand. It was extremely painful and near impossible to carry out my duties, so I went to see the Chief Officer who took a look and said, "Mm, that looks nasty, I'll speak to the Captain about it." Later I was given a note to see the Medical Officer at the Merchant Navy Pool, Hull. Already I was visualising the prospects of being found unfit for sea and missing a Russian Convoy. Perhaps, later, I would be given another ship going to exotic places. The thought warmed me and eased the pain in my throbbing hand.

The Federation Doctor was a small, elderly man who looked desperately tired. I was not to know that apart from dealing with lead-swinging merchant seamen, he had been up all night dealing with air raid victims, for Hull had been heavily bombed that night. Removing the bandage he picked up a scalpel. "Look at that wall, man." I felt a searing pain as the scalpel sliced the abscess, the room spun round a couple of times and it was all over. While he bandaged the hand I asked innocently, "I suppose this means I'm unfit for sea?" "Of course not, man. Three days light duties." He snapped.

Leaving the Federation office I made for the nearest pub and ordered a whisky. "Sorry, mate, only beer." Nodding wearily, I unconsciously placed my bandaged hand on the bar. The wound was already staining it crimson. "Got caught in the air raid last night, did yer, mate?" enquired the barman. Lost for words, I merely nodded. "Ah, it was a reet bugger, weren't it." Giving me a conspiratorial wink, he beckoned me down to the far end of bar. Furtively reaching under, he slipped me a large whisky. "Just happened to have one left, mate." I assured him he was a Prince among men. The golden liquid fired its way through my body, easing the throbbing pain and lifting the depressed state of my mind.

Chief Officer Fowler looked sourly at the Doctor's Certificate. "Light duties! Where the bloody hell do you think I'm going to find you light duties with the ship about to sail?" Sydney Fowler was a young Chief Officer, being only 26 years of age. He was not a man to stand on his dignity, being very approachable and friendly. It's all right, Sir, since the Doc. lanced it it's feeling much better. I'll carry on as usual." No doubt about it, that shot of whisky was working wonders. I saw a flicker of relief on the Mate's face. "Alright Mills, but you be bloody careful." Of course I could have stood on my rights and had a cushy three days, but then he would have made my life hell. I may have been young but I was not stupid!

Early the following morning the ice lorry arrived, and all hands were turned out to off load the large blocks of ice and store them in the ship's icebox. There was no refrigeration in tramp ships of that era. The ice was stored on shelves around the compartment, on which fresh meat and vegetables were stored. Salt beef, pork, and dried fish came aboard like sheets of hardboard. With any luck, the fresh provisions might last a week, after that it would be down to hardtack.

Pre war days, ships and companies were known amongst seafarers as good or bad feeders, and played a large part in the recruitment of crews. The ships were known by the logo on their funnels, for example, H. Hogarth & Co. had a large 'H' on their funnel and were known as Hungry Hogarth's. My own company, Reardon Smith & Co. had a prominent black 'S' and were referred to as Starvation Smiths. It was my experience that while the food might have been rough and ready - depending on the skill of the cook - there was always plenty of it and I never went short.

With stores aboard we guessed we would be leaving the following morning. At 0500hrs the door was thrown open admitting an icy blast of snow laden air. A pot of steaming coffee was banged onto the table and we were given a rough shake. "Wakey - Wakey - boat leaving stations 0530hrs." Grumbling, stumbling and swearing, we dragged ourselves out of warm bunks, and put on our sea going gear; thick woollens, sea jerseys, donkey jackets, sea boots, oilskins and so'westers. A quick mug of coffee while we smoked a cigarette and reflected on our future. No more leaves for a few months, goodbye families, wives and sweethearts - we are off to the frozen Arctic.

It was pitch dark and slushy snow lay over the deck. My station was on the stern where I found the 2nd Mate and some sailors engaged in desultory conversation, stamping their feet to keep warm while they waited for something to happen. Out of the darkness a tug slipped under our stern, in response to a shout we lowered a heaving line to which a stout towing rope was attached. A period of inactivity followed during which our eyes became accustomed to the night. Below we could just make out the figures of the tugboat men who, like us, were huddled into their oilskins sheltering from the squalls of snow. Now and then a shower of sparks would erupt from the tugs spindly funnel, casting a flickering light over the scene revealing the shore gang on the quay, patiently waiting to cast off the mooring ropes from the bollards.

There were no such things as cellular phones, or intercom, on tramp ships in those days; communication was by megaphone, whistle or siren. "Let go fo'ard - let go aft." Came the stentorian bellow from the bridge. Steam winches began to chatter as they took the strain off the ropes and the dockers immediately slipped the ropes off the bollards. Into reverse went the winches and slowly the heavy, water-laden ropes come inboard to be coiled in large loops on the deck. A spring wire now held the ship fore and aft. "Let go your aft spring". Slowly the stern moved away from the dockside. "Let go fo'ard." The tugs now had us under control easing us sedately down the dark shapes of moored vessels into the sea lock, where the whole process was repeated. Clear of the lock the tugs surrendered their hold; we felt the deck tremble under foot as the engines slowly turned the propeller in a rhythmic - trash - thrash - thrash. After many weeks of inertia in the dock, having to suffer the onslaught of dockers and workmen, the ship became a living creature with a beating heart. Steam coursed through her veins of pipes, and hot breath belched from her funnel. We were too busy to notice the outskirts of Hull fade into the semi-darkness. By the time we were knocked off for breakfast we were well down the river Humber heading for Spurn Head and the open sea.

CHAPTER 7
UNDERWAY

Pausing for a moment before going into the cabin, I leaned on the rail and took in the gloomy scene. The water surging down the ship's flanks was a dirty brown, flecked with oil and debris; the early morning mist rising from the river gave off a dank odour. The bow wave, just visible, washed along the riverbanks stirring up the mud and beyond, a bleak, flat landscape was just discernible. It was a depressing outlook and, as though in sympathy with my mood, my mind was transported back to a lovely, hot sunny day in August. I was on leave taking my girl boating on the River Ouse. I had hired a rowing boat from the boat yard near to the old Huntingdon Bridge,

With uniform jacket and cap nonchalantly thrown over the back seat - but not so nonchalantly as to hide the gilded crown and anchor badge - I pulled steadily up river leaving the town behind, to enter a pastoral world. Lush meadows lined the banks, with grazing cattle. Weeping willows spread their fronds over the river-creating cool, green, secret tunnels. The boat, slicing through the crystal clear water, disturbed the water plants that swayed in the river's current. Herons stood motionless on one leg in the shallows, one eye open for fish and the other on our passage. Families of Coots darted in and out of the reeds seeking insects. The air, filled with the sound of buzzing insects, shimmered in the heat. It was, in every sense, idyllic. A scenario set for lovers.

Alice, reclining on the cushions, head thrown back with gloriously wavy brown hair cascading over the back seat, was soaking up the sun. Placing her hands at the back of her head caused her light summer dress to rise well up her thighs, revealing her shapely legs encased in silk - a present from New York. The movement also thrust out her firm, full breasts. Her eyes were shut against the sun's glare, but I knew full well that she was aware I was closely studying her. Her coquetry was not lost on me, "Alice." "Yes, Morris." "You're a witch." "I know, Morris."

We had been sweethearts, and lovers, from the age of fourteen, and the relationship was getting serious. It was obvious Alice expected us to marry and it was not a question of if, but when. We had discussed and agreed marriage was not possible until I had completed training and been promoted, but still she kept pressing the issue. It disturbed me. Of course I loved, and desired her, but marriage was not in my plans at that stage.

Feeling the motion of the boat change, she raised her head and in a quizzical, teasing voice asked, "Why are you going into those trees?" "Ah, but that is another story!" Thinking back on that glorious day filled me with remorse that we had so recently parted on such bitter terms. What a bloody fool you can be sometimes I thought, as I dragged myself back to reality.

Breakfast over, it was back to clearing all the rubbish, dunnage and stokehole ashes that had accumulated during our long stay in port. In those days there was no such thing as Greenpeace, or Save our Oceans, the garbage was simply dumped into the North Sea. We joined a small coastal convoy bound for the Tyne to replenish our coalbunkers. We were designated Commodore ship, our only escort being a small Navy trawler. The New Westminster City, with all her weaponry, stood out like a battleship amongst the small coastal vessels.

About midday, having thrown all the gash overboard, we were coiling down ropes and generally tidying up when we heard a dull explosion. Looking up we saw a column of water rise out of the sea, followed by the jangle of action stations. Dropping everything I raced for my gun nest, ripped the canvas cover off, slammed a shell canister in, and cocked the gun. Barely ten seconds had elapsed. I spun round to face the enemy. Nothing! No screaming dive-bombers, no gunfire, just the small ships butting they're way through the seas. I doubt there was as much as a rifle on any ship.

It was a cold, peaceful scene. Below me on the bridge, the Captain and Chief Officer were chatting and I overheard, "Yes, Mate, I think it was just a tip and run raid. Best keep the gunners closed-up for a while." So I spent the next hour stamping my feet, and flapping my arms, trying to keep warm in a stiff North East gale.

The following day we entered the River Tyne and tied up under the coal tips at North Shields. This was a rickety, wooden structure that towered over the ship. Rail wagons shunted to the top and emptied their loads down shutes into our coalbunkers. It was a filthy, messy business and coal dust infiltrated into every nook and cranny of the ship. We breathed it, ate it and drank it. We did manage to escape it for a few hours with a run ashore. MacGowan, Bartlett and I decided to catch a train for Redcar, in peace time a popular holiday resort for Tynesider's. In war time, and mid-winter, it had lost all its charm and attraction. Everywhere windows were closed and shuttered. The promenade was closed off with barbed wire, and sentry boxes posted. The town had an air of being under siege. We tried to find a decent place to eat, without success. There was a Victory Restaurant where no doubt we could have got sausage and mash - if we had the necessary coupons. It was all so incredibly depressing. We had a quick pint and caught the next train back. Somehow, even the ship seemed more attractive after that run ashore.

We were raring to go, and the following morning we slipped down the Tyne and joined a North Bound Convoy through the Pentland Firth for Loch Ewe, arriving 2nd March 1942. There is not a lot to say about Loch Ewe, other than it was the main assembly point for convoys. This was my third visit and each time it had been in the dead of winter. I suppose in summer time it could be considered magnificent with mountains surrounding a vast stretch of water. I found it a grim business swinging on the anchor with nothing to do. Usually, a strong Nor'Easterly wind laden with snow would sweep down the mountains, creating a stramash of flying spume, and obliterating the ships at anchor.

On one rare occasion the wind dropped, and a sickly looking sun broke through. This was an opportunity for the Old Man to further our nautical education. Calling out the 3rd Officer, he ordered him to lower the Jolly boat and instruct us in the art of sailing. The whole episode was quite hilarious.

Procedure for lowering the boat is fairly simple, and we might have made a good job of it but for the baleful presence of the Captain observing from the bridge. We could clearly hear his sarcastic remarks two decks up. In lowering a boat it is important that both falls are lowered evenly otherwise there is a danger of tipping either end and throwing the occupants out. We very nearly achieved this distinction!

It is equally important to lower the boat steadily onto the water. In our case we allowed it to go with a rush and it hit the water with a resounding smack, evoking a groan of anguish from God on High. By this time we were so flustered we hardly knew what we were doing. We unshipped the oars and staggered away from the ship like a drunken beetle. Once clear of the ship we settled down and rowed, and sailed, like jolly jack tars.

We had an enjoyable time until mist laden fog swept down from the mountains and shrouded the ships from view. Taking a compass bearing we headed in the general direction of our ship, creeping past numerous vessels that loomed out of the enveloping mist like gigantic steel walls. It was a nerve gangling experience, quite impossible to distinguish one ship from another other than hailing, "What ship - Ahoy?" We were now seriously overdue and Peter, our 3rd Mate, was becoming agitated. He could visualise the Captain putting out an SOS and the pandemonium that would cause; therefore, it came as a surprise when we eventually came alongside a dark, and silent, New Westminster City. The lookout answered our hail and thankfully we mounted the Jacob's ladder, raised and secured the boat on its chocks, before retiring. Captain Harris was absent, and we heard no more about the incident.

On the 10th March we weighed anchor and slowly left the Loch to join a convoy to Iceland. This would be my third visit. I was not impressed by the place, and thought it grim and forbidding. Strange to think that today people pay large sums of money to holiday there. The Icelanders considered us to be foreign occupiers, which, of course, we were, and we were shunned wherever we went. This time we did not go to Reykjavik but anchored in Hvalford while Convoy PQ13 assembled.

The fjord was a vast anchorage surrounded by snow covered mountains. Isolated buildings were scattered along the lower regions. The air was like champagne, it was a joy to leave a stuffy, smoke filled cabin and fill one's lungs with pure, cold, invigorating air. Sound reverberated around the fjord and echoed stereophonically around the mountains. Conversations on distant ships were carried over the water compelling one to eavesdrop. By this medium, several ships arranged a fishing contest, the winner being the one who caught the most fish. With the greatest ingenuity, fishing tackle was manufactured out of the most unlikely objects and soon the whole crew was dangling a line - of some sort - over the side. The fish, mainly cod, were hell bent on giving themselves up. I have no idea who won, or what the prize was, but we greatly enjoyed ourselves. As a bonus, we enjoyed delicious fresh cod on the menu for several days.

CHAPTER 8
CONVOY PQ13

We sailed 0645 hrs 18th March 1942 and were well out to sea with the coast line just visible when two days later, off North Cape, we noticed a lot of activity from the escort. Destroyers were dashing through the convoy with Aldis lamps frantically winking away. Something is up we thought. The Commodore ship hauled up a line of pennants, and after referring to the signal book found we were to reverse course and return to Reykjavik, and anchor. This was not only astonishing but also very worrying. To reverse a whole convoy and send it back was a portent of something very serious and nasty ahead.

There was much speculation about this unexpected manoeuvre. Some suggested it was an exercise to test the co-ordination of the merchant ships. Others thought the German Battleship, Tirpitz, was about to attack. One wit suggested the Commodore had forgotten his 'Baccy'and we were going back to fetch it. The truth, unknown to us, was the Admiralty had intelligence that a Line of U-boats were waiting for us off the Norwegian coast. Our naval forces stationed in Murmansk were ordered, together with our Russian Allies, to try and disperse them, or at the very least make them keep their heads down. I guess any escort commander would have known this was a forlorn hope, but orders are orders.

After 48hrs at anchor off Reykjavik Convoy PQ13 weighed anchors and was truly on its way to meet its destiny. The convoy consisted of nineteen ships sailing in six short columns, at seven & half knots - a walking pace! Close escort was two destroyers, two minesweepers and two whalers.

The whalers proved more of a handicap when they ran out of fuel and had to be towed.

Distant escort comprised a battleship, cruisers and a host of destroyers. Their purpose to protect us if the Tirpitz left its Norwegian lair to attack us. Of course, we never saw them. What a welcome sight they would have been when we were fighting off the bombers. No doubt, their Lordships of the Admiralty considered these units of the Fleet too valuable to risk in close contact with the convoy. Many years later some Naval Historians seriously put forward the theory that the Admiralty deliberately trailed this weakly defended convoy across Hitler's Norwegian doorstep as bait, hoping the Tirpitz would be tempted out and our battleships could engage, and sink her. If this was the plan - and it sounds feasible to me - then it badly misfired. Tirpitz did not take up the challenge. PQ13 was savagely mauled and the Navy lost a brand new cruiser, with two destroyers damaged.

On the 23rd March HMS Trinidad and her two escorting destroyers joined us, and slowly steamed through the convoy. At ten thousand tons she towered over the merchantmen, and a glow of pride and confidence spread through the ships as we surveyed her six-inch guns, and batteries of anti-aircraft guns. The unspoken thought passed through all our minds -'We'll be alright now. 'Having shown herself the water boiled under her stern as she sped off to patrol on the outskirts. A seven-knot convoy was no place for a thirty-knot cruiser to dally.

The convoy steadily ploughed on into mounting seas, with the temperature dropping dramatically by the hour. Shipboard routine was well underway, with four hourly watches on and watch off. On the third day, Vernon coming off watch casually mentioned, "It's arrived." No explanation was necessary, we knew that harbinger of evil, a long range German reconnaissance plane was circling the convoy reporting our every movement. They always circled just out of gun range. On one occasion a destroyer signalled the plane, "You're making me dizzy, would you mind going round the other way." Which the German pilot immediately obliged proving he had a sense of humour.

On the 23rd March, to avoid dangerous areas, the course was altered to latitude 0.5 west with instructions to keep as far to the

Northeast as ice conditions would permit. With the close proximity of the Polar Ice the temperature dropped as low as 40F below freezing. It became a constant battle clearing ice and snow off the deck and superstructure. Mast stays assumed gigantic proportions as ice encased them six to eight inches thick, and they had to be attacked with sledge hammers to free them of ice. The ship, itself, was grinding through pack ice with a growling, cracking noise.

In these conditions, a small drama occurred in our cabin. Situated on the main deck, aft of the bridge, access to the wheelhouse was gained by passing our door and ascending two flights of ladders. It was the lookout man's duty when coming off watch to make a pot of coffee, and wake the next man on duty. AB Pooly, the obnoxious character I had rousted from his bunk in Hull, took to coming into our cabin and helping himself to coffee and cigarettes, before going to his quarters in the fo'c'sle. Apart from the fact we could not stand his foul mouth, and bullying attitude, we were trainee officers and not allowed to socialise with the crew.

Several times I had asked Vernon, our senior, to tell Pooly to keep out, to no avail. I suspect he had no desire to tangle with the guy, so the next time Pooly came in I said, "Pooly, you're not allowed in this cabin - bugger off." He froze in the act of reaching for the coffee-pot; his face mottled with rage came within inches of mine. "And who bloody well says so." He snarled. "I do, Mate." For a few seconds his tiny brain wrestled with the problem. "Oh! I suppose that means your fucking well going to report me to the Old Man?"

"No need Pooly, we'll sort this out on deck." A smile of anticipation lit up his bloated face. "Christ! Mate, that suits me fine. Come on."

I was almost eighteen years old, six foot three and around thirteen stone. What was more to the point I had been a boxing fan all my young life, and had been a regular member of an amateur boxing club. I had boxed in a number of amateur contests and, because of my physique, was always matched against older, and more experienced opponents. I occasionally took punishment, but generally I won.

Of course, Pooly knew none of this, he just saw me as an over-grown kid - easy meat! Before going on deck I took my jacket off for easier movement. Pooly couldn't be bothered to take off his oilskin; he came at me like a windmill, arms flaying wildly. It was just too easy, I took a step back and hit him with a crashing right to his jaw, down he went as though pole-axed into the scuppers. He lay for several seconds unconscious until an incoming sea washed over and revived him. Dragging himself up right he wiped a trickle of blood away from his mouth, his glazed eyes focused on me, then, "Ah! Fuck you mate." And he staggered off to his quarters. I was not to know he would be dead in two weeks, or that I would never box again.

Standing on the open deck with no jacket or gloves in temperatures as low as 40F below freezing was madness, yet the adrenalin from the encounter flowed through me producing a warm glow. When I re-entered the cabin I expected some congratulation from Vernon, after all I had really done his job for him, but it was not to be, massaging my bruised hand, I said, "I don't think Pooly will bother us again, Vernon." Barely looking up from his book he merely said, "That's good." We had been shipmates for a long time but I never really fathomed him. With nearly four years sea service he could have been a great help with my studies, but he never showed any interest.

March 25th, the weather deteriorated rapidly and a ferocious gale blew up from the Northeast, roaring down from the North Pole. This was no ordinary gale, this was the mother and father of all gales. The deeply laden ships pitched and rolled in the mountainous seas, and would sink into the valleys of enormous waves with just their topmasts visible. Then the tortuous climb to the next wave pinnacle revealing their salt encrusted, scarified hulls with racing propellers before falling with a shuddering crash into the next trough. Thunderous seas poured over and down the decks finding their way into ventilators and cabins. To open a door at the wrong moment was to invite a flooded cabin. Eighteen-inch weatherboards barely kept out the torrents of water washing down the decks. Consequently, we lived with several inches of water swilling around the cabin. We wore our main clothes and sea boots all the time but inevitably some article would fall, or be thrown by the violent motion, into the wet stinking mess. There were no means of drying anything; you simpy put them on again.

Bedding became sodden through getting into bunks with wet clothing. The heat of our bodies reacted with the freezing cold to form a mist that floated round the cabin like a poltergeist. Every thing was covered in a green slime, what little food we had in our locker turned rotten - even the cockroaches hid themselves in the depths of the piping. Regular hot meals were out of the question; we existed on coffee and sandwiches. Even this had to be brought from the galley and was a death-defying act. One waited until the ship gained some sort of equilibrium and then made a mad dash across the deck. With any luck you might make it without getting soaked. The difficult part was returning with a can of coffee and sandwiches in one hand and still keeping a hold on the lifeline.

I observed an Arab fireman returning from the galley laden with mess kits for the fo'c'sle, he had left the shelter of the bridge and was half way along the deck when the ship buried her head into an enormous wave. The Arab fireman hesitated, undecided which way to go - back or forward - if he had made a dash for it he might have made it. Too late, the ship lifted her head throwing tons of water over the deck and he was engulfed in a tidal wave. My God! We all gasped, he's gone. When the water subsided there he was hanging onto the lifeline, willing hands dragged him into the fo'c'sle but the real tragedy was their evening meal was gone. There would be no food for the firemen until the next meal.

The noise of the wind was indescribable; howling and screaming like a banshee. The air laden with flying spume froze as it struck the ship turning it into a white, ghostly, spectre labouring through this hellish frozen world. Watchkeepers and gunners rapidly became ice-sculptured silhouettes, moving lethargically. The warm air they breathed out immediately froze into tiny icicles around the slits of their headgear. Eyelids were constantly brushed to stop them freezing together; hairs in the nostrils became icicles that pierced the nose when rubbed. Only later, after thawing out one felt the pain.

Bartlett came off watch at 0700 hrs and gave me a shake. "I've got some coffee, Boyo, but the galleys out of order - no breakfast." With a groan I swung my legs over the bunk. The cabin was going crazy; various articles of clothing were sloshing about in several inches of water. The bulkheads gleamed with a sheen of ice and our breath pumped out in bursts of steam. In a corner, Bartlet's oilskin, which he had taken off, stood like some frozen, headless man. In an adjoining bunk, Mac's body slid backwards and forwards with the violent motion of the ship, totally oblivious to the mad, gyrating world he inhabited, he slept the sleep of the dead.

It was impossible to sit at the table so we jammed ourselves into a corner of our bunks, drank our coffee and ate some dry biscuits. Bartlett, totally exhausted, rolled into his bunk fully clothed and was instantly asleep. I was already half clothed and finished dressing by putting on a fleece lined leather jacket wound a towel round my neck to absorb some of the water. Next a duffel coat and oilskins, woollen gloves under leather gloves, and finally a leather type helmet with slits for eyes and mouth. I was now your true Michelin man, ready for the elements.

Outside, the fury of the storm made me gasp for breath as I struggled to close the cabin door. The sea swirled about my legs as I leapt for the bridge ladder. Reporting myself to the duty officer I climbed into my raised gun nest. From this position the scene was terrifying. In the half-light horizon and sea blended into a maelstrom of boiling seas barely visible through raging snowstorms. The screaming wind from the North Pole tore the tops of forty to fifty foot waves filling the air with flying spray that hit one like frozen bullets. It was awesome to see the ship drive into, and under, these gigantic waves then, slowly, agonisingly, shuddering like a trapped animal, struggle to lift her head from under the colossal weight of water. Huge seas cascaded over her fo'c'sle and poured down the length of the ship. At times I really thought we had been overwhelmed and were sinking.

We were no longer fighting Germans but King Neptune himself. That usually benign figure sitting on his throne with smiling features and flowing locks, trident held high had been transformed into a raging monster. Face contorted with rage, eyes flashing sheets of lightning, crown encrusted with ice and trident held at the charge, he roared down on us from his icy kingdom determined to erase us from his realm. Fancy thinking you may say! But in my gun pit I was already beginning to freeze to death.

Fortunately, the Captain quickly realised there was no point in keeping the gunners in their exposed positions. There was not the remotest possibility of the Germans attacking; they would be suffering as badly as we were. Barely recovered it was soon my turn to take the wheel. The helmsman gave me the compass bearing, which I repeated and he gratefully disappeared below. Steering a ship these days must be an easy job. On modern vessels there is a small wheel - scarcely larger than a car wheel - in many cases a joystick is used, instructions are conveyed electronically to the rudder. Not so on the New Westminster City. The wheel was made of solid oak with brass inlaid, and was some four feet wide. The steering mechanism consisted of rods, chains and links that ran the whole length of the ship. It was a hard physical job at the best of times, in these conditions it was a nightmare.

Taking the wheel felt like grasping the heart of a wild beast fighting for its life. Eight thousand tons of ship and cargo rising and falling like a lift with a shuddering crash into each trough. Colossal pressure of wind and water forcing her onto her beam ends, submerging deck rails. That terrifying moment when her head swings off compass bearing and you fight to bring her back on course, then the struggle to stop her swinging to far back. "Will she stop." You ask yourself, "Please stop - stop you bastard."

The wheel house door slid open letting in a blast of icy air with swirling snow. Captain Harris, gripping the binnacle to steady himself stared intently at the compass card with its spinning needle. In the semi-darkness the binnacle light illuminated his red, raw face. The tarnished gilt of his peak cap showed under his oilskins. "Good, God! Mills, carn't ee do better than that?" Desperately spinning the wheel to check another swing, I snapped, "No, Sir." There was a stillness in the wheelhouse that transcended the storm, I awaited the explosion. It never came, with a muffled grunt he left me to carry on.

Shortly after, the sliding hatch connecting chartroom to wheel house slid open and the 2nd Mate said, "For Christ sake, Mills, keep her head Nor-East, your playing buggery with my navigation." Thoroughly exhausted, I snarled under my breath, "Go to bloody hell!" Snap went the hatch behind my head. When I was relieved I went into the chartroom for a chat with the 2nd Officer, who I found grimly holding onto his chart table while trying to retain a grip of his instruments. Looking up he said, "I suppose you know the convoy has been scattered by this bloody gale. We're all on our own now." I realised that in the period I had been on the bridge I had not seen another ship but that was not unusual in the weather conditions prevailing. "Christ! 2nd, things are looking bad." "Aye, lad, but it will get a bloody sight worse when this gale moderates - we'll be easy picking for the U-boats." Breaking off the conversation he slid the hatch to wheelhouse back. "Come on man." He shouted at the helmsman, "Keep her Nor-East, you're playing buggery with my navigation." Slamming the hatch shut, he turned and gave me a broad wink.

The gale continued with undiminished ferocity throughout the 25th and 26th March. It was a horrendous experience; continually soaked to the skin, frozen to the marrow, half starved from lack of hot food, physically exhausted from the sheer effort of trying to stay upright. We were reaching the limits of physical endurance when the gale moderated on the 27th March. The number of distress calls intercepted on the wireless tempered our relief. Harpalion bombed 1438hrs. - Empire Ranger bombed 1438hrs. - Empire Ranger sinking. Am abandoning. 1818hrs. - Induna torpedoed on fire and sinking - Cheerio. - Signal intercepted from unknown ship. S.S.S.S. torpedoed and sinking. - Mana. Submarine attack 0844hrs.

It was grim news as we waited our turn to be blown into oblivion. We had no doubt our expected demise would be spectacular for we were carrying tanks, shells and ammunition. At 1450hrs. on 29th March we sighted a large submarine on the surface about five-miles distant, and altered course to starboard. Visibility was poor with frequent snow flurries, and we thought we had evaded him. At 1615hrs he again appeared three miles on our stern. There was no point in attempting to man, and fire, our 4.7pdr gun as it was frozen solid, as no doubt was the German's gun. Course was altered to port and zigzag carried out. Again we lost him in the snow flurries. It was a nerve-racking time and undoubtedly he could easily have sunk us. The only logical explanation being he had used up all his torpedoes.

Later that day we met up with HMS Eclipse and two other merchant ships. From the destroyer we learnt three heavy German destroyers, each with five-inch guns, were fast approaching to attack and could be expected any time. Now was the time to start praying. Shortly after, two small destroyers escorting four merchant ships joined us. We were now a small convoy of six ships and three escorts. The odds against us were ludicrous; our escort each had one 4 inch gun while the enemy had a combined armament of twelve 5 inch guns. By the laws of averages they were capable of blowing all of us out of the water.

When the alarm gongs sounded I raced to my gun pit. Of course I realised that apart from the gun being frozen, it would be useless in a naval battle, but I guessed I had to be somewhere. From my high position I had a clear view of our small convoy rising and falling in a moderate sea. The sky was overcast and there were frequent snow squalls. Efforts to keep warm by flapping arms and stamping feet were arrested by the sound of heavy gunfire. A dull glow occasionally lit up the horizon. We knew we were sailing into a naval battle but at that young stage of my life I had no conception of fear. I was sailing into battle and from my elevated position had a panoramic view. The Captain and Chief Officer paced the bridge in deep conversation. This was 'Boy's Own stuff' straight out of an adventure book.

Then, hull down on the horizon were the silhouettes of three German destroyers as they raced out of a snow squall. There were gun flashes followed by the rumbling whine of shells as they passed overhead to explode harmlessly in the sea. The last German ship had already been badly hit and was on fire astern. Within seconds they vanished into another bank of snow. It was like a dream sequence, we could hardly believe what we had seen. If this is war then it wasn't too bad.

The reality of the situation became apparent some thirty minutes later when emerging from a snow storm we came upon the cruiser HMS Trinidad, lying dead in the water with a huge hole in her side from which smoke and flames poured. There was great consternation as we viewed the stricken ship. How was it possible the smaller German ships had beaten this powerful ship? Only later did we learn that by a million to one chance, she had torpedoed herself. Apparently, one of her own torpedoes had malfunctioned - possibly a frozen gyro - had run wild in a circle striking the ship. Slowly we steamed past the stricken cruiser with her attendant destroyers to ward off any U-boats. I was filled with excitement as I viewed this spectacle, what a story I would have to tell when I got back home.

Oh, yes, I knew men had been killed and wounded, but death and dying were ever intangible, ephemeral subjects to the young. Impossible to imagine that would ever happen to me. So, I may be excused my unthinking excitement, all too soon I would be experiencing the stark horror of the scene I was witnessing.

We left the Trinidad in what appeared to be a sinking condition, heeled over, shrouded in smoke and flames she looked a doomed ship. In fact, the crew managed to contain the fires and get the engines started and she made Murmansk before we arrived. With the absence of the cruiser and her attendant destroyers we felt naked and undefended. Especially as we were approaching the most dangerous part of the voyage - the Kola Inlet. A line of U-boats lay across our path and German bombers were barely fifty flying miles away. Here was our most vulnerable point.

Later, two Russian destroyers, the Gremyashchi and Sokrushitelny, reinforced us. Fleet Minesweepers Gossamer, Harrier and Speedwell, also joined us and began circling the convoy dropping depth charges to keep down submarines. The morning was fairly quiet - that is, until I fired a rocket. How did I manage such a stupid thing? - Easy! PA rockets were fitted both sides of the wheelhouse and was fired by a lanyard looped from the top of the wheelhouse. These rockets were intended to be fired at dive bombers, the theory being the rocket shot skyward trailing a metal cable which brought down the bomber (Hollow laugh). Now, I am normally six foot three tall but the addition of the head visor and so'wester added inches to my height, and somehow my headgear snagged the firing lanyard with devastating results. There was almighty 'Bang', a sheet of fiery sparks, and I found myself lying in a corner of the bridge hearing the scream of metal cable as it left the drum on its way to the heavens.

Gunners on other ships, half frozen, nerves stretched to breaking point, searched the sky for bombers. Here and there, was spasmodic gunfire at imaginary planes then, like a storm passing all was quiet. The enormity of what I had done struck me like a blow - at the very least this had to be a hanging job! I became aware of Captain Harris standing over me, his expression changing from rage to utter dejection, as though to say, "What have I done to deserve this?" Turning, he entered the chartroom without a word, and there it rested.

March 30, we were approaching the mouth of the Kola Inlet. Already, we could smell Mother Russia, the pungent odour of forests, sawn timber, and that indefinable earthy, mustiness.

Today, the evocative music of Sibelius's Finlandia can vividly bring the memories and sensations flooding back as though it was yesterday.

With the voyage nearly over the Germans mounted a final air attack on the convoy before it entered the Kola Inlet. The sea was moderate with low patchy cloud. Their tactics were different to previous attacks when they had swept in low over sea level. This time they remained above cloud level diving through the breaks. "Concentrate on the holes in the cloud." Shouted the Mate. Over on the starboard side I saw the S.S.Tobruk being attacked. She put up a fierce defence, and even claimed a bomber shot down. Then it was our turn as a JU 88 dived through the cloud straight for us. Every gun on the ship opened up with a roar. Here was my moment of glory; I was eyeball to eyeball with a German bomber. The bloody thing filled my gun sight; I could see its cannons rippling along its wings. I saw the bomb leave the plane, wobble then straighten up. To this very day I bitterly regret not having hit the bloody thing. I should have done. What satisfaction it would have given me. Of course, I forgot every thing the Gunnery Instructor at RAF Beverley had tried to teach me. I started firing when it was hopelessly out of range; I aimed at the bomber instead of just in front of it. Even worse, as the plane flashed overhead I followed it round still depressing the trigger with the result a stream of tracers flashed over the bridge.

I still have a vivid picture of the Captain and Chief Officer's back-sides scuttling into the wheelhouse! Such was the excitement I completely forgot about the bomb, which must have exploded in the sea. The Captain who was literally dancing with rage brought me back to earth. In the most violent language possible he swore that if the bloody Germans didn't kill me - he bloody well would. Fortunately, for me, another attack developed and he had more pressing matters to attend to. When we later appraised the action, I realised I had not exactly covered myself in glory.

However, common sense prevailed, after all, I only had a few days training at the start of the voyage, and none of the military gunners had done any better so perhaps I was being unduly critical of my self. But what a moment to have cherished if I had hit it!

CHAPTER 9
MURMANSK

Entering the broad Kola Inlet the ship slowed down to pick up the pilot, a squat figure bundled into a ragged naval type coat, a fur hat with long flaps that almost hid his Mongolian features. He bustled up to the bridge and wedged himself into a corner. There were no civilities; his English was limited to starboard and port. Oh, yes, one other word, "Paparosi." (Cigarette) A carton of cigarettes already placed on the wheelhouse sill was duly passed over. The fact he could speak no English in no way worried Captain Harris, who had traded in these waters many times. He needed no pilot but was compelled by law to carry one. When we arrived at Murmansk the Captain took the pilot below and filled him up with whisky. That was the extent of their socialising

The ship secured to a rough wooden quay. There were no brass bands, no cheering crowds or flag waving. The shore gang resembling bundles of old rags sullenly took our ropes and wires to the bollards avoiding eye contact. It was as though we didn't exist. Were they aware we had been through hell to bring them these vital war supplies? Who could say? This was a country that only told its citizens what the State and KGB wanted them to know.

No sooner were we tied up than a squad of armed soldiers came aboard and stationed themselves around the ship. We could not fail to notice the two sentries posted on the gangway. God! What a welcome - what a country. The view ashore was equally depressing. Murmansk lies along the Eastern Shore of the Inlet and is ringed by snow covered hills. Murmansk was possibly the most severely bombed town in WW2. The German airfields were barely fifteen minutes flying time away in Finland, and they regularly made several raids a day.

They would come swooping over the hills dropping down to water level; sweeping across the large expanse of the Inlet criss-crossed with shells and tracers before dropping their bombs and lifting up and away over the hills.

The town, itself, was a shambles. The wooden structure of so many buildings and almost all the quays rendered large areas of the town only too susceptible to incendiary attack. Owing to the unreliability of cement in Arctic conditions, many larger buildings were in a terrible state; some simply collapsed from the shock of near misses. The Northern end of the town appeared to have been completely demolished, of the remainder, approximately one third were unfit for habitation. Not a single building had glass, their windows being boarded up. A heavy pall of smoke continually hung over the town. I was surprised to see a windowless shop with an appetising display of hams, sausages and fish - all made of wood. Psychologically, I failed to understand how that display helped the starving population's morale! Crude war posters depicting the gallant Red Army soldiers were everywhere, while martial music blared out of a speaker attached to buildings and suspended from poles. The only entertainment for the visiting sailors was the International Sailors Club; here one could get a meal - of sorts - an occasional film and dance. They were strictly organised by the Russians who provided English speaking hostesses. We were strongly advised the hostesses were probably KGB Agents and to be guarded in our conversation.

Working conditions on board ship were atrocious. It was winter and the sun never rose above the horizon, there was a brief period of twilight midday but this was often obscured by snow blizzards. Artificial light was necessary to work the cargo in the holds, but this was kept to a minimum for fear of constant air raids. Machinery had to be constantly watched and warmed through with steam pipes to prevent it freezing. Gloves could only be removed for short spells so the simplest task such as screwing a shackle bolt into a cargo sling, or passing a wire strop assumed Herculean proportions.

We were berthed at No 11, Commercial Quay, which was timber floored with a single rail track on which ran a small crane. Its lifting capacity was totally inadequate for off loading our tanks and we had to organise a jury system with our derricks. It was a very antiquated and unsafe method, but we just had to improvise. There was a large warehouse directly opposite the ship that was already full, so our cargo was landed on the quay where it was quickly buried in snow. Further up the quay was an air raid shelter. Berthed immediately in front of us was the Empire Starlight.

Each morning we witnessed the pathetic sight of manacled prison labour - mostly women - being marched down to unload the ship. They were grossly inefficient and had little idea of cargo work. For some strange reason they insisted their labour drove the winches. This had severe and unfortunate consequences. They had no idea of taking the strain gradually and simple opened the throttle wide when the top man indicated lift. Crack would go the wire whipping viciously across the deck. Their stupidity greatly annoyed us, especially as we had to repair and replace broken wires. Things came to a head when a heavy lift failed to clear the hatch combing and fell on the deck, striking our ship's carpenter who happened to be passing, breaking his leg. Captain Harris flew into a terrible rage and had a violent row with the Head Stevedore, threatening to stop all cargo work unless his sailors drove the winches. In the meantime, an ambulance was called and poor old 'Chippy' was taken to hospital. The date, 3rd April 1942. A very significant date for me.

We commiserated over the fate of our carpenter. Poor old sod." Said one AB. "Bugger'd if I'd like to be in a Russian hospital." Another said, "I wonder if we can go and see him tomorrow?" The grim reality was that most of us would be in that hospital that very night, but in no condition to visit 'Chippy'.

We had off loaded cargo from main holds and started on the ammunition and shells in lower holds. Living conditions on board were harsh. It was bitterly cold with intermittent snow blizzards and semi-darkness. The ship's machinery was working at full pressure to maintain steam for the winches. There never seemed to be any heat in our small radiator, and with the door being constantly opened and shut there was as much snow and slush inside as outside. Food was very basic and getting less every day. Obviously,

101

the Chief Steward was conserving supplies. Normally, when a ship arrives at a foreign port stores are replenished. Here, in North Russia, that was out of the question. The people themselves were starving. Russian workers would gather round the galley door in the hope of scrounging a morsel of food. They would quickly, and brutally, be dispersed by their own soldiers with rifle butts and kicks. Our crew were incensed by this and attempted to intercede only to be threatened in a similar manner, and so learnt not to interfere. Some of the women managed to escape the scrutiny of the soldiers and entered the fo'c'sle where they sold themselves for a crust of bread. To be caught would have led to the most severe penalty - possibly being shot. As for our crew, how they could consort with these haggard, filthy women defied my imagination!

Unloading continued at a slow and erratic pace, mainly due to constant air raids. There was an air raid shelter on the quayside and when the sirens sounded shore labour and crews would make a mad dash for it. However, as we had as many as eight to ten raids a day this exercise began to pall and we became fatalistic and took our chances where we were.

Having finished work on the evening of 3rd April, I decided to have a run ashore to break the monotony. I changed into uniform knowing the only thing Russians respected was a uniform backed up by lots of official passes. On the subject of passes, we had already been exasperated by the need to produce a pass simply to go onto the quay to check our own mooring ropes. Finally, our patience ran out and we got the Chief Steward to concoct a set of official looking passes from ship's papers, such as; store lists, weather reports, wine lists, Marconi wireless pads, etc. These were heavily endorsed with ship's stamp, date stamps, receipt stamps and others I can't remember. These we would present to the gangway sentries who would carefully examine them from every angle, nodding in a knowledgeably fashion they would say, "Korosho." (Good) and let us pass. They must have thought we were a happy lot always laughing. I doubt if they understood Russian never mind English!

Going ashore on my own was a different matter, so I made sure I had my Seaman's Discharge Book and Identity Card with me. I was well aware of the propensity of the Police and military to stop one and demand Identity papers. I had decided to go to the International Club but couldn't find it and after wandering around rubble-strewn streets I had enough of the delights of Murmansk, and returned to the ship. The cabin was empty. I would have enjoyed some company but guessed the others were probably in other cabins yarning. I toyed with the idea of seeking them out but it had been a hard physical day, I had a boring run ashore, so decided to turn in early and catch up on my sleep. It was a fateful decision, although who can say what may have happened had I been elsewhere? It had been a quiet night without any air raids. The rumble of cargo being worked in the bowels of the ship sent tremors through the vessel. It was strangely soothing and I was soon fast asleep.

At 2100hrs a bomber evading detection dived on the New Westminster City and four bombs struck the ship igniting her into a blazing inferno. Over thirty Russians working in the holds were killed, as were several crewmembers and two Army gunners. The bomb that struck the bridge penetrated three decks before going through my cabin and exploding in the hold. The detonation of a five hundred pound bomb within feet of one's self beggars description. A column of flame blasted through the accommodation, followed by a colossal roaring sound as the cabin disintegrated. The opposite bulkhead ripped apart like tissue paper revealing, for a split second, the horrified face of the Radio Officer. I was hurled into a corner and showered with burning debris.

The conflagration of flames, the hideous sounds of metal being torn apart, mixed with the cries and screams of the wounded drove me to a mad desperation. Frantically I tore myself free of burning wreckage and hurled myself through a jagged hole where once the door had been. Out on the open deck, I ran blindly for several yards before collapsing in an alleyway. All around me the bridge was a blazing inferno and I could feel my skin scorching. I was quite rational and knew I had to get somewhere safer, so pulled myself upright only to fall down. "This is bloody stupid." I thought, what's wrong with me? Then I saw my left foot had been smashed to a bloody pulp and was only connected to my leg by strips of sinew, the white bone protruding at the bottom. Then the waves of agony raged through me in torrents. I may have screamed in my torment, if so it was a silent scream for I heard nothing. I was terrified the foot was going to drop off and sat cradling the bloody object in my hands, the hot blood pumping out through my fingers.

The Captain found me in this condition, at first he had difficulty in recognising me, wiping the blood from my face he exclaimed, "Good God! It's Mills, he's in a bad way, if we don't get him ashore he'll bleed to death." The problem was the bomb blasts had blown the ship several feet off the quayside destroying the gangway. "Quick men, get a heaving line round him and we'll lower him over the side." Several figures on the quay were warned to receive a wounded man. Barely conscious, I was lowered over the ship's side down to quay level, but tantalisingly, several feet away from out stretched hands. There I spun like a top, my world a crazy kaleidoscope of burning, exploding ship, glimpses of a dark void lit by flashes of gun fire like some gigantic fire work display. Below the freezing water deceptively coloured a molten gold from the blazing fires.

I don't believe in hell, but if there is such a place then I have truly been there!

Below a group of people was trying to reach me, without success. Only thing to do was to swing me like a pendulum. Back and forth I swayed like a bloody sack on the end of the rope with the grotesque remains of my foot flopping uselessly. Every now and then striking the glowing sides of the ship until I had gained sufficient momentum to be caught. I was landed on the quay with a thud, has my helpers were untying the rope the next wave of bombers swept in. I had the impression of a large black shadow roaring down the quay spitting fire. The cannon shells rippled down the quay in flashing explosions, sending lethal shards of timber flying through the air. All around, Russians were going down like ninepins as they dived for shelter. I was left a helpless witness to this carnage, and saw the plane at the end of its run bomb the Empire Starlight, which immediately burst into flames.

In a strange, hallucinatory sense, the scene unfolded like a slow motion picture which has replayed its self in my mind ever since. In actuality, it was all over in seconds.

Pandemonium reigned as the Russians attempted to deal with a multitude of tasks, fighting fires, collecting wounded and removing bodies. It seemed an age before I received attention. I was half

104

carried and dragged into a nearby warehouse; inside the lurid light of burning ships piercing the cracks and holes in the decrepit old wooden building broke the darkness. A group of women workers were huddled in a corner crying and wailing. When I was brought in some of them came over and tried to comfort me, wiping blood away from my face, and speaking soothingly has they restrained me in my agony. I have a vague memory of being carried out and placed in a truck - then nothing.

When I regained consciousness I was in a white washed room, lying on an operating table. White coated figures bustled about removing the burnt and tattered remains of my clothing, and washing me. With the return of consciousness, waves of pain flooded my body. Attempts to rise were roughly resisted. I became aware of a blue uniformed figure standing by my side, who I later learnt was a Russian Merchant Navy Officer. He was gripping my hand very hard; his face inches from my own. "You very bad." He said in broken English. "Me very sorry." Shaking his head, "Foot bad - must cut." He made a chopping motion with his hand. "Me very sorry." His round Slav face full of genuine sympathy. "You lose much blood - I give you blood - me very sorry." He kept repeating 'Me very sorry.' As though he was personally responsible for my condition. "You have gas - feel better - me very sorry." His face vanished and an ether mask was clamped firmly on my face.

Up to this stage I had received no morphine or any other painkillers, there just weren't any. I knew they were putting me under and welcomed it as a relief to my suffering. I sucked deeply at the ether until I could no longer breath. I was suffocating. They were trying to kill me and I fought desperately to tear the mask off. It seemed an army of people was weighing me down intent on choking me to death, and then, oblivion.

Coming to the following morning was a surrealist experience. I appeared to be in a large room with many beds crammed together. Figures were moving rapidly to and fro, occasionally bobbing as though in obeisance to some higher deity. Faces would float into view and mouth silent questions. There appeared to be a cloud floating in the sky, and the bed was trembling. It was as though some silent pantomime was being performed for my amusement. Bemused I lapsed into unconsciousness.

I was, in fact, in the Assembly Hall of a school that had been turned into a hospital. Several air raids had taken place, and bombs had fallen near to the hospital causing the medical staff to involuntarily duck. My cloud was dust and plaster descending from the ceiling and walls, and the silent fantasy induced by temporary deafness due to my proximity to the bomb the previous day.

Returning to the real world later in the day my first reaction was one of searing pain. I knew I had lost a foot even before I saw the stump. I tried to take in my surroundings. It was a large hall containing some sixty beds, inches apart, occupied by merchant navy survivors from various convoys. Painfully turning my head I was startled to see Captain Harris sitting by my bed. He was a pathetic figure; always small in stature he now appeared to have shrunk into his dishevelled uniform, his florid features now ghastly pale. Head bowed he sat staring at the floor. Was it any wonder, ship sunk, crew killed and mutilated. I tried to speak but no words would come from my battered and lacerated lips, and I lapsed into unconsciousness. He had gone by the time I regained consciousness. The following weeks were a nightmare. Gradually I became aware of my situation. Pain, misery, and the realisation I had been crippled overwhelmed me. All around were cries and groans of the wounded. The foul stench of suppurating wounds, and the stinking, sickly smell of amputated frostbitten limbs bore down on one's senses. The constant barrage of anti-aircraft guns, the thunderous explosions of bombs that rocked the building, washed over me leaving me with an earnest desire that one would quickly dispatch me from this place of torment.

Murmansk was barely thirty miles from the battlefront, and on one occasion the Germans made a push that brought them within fifteen miles of the town. The sound of battle was clearly heard and casualities poured into the hospital, which was already filled to capacity. Wounded lay on stretchers in the corridors, hallways, and eventually rough shelters were erected in the hospital grounds - and this in sub zero temperature. There were no medicines, painkillers, or bandages. I recall a soldier who had been bayoneted several days ago and had received no medical treatment. Stripped in the dressing room, he had an evil sack of puss hanging from his stomach wound. The woman Army Doctor ordered him to stand to attention, then taking up a surgical knife slit the stomach releasing the stinking puss to run down his leg. The man swayed, but pulled himself together when the doctor snarled at him. A rough dressing was applied and he was dismissed. I was to see many such incidents, and marvelled at the Russians ability to stoically withstand pain.

Not only were the Russians without medical equipment and drugs, they were also on the verge of starvation. Our food was just sufficient to sustain life. The main meal was a thin, watery soup resembling pigswill - though perhaps not so nourishing! - A thick slice of rock hard black bread accompanied it. It was always cold by the time we received it.

Very occasionally one might find a morsel of meat or fish floating in it. There were many arguments as to the origin of the meat - horse - dog - cat - even rat. Whatever, we hungrily devoured it. This led to an ugly incident between a Liverpool scouser and myself. Several Arab firemen from my ship occupied beds nearby, and the first time we had meat, the scouser knowing Arabs were Mohammed's, and would not touch pork, shouted over, "Ali, that's pork - pass it over." Which they did with alacrity. This was treated as a joke but when it happened a second time I really lost my temper, "Ali, you listen to me - you know me - all the same ship -not pork - good meat you eat." Then to the scouser, "Listen, Mate, you try that again and I'll bloody well crawl out of this bed and bash your fucking stupid head in!" Such was the ferocity of my tone I had no further trouble with him.

Thereafter, my Arabs refused to be parted from me, and throughout our travels in North Russia were constantly with me. Whenever I was being moved from A to B, I would hear their frantic cries, "Where you go? I come with you." Such were their entreaties the Russians automatically moved us as a party. So it was for well over six months until we eventually arrived back in Scotland.

Before being wounded, I had a poor opinion of the Russians. They were generally ill clad, dirty, brutal, suspicious, and anti-British. Gradually, I came to view them in a different light. They had little enough reason to like us. True, we had risked life and limb, and suffered the most appalling hardship to bring them vital war material but compared to their gigantic war effort, shocking casualities, and daily suffering, it was little enough. As to their suspicious nature, they had not forgotten that in 1918 we had sent an Army to fight the Bolsheviks - hardly a friendly act!

Doctors and nurses with non-existent medical supplies did their best. Of course there were times when nerves snapped and tempers flared. One such incident occurred when I was taken down to the dressing room (torture chamber) to have my stump dressing changed. The smashed foot had been taken off by guillotine amputation, that is to say, sawn off several inches above the ankle. Visualise, if you will, a leg of lamb lying in a butcher's window, except my stump bore no resemblance to a nice juicy piece of meat, it was a suppurating mass of puss. The Russians had no cotton bandages or stump pads, but used a stiff paper like material. This had to be daily taken off and changed. Bits of the material would be left adhering to the stump that had to be swabbed and picked off. It was a ghastly experience. The most hellish torture devised! There were no anaesthetics or painkillers, one simply lay there and tried not to scream too much. It normally took three nurses to change the dressing, one to hold you down, one to hold the stump in a vice like grip, and the other nurse to swab and pick away at the stump.

On this occasion the nurse poked a particularly sensitive nerve causing the stump to give a violent, and involuntary jerk, catching the underside of the trolley with an almighty crash, sending the instruments flying all round the room. The Army Doctor in attendance came rushing over in a terrible rage, fumbling under his white coat he withdrew an enormous service pistol pointing with a trembling hand straight between my eyes, screaming a torrent of abuse. I tried to shut my eyes to blot out the spectre of having my brains blown out, but could not dragged my hypnotic gaze away from the trembling finger curled round the trigger. Insanely, I wondered if I would see the bullet before it hit me.

Then, regaining some semblance of control he stormed out of the room. The nurses, who had been cowering in the corners of the room collected the various instruments and, patting me on the head, said, "Nichivo." (It's all right) The dressing was finished off without any further disturbance. I had no sensation at all - I was petrified with fear!

The following morning the same doctor did ward rounds, my heart stopped beating when he paused at my bed. Pointing dramatically at me he said, "This one, 'John Bull' Uchin Ploka (Very Bad)" then burst into a roar of laughter, passing, much to my relief down the ward. Thereafter, he was most kind and considerate to me, which proved his conscience must have troubled him.

There were precious few moments of humour, it was unremitting pain, fear, cold and hunger. The nights made hideous by numerous air raids on the docks and town. The wailing sirens would send shafts of fear into the pits of our stomachs; the one thing we never suffered from was constipation! Above the thunder of anti-aircraft guns we could distinguish the Stuka dive-bomber with their special screaming device to strike terror into the populace. Above droned JU 88's dropping five hundred pound bombs. The hospital, a large white building standing on the hillside seemed to be their main target. God, alone knows why it took them so long to hit it! One night, eight bombs fell within a two hundred-yard radius of the hospital. Inside bedlam reigned. Iron beds shook and rattled both from the explosions and patients shaking in sheer terror. Cries and screams rent the air as some men lost control of their senses. Some fell out of their beds in a futile effort to hide underneath. Clouds of smoke and dust rolled through the wards as the building rocked and swayed, as though in an earthquake. Large statues of Lenin, Stalin and other Bolshevik heroes placed in alcoves around the ward rocked and swayed alarmingly, as though intent on crashing down on the capitalistic swine below them.

During these air raids the medical staff would disappear, and shouts and screams from terrified patients went unanswered. One night a Polish seaman with terrible stomach wounds fell out of bed and lay writhing in agony on the floor, his life blood spreading an obscene stain.

No one was able to get out of bed to assist him. We shouted, screamed, bang objects on the floor, to no avail. He took an incredibly long time to die, ranting and raving as his lifeblood flowed away. Those nearest to him, overcome by the trauma of the tragedy, shouted obscenities at him. "For Christ sake shut up you Polish bastard. Why the fucking hell don't you die and get it over?" It was mindless, unthinking, born out of a deep fear they were witnessing their own fate. Bad enough contemplating one's own death without watching the nauseating spectacle being played out in slow motion before your eyes. In the morning the nurses came and took the body away without fuss or question. He might never have existed.

The nurses on the whole were a nondescript bunch; mostly they were of small stature with thick round bodies.Their features mainly Slavic, Mongolian, even Chinese. Some were just plain ugly others positively repulsive. Apart from the interpreters one rarely saw an attractive woman. Initially, they appeared afraid to make any social contact with us, no doubt fearful of the ever oppresive prescence of the Political Commissar. Nevertheless, the British Tar is an incurable optimist and no way was he going to let Political Commissars, or restriction to bed, limit his amorous inclinations. He was bent on having his fun with the nurses - or should I say at their expense! So we started to learn a few words of Russian such as, "Ya Lluba Vos." (I love you) "Eta krasseva." (You are beautiful) and I've forgotten what "Would you like to come to bed with me?" was. It was hard going at first as we called out these endearments and watched their stony expressions, but gradually we forged a link in their Soviet armoury - after all they were only human At first they tried to hide their smiles, then came laughter and no doubt uncomplimentary repostes which , perhaps fortunately, we did not understand and to emphasise their point they would give us a friendly dig - well more like a punch! These antics helped to relieve the constant tension of boredom and fear.

Later, as the nurses relaxed they would, if unobserved, sit and chat with us and our Russian rapidly improved. Two nurses stand out vividly in my memory, Bolshoi Vera (Big) and Malenki Vera (Small). Bolshoi Vera was built like a Japanese Sumo Wrestler, strong as a horse with features to match. She had a boisterous manner, always laughing and shouting she appeared to be in awe of no one. When it was time to have dressings changed, Bolshoi Vera would come thundering down the ward and with one easy sweep lift you bodily - there was no need for a trolley. On the rare occasions they change the bed sheets Bolshoi Vera would simple pick you up while the sheets were changed. This was not done gently and the helpless patient would shout and curse her, and she in turn would laugh and shout back. It could have been quite hilarious had it not been so painful.

Malenki Vera was entirely different, small, petite, and rather pretty. By nature she was shy and reserved. Always had a smile and

110

handled her patients with care. She stood out as a shining star amongst the other nurses. One morning, after a particularly heavy air raid, Malenki Vera reported for duty, it was obvious something was wrong for her normal, pleasant face, was haggard and tear stained. We asked the nurses what was wrong and were deeply saddened to learn her home had received a direct hit, and both her parents killed. It was a miracle she had escaped unscathed. Such was the indoctrination of Soviet propaganda to duty, and Joe Stalin, that despite the horror she had been through, and the grief of losing her parents, she had reported for duty. We could only marvel at her fortitude and courage. But then, she was a creature of the overpowering, insidious, all pervading propaganda of the Communist State. One had to live in Russia at that time to understand how Stalin had narcotised his people into mindless robots. Every minute of every day, blaring martial music and patriotic speeches poured out of the radio, tannoys placed in works, on street corners, in shops and offices. Enormous pictures of the Great Leader peered down from every conceivable vantage point.

The following days saw the steady arrival of survivors from other ships sunk in Convoy PQ13. The Induna, Empire Ranger, Raceland and Bateau. They had spent days cast adrift in the Arctic Ocean. Some landed on desolate coasts seeking shelter from the freezing conditions, hoping and praying to be rescued. All were terribly frostbitten and their relief at eventually arriving in hospital was tragically shattered on learning that in order to save their lives limbs would have to be amputated. - not that many were in any condition to comprehend their fate.

Today, more than half a century on, the nauseating stink of hundreds of bodies lying crammed within inches of each other with gangrenous limbs; suppurating wounds, filthy dressings that were too infrequently changed. Patients defecating and urinating in their beds because there were insufficient nurses to cope, or losing control their bodily functions during the terrifying air raids - I can still hear the pathetic cry, "Sudna Pajalasta. (Bed pan - please)" - that seemed never to come! That horribly foul, stomach churning stench, hung thick and stagnant in the confines of the ward, from which all clean air had been excluded by the boarded-up windows. That putrid odour pervades my senses as I write.

Nothing I can say will adequately describe our appalling conditions, but, an Official Report from the Senior Royal Navy Surgeon, North Russia to the Admiralty, dated 23rd July 1942, of which I quote a brief extract, does give a medical view of what we had to endure: -

ROYAL NAVY SURGEON'S REPORT TO ADMIRALTY

"This hospital is a converted school and stands on a hill dominating the town; its vast white walls make it an obvious landmark. This presumably accounts for the fact that in two days, June 12-13th, the hospital had sticks of bombs within 200 yards on three sides of it. No visible Red Crosses were shown on the roof. There are about three hundred beds. The Administrative Services and Departments are on the ground floor. The Russian wards are on the first floor and in what was the school hall on the second floor are housed the PQ and QP survivors. 99% of the window space was boarded up and therefore fresh air was non existent. Incidentally I had great difficulty persuading the authorities to remove various pictures and busts of noted Bolsheviks and weighing upwards of 10 cwt from the walls. These swayed about in a most alarming manner during air raids and in themselves were capable of proving lethal weapons.

No words of mine can describe the deplorable conditions under which the patients were treated. "Bloody awful," in its literal sense, is the nearest I can get to it. The cots were placed together in twos, with an eighteen-inch gap between each pair. There were no smoking restrictions, not even among the staff. If a patient wanted to open his bowels during a mealtime, then he did so, without screens around the bed. Should epidemic disease occur under these conditions it would have been impossible to control it. The sixty patients in this hall were indiscriminately mixed both regard to race, rank and disease. Poles, Americans, Hindu, Portuguese and English with diseases as variant as pneumonia, clean compound fractures (at least so on admittance), fractured spines, with amputations following frostbite.

Dressings are usually done on the ground floor out of the ward. Here incontinence and bed sores, malaria and about 15 cases of gangrenous extremities, conditions vaguely simulating a dungeon, where no screams could be heard, major dressings such as those involving the packing of shoulder joints with reapplication of plaster of Paris would be conducted without anaesthesia. Young cabin boys, of whom I saw three aged 14, 16 and 16 respectively, with arms or legs missing and with unhealed stumps were subjected to this medieval medicine."

It was tragic to observe these emaciated patients, with no hope of cure under these conditions subject to an average of eight air raids a day including three severe air raids during which the building literally rocked. Naturally they were terror-stricken to such an extent that the absence of arms and legs proved no hindrance to their diving under their beds, as a result they often as not injured themselves and would have to have their wounds redressed.

The operating theatre contained two tables and two benches and here, following the arrival of a convoy, or air raid the wounded were operated on en masse. I saw following one blitz, cases of compound fracture of the spine, shrapnel wounds to the abdomen with evisceration and a lacerated wound involving the elbow joint and a compound fracture of the lower end of the humerus, all operated on at the same time from a communal table of instruments.

I have already made mention of the food but at Murmansk especially its poorness in quality and unappetising way in which it was served defy all description. Where it not for the illicit traffic of food into the hospital by friends from ships in the harbour, supplemented by intermittent supply from official British sources, the patients diet would have been a starvation one.

This Report goes into great detail but I think this extract paints a frightening picture of what we had to endure, and makes my blood cold reliving it.

All around agony, misery and despair, and it was in this slough of utter despondency that I noticed a Royal Navy seaman advancing down the ward looking closely at each patient, he was muffled up in a greatcoat and yet something about him was vaguely familiar. Was I dreaming? He looked just like my Uncle Jim! Recognising me, he rushed over and we emotionally embraced. I had last seen my Uncle in August 1940 when my ship was in Surrey Commercial Dock, London. I had managed a weekend leave and had stayed with him and my Aunt Eileen in their Finsbury Park flat.

My Aunt Eileen, in 1940, was a most attractive woman in her late twenties. She was a theatrical performer with a fine singing voice. I idolised her and considered her a star and celebrity. Of course she was not quite that, but I thought so, especially when she took me back stage to see her perform at the Finsbury Empire. It was my first taste of the glamour of the theatre. Standing there in the wings, in uniform, with all those gorgeous chorus girls with heavy make-up and minuscule costumes, pushing past me to make their entrance made me feel very sophisticated. Centre stage, in a spotlight, my Aunt in a shimmering dress singing beautifully. It was a memorable moment. Later, she joined ENSA and entertained the troops.

My Aunt and Uncle were two diametrically opposite personalities. Eileen, effervescent, self confident with more than a touch of swank, as if to say, "Look at me - I know I'm the tops." Excellent qualities in someone making a career in 'Show Biz'. Her bad points were she was dominating, had a quick temper, and was inordinately possessive of her husband and possessions. Her flat was a temple to art nouvelle, a place she could bring her friends round for a drink after a show. God help, Jim if he replaced an object in the wrong position, or in anyway disturbed her arrangements. I know I felt uncomfortable the few hours I stayed!

My Uncle was quite the opposite. Quiet and serious, a pin striped city gent. Every morning off he would go with his rolled unbrella to perform whatever mysteries he did in the city. Now, as though by a miracle, he was transformed into a Jack Tar, bell bottoms, round cap pushed back on his head and a silly grin on his face, greeting me in a Russian hospital. I was dumbfounded. When I had collected my wits I asked him what he was doing in the Navy? He was in his early thirties and in no danger of being called up. "Well, Morris, I felt so useless going to the office, I just thought I should be doing more for the war effort - so I volunteered." It was not said boastfully, but with a quiet conviction that there was no other course of action opened to him. He told me he was serving on the Fleet destroyer Somalia and had just arrived with the latest convoy, and was at anchor. "I'm sorry I can only stay a few minutes, Morris, we're on standby to sail. I'll try and see your Mum and Dad and put their minds at ease. Keep your chin up old lad." So saying, he gave me some bars of chocolate, a big hug, and was gone. Seeing him go nearly brought me to the point of a complete breakdown. I wanted to shout after him, "For God's sake, don't leave me here - take me with you!"

How he managed to get ashore and find me I shall never know. I suspect he broke (left) ship unofficially. I also never knew whether he managed to contact my parents because some time later I learnt HMS Somalia had been torpedoed, and although badly damaged there was a possibility of saving the ship. The Captain called for volunteers to stand by the ship in an effort to save it. Once more my Uncle volunteered and was lost when the ship was overcome by heavy seas and sank taking the volunteers with it.

It was a heroic act on my Uncle's part - although he would never have seen it as such - there was no need for him to have stayed with the ship, he could have gone onto the rescue ship with a clear conscience. He was a 'Hostilities Only' seaman, middle aged and married, but for some men the concept of duty transcends all other considerations.

It had been wonderful to have seen him - however briefly - but his visit had stirred powerful emotions. There was the pleasure and joy of talking about the family and home, creating the illusion he had just popped in to see me from there, and equally, I would be going home soon.

This wild and irrational thought soon evaporated. It was as though a rope of rescue had been thrown and was now slipping out of my grasp, I was falling deeper, and deeper, into a morass of despondency. Slowly my head was sinking below the mud!

It took several days to drag myself out of this black mood of depression. Then, to our intense joy we received a visit from a Naval Officer, who told us we would shortly be going home. The excitement and anticipation was almost too much to bear. Came the great day, the 27th April, and we were carried out into ambulances - in reality, battered old Army trucks with a canvas top and open back - they managed about six patients to a truck. We had not gone far before a ferocious air raid occurred. The vehicles came to a shuddering halt; the drivers jumped out and made a mad dash for the nearest building leaving us totally defenceless in the middle of the street. From the back of the truck we had a panoramic view of the raid. The air was full of bursting shells and shrapnel scythed through the air with a vicious whistling sound. From our grand-stand view we saw buildings disintegrate in clouds of smoke and flames. One building received a near miss and, like a very old man, collapsed in on its self, leaving two Gothic pillars standing, revealing they were only stucco facing on wire. Strange how, even in a blind panic that image remains in my memory.

It was a miracle we survived that storm of shells and bombs, I can only liken it to being out in torrential rain and not getting wet. When the raid eased off, our drivers returned and looked into the back of the trucks, as though disbelieving we were still there. They must have gauged the depth of our feelings from the vitriolic manner we shouted and swore at them. Totally unabashed, and in typical Russian fashion, they merely shrugged their shoulders and said, "Nichivo (it's nothing). We had not gone much further when the next wave of bombers came in, again the ambulances screeched to a stop. This time, however, they did not desert us.

In a mad haste we were rushed into a large building and laid in every conceivable space, corridors, hallways and tops of tables. To this day I have no idea what type of building it was - hotel, office block or barracks. I suspect the latter because it was crammed with soldiers destined for the Murman Battle Front, then only twenty miles away. Our unexpected arrival caused them to bunch up to make room for our stretchers, this they did with good humour as they helped with the lifting. The building rocked and shook to the concussions of the bombs, dimmed lights flickered on and off. As we lay terrified, a Russian soldier came over and squatting down beside us, producing a balalaika, began singing haunting Russian songs, soon his comrades joined in. Before long, the mood changed as they broke out into rousing martial, marching songs, which they sang with such gusto they almost drowned out the dreadful din of battle. When it was time to leave my Russian placed the balalaika in my hands and said a few words, which I roughly translated as, "Good luck - this is a souvenir." I thanked him

The Author aged 25, an Official with the Merchant Navy Reserve Pool, Glasgow.

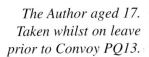

The Author aged 17. Taken whilst on leave prior to Convoy PQ13.

New Westminster City

An Ice Ship

Sir WILLIAM REARDON SMITH & SONS,

LIMITED.

TELEGRAMS: SMITHCRAFT, CARDIFF.
TELEPHONES: 5116 (4 LINES)

DIRECTORS
SIR W. REARDON-SMITH, BT. DOUGLAS SMITH.
A. J. POPHAM. W. G. LILEY. D. A. LOW.
W. R. REARDON-SMITH.

MERTHYR HOUSE
JAMES STREET
CARDIFF.

AND AT CREECHURCH HOUSE, LONDON. E.C.3.

DS.

10th April, 1942.
(Friday).

Detective Sergeant T.O. Mills
Police House,
St.Johns Street,
HUNTINGDON.

Dear Sir,

We regret to have to advise you that information
has been received here to the effect that the vessel on which
your Son was serving has been in action with the enemy. The
Admiralty Casualty Section today advise us that during this
action your Son was wounded with the result that he has had to
have his left foot amputated.

The Admiralty further states that he is recovering,
and therefore you can rest assured that he is receiving every
care and attention.

As soon as there is any further information, we shall
be pleased to pass same to you, although such information may be very
slow in coming through.

We have no doubt, however, that as soon as your Son is
fit to travel, arrangements will be made accordingly.

Yours faithfully,

Superintendents Dept.
(W.G.Liley).

Letter from New Westminster City's owners to the Author's Father

СПРАВКА

Дана _____
Тов. _____ г. _Миле Марис_____
       (военное звание)   (наименование войсковой части)
                                        (фамилия)
_____
   (имя)   (отчество)
в том, что означенный _был_ г. _Миле Марис._
                                    (фамилия и инициалы)
находился на излечении в _Ф. Г. № ._
                              (наименование медицинского учреждения)
с "_1_ _июля_" 194_2_ г. по "_5_ _августа_" 194_2_ г.
по поводу (писать по-русски) _Осн. диаг. сл. ранении_
                              подробный диагноз ранения(болезни травмы и т. д.)
2. Неактивная артерия след из отм
после ликвидации
ранение (заболевание, травма) связано, не связано (подчеркнуть) с пребыванием на фронте (при-
вести мотивировку) _____

_____

врачебней комиссией признан по ст. _____ гр. _____ расписания болезней приказа НКО
СССР № _____ 194 года _воспитание курсанти_
для приезда.

_____
_____

Место
для
печати
                          Начальник лечебного
                          учреждения _Л. Сем. У._
_5 бю 42 г._

Нач. слан. отд.
Л. Кокур. Лос.

The Author's Official Hospital Discharge,
Archangel, 5th October 1942.

Murmansk Docks

H.M.S. Edinburgh (Imperial War Museum)

H.M.S. Harrier taking off survivors from
H.M.S. Edinburgh (Imperial War Museum)

H.M.S. Edinburgh sinking (Imperial War Museum)

U.S.S. Tuscaloosa

Painting commissioned by the Author depicting
New Westminster City under air attack

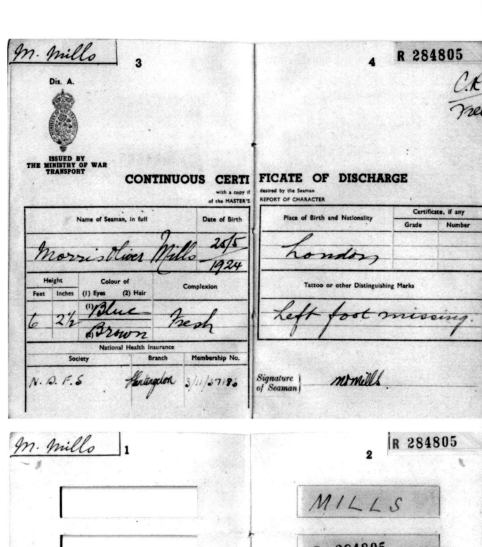
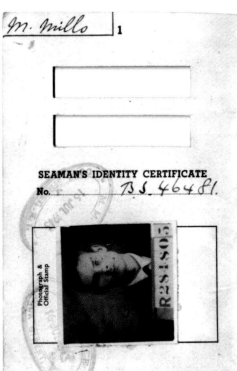

Author's seaman's papers.

Alice aged 16

*Alice in Wartime
A.T.S. uniform*

*The Author disharged MN 1943
and engaged to Alice.*

*New Westminster City salvaged and refitted as
cargo passenger vessel Dingle Bay. (J&M Clarkson)*

New Westminster City as built (J&M Clarkson)

Alconbury airbase post-war.

Post-War Murmansk.

*The Murmansk
hospital building
where the Author
spent many months*

The cemetery at Murmansk where many British Merchant Seamen lay buried.

Letter from Soviet Authorities

Medals awarded by the Soviets.

Model of the New Westminster City built by the Author

The Author with his family today.
L to R - Clive (son in law) Aileen and Avril, Robin (son in law)

CHAPTER 10
HMS EDINBURGH

We arrived at the dockside and boarded a Fleet Minesweeper, I think it was HMS Gossamer, and taken down river to Vaenga, where the cruiser HMS Edinburgh lay alongside the quay. I was in a bad way and cannot remember too much about it, but I had an impression of this magnificent 10,000-ton cruiser towering above me as I was carried on board. Here was the very pinnacle of British Naval power. Two 6" triple mounted gun turrets fore and aft, a mass of anti-aircraft guns, a Walrus aircraft amidships, and in excess of thirty knots speed at sea. The Russians had nothing like her and must have been impressed.

There were some thirty to forty badly injured patients from Murmansk hospital. The ship's hanger had been turned into a temporary hospital, and most survivors were accommodated there. The most severe cases were taken into the ship's hospital, a small area with six cots, and as I found myself there it is reasonable to presume I was in a bad way. My verminous clothing was taken off and after being washed I was put into a clean cot. Shortly afterwards, the ship's surgeon came down and said he wanted to have a look at my stump. He must have read the fear in my face for he said, "Its allright, lad, I'm going to give you a shot to kill the pain." This was another world to what I had so recently left, everywhere efficiency, cleanliness, order, good food and medicine. Above all, the wonderful, cheerful, esprit de corps of the Royal Navy.

The cruiser lay alongside the quay a few days. The Germans made several unsuccessful bombing attacks that were driven off by the barrage of anti-aircraft fire. Two decks down, the sound of battle was muted, and an air of quiet confidence reigned. One of the reasons for the ship's temporary stay was to load a large quantity of gold bullion, payment by the Russians to the Americans for war supplies delivered. Even at that early stage of the war, the Americans, having taken most of Great Britain's gold reserves, now demanded their pound of flesh from the Russians. Was it any wonder America ended the war richer, and more powerful, than she entered the war?

The gold estimated value £12,000,000 came on board in large wooden cases that were heavily stencilled with red paint. When the cases were dragged over the slushy snow they left streaky, blood red trails over the decks. This was a bad omen, and the sailors, ever superstitious, were not happy.

Convoy QP11 left the Kola Inlet on 28th April 1942 for the return voyage to the UK, and a few hours later HMS Edinburgh sailed from Vaenga to join it. Laying in my cot, warm, fed, and partially sedated, I felt the ship dip her head into the seas, and felt a wonderful sense of suffocating joy surge through my body, such as almost made me fight for breath. I was going home on one of the most powerful warships in the British Navy. In my mind's eye I could see that dark, evil, shore receding into the distance. The following morning, Rear-Admiral Sir Stuart Bonham-Carter KCB, CB, CVO, DSO, commanding 18th Cruiser Squadron, paid us a visit in the sick bay. A burly figure in a heavy naval coat without out any insignia of rank - apart from his gold braided cap. His Flag Lieutenant, Wilfred Parker, a very superior young officer destined to be knighted, and promoted a Vice Admiral, accompanied him. The Admiral was full of bonhomie and confidence as he spoke with each of us. Before leaving he made a short speech. "Well, lads, you know we are escorting Convoy QP11 back to England. I don't think our German friends are going to let us pass without a fight, so you must prepare yourselves for action, but never fear, you are in the hands of the Royal Navy and we'll get you back safely." Stirring words.

My only other recollections of the next two days were of a Merchant seaman suffering from frostbite. His condition deteriorated rapidly as the gangrene spread through his leg. The surgeon decided he had no other course but to amputate the leg. A screen was drawn around the table but from my position, second cot high, the surgeon and his assistants were clearly visible as they performed the operation. The sickbay was deathly quiet except for the clink of instruments and the subdued voices of the medical team. Then came the harsh rasp of the saw as the surgeon cut through the bone, invoking a visceral stabbing pain to shoot through my stump as I suffered with the patient. The blackened limb, resembling a fossilised piece of wood, was dropped into a container and quickly taken out - no doubt to be dropped over the side.

For some time afterwards, I lay staring at the white deckhead. Wild, irrational thoughts coursed through my head. I did not know the poor devil just operated on, I felt no pity, or emotion for him, quite the reverse. I almost hated him for being the means of demonstrating what I had so recently endured. The sight of the severed limb being taken away not only sickened me, but drove me into a frenzy of self-pity. The awful reality of my own physical condition struck me like a blow. From being a fit, healthy, eighteen-year-old, bursting with energy and full of the joys of life, I had been reduced to a helpless cripple. At that moment I did not care much whether I lived or died. Within hours I was to discover how strong the will to live could be.

High on the bridge of the cruiser, Admiral Bonham-Carter received intelligence reports indicating submarines were moving into position to attack; also three German destroyers had left their bases in Norway. German aircraft had already been sighted circling the convoy. This was no time for a fast cruiser to be idling in the centre of a convoy, and the Admiral ordered the cruiser to patrol some twenty miles ahead of the convoy. Tragically, and for reasons never fully understood, he left his two escorting destroyers with the convoy and adopted a steady zigzag course. This action must be questionable, especially as it was known U-boats were in the area. To make matters worse, it was stated the Asdic operator reported a U-boat contact, which the Admiral dismissed as being much too strong, and must be a nearby whale. This may be an apocryphal story emanating from the 'galley wireless but it has the essence of truth in it!

Kapitanleutnant Teichert of U-boat U456 must have been astonished at what he saw as he peered through his periscope. There, in a moderate sea, was the latest addition to the British Fleet, the cruiser HMS Edinburgh; steaming at a sedate twenty knots on a regular zigzag course, totally unescorted. Truly a gift from the Gods. Teichert's problem being he only had two torpedoes left and could not afford to miss - but then, how could he?

Four o'clock, 2nd May 1942, the Sick Berth rating had just brought us tea and sandwiches, and I was propped up sipping tea watching the ice flecked seas racing past a porthole, when there was an enormous explosion as a torpedo blasted its way into a seaman's mess two decks below the sickbay, killing all the occupants. Before our senses could comprehend what had happened a second torpedo struck the stern disabling the ship. The vessel seemed to leap out of the water before settling on its port side with a 17 to 20 degree list. Following the catastrophic explosions there was a split second's silence, the ship trembled like a wounded animal as the seas rushed into her gaping wounds, and then the all too familiar cries and screams of the wounded. Panic broke out in the sickbay as thick oily smoke reeking of cordite belched through the alleyways, filling our confined space. I felt sure I was about to die, but was terrified of dying like a rat caught in a metal box, sinking into the icy depths of the Arctic Ocean. Please, God if I am going to die let it be under the open sky.

In a blind panic, I desperately struggled to pull myself over the cot side in order to fall to the deck and crawl out of this death trap. I had almost made it when a sailor rushed in and hoisted me onto his shoulder, "It's allright mate - I've got you." With superhuman strength he battled his way over a tilting deck, through a milling crowd of seamen, up several iron ladders, and laid me on the open deck. He didn't wait to be thanked, even supposing I could have spoken any words through clattering teeth, but returned below to rescue others. A true, unsung hero. Owing to the violent manner necessary to get me from below, my various wounds had all burst open, yet again I could feel the hot blood pumping from my stump. I might have bled to death, but for the fact I was laying on an open deck clad only in a hospital night-shirt, in a snowstorm, and minus 20 degrees F. the blood was literally freezing in my veins.

The wounded, bodies blackened by the oily smoke they had emerged from, were being attended to as best as circumstances allowed. Propped, and laid, against obstructions to prevent their

120

rolling down the listing deck, and overboard. Surgeons, and sickbay attendants, were working miracles; here injecting morphine, there applying a tourniquet to a smashed limb. Apart from the involuntary groan of agony most of the injured suffered in silence.

There was a moderate sea running, but the water looked menacingly evil as it rolled down the ship's sides, lapping at the guard-rails that were almost underwater. Occasionally, a wave would break on deck like the finger of nemesis, anxiously beckoning us into its cold bosom. Laying in this semi-conscious state looking over the vast bleak expanse of ocean, I was barely capable of rational thought, and yet it came into my head only a few weeks had elapsed since I stood on the deck of my ship, the New Westminster City, wildly excited at the sight of the cruiser, HMS Trinidad, torpedoed, on fire, and apparently sinking. What a story I would have to tell when I got home. Now, after having my own ship sunk, losing a foot, and having endured days of continuous bombing, by a Machiavellian twist of fate, I was transported into an identical scenario. Imminent death was staring me in the face, I was not conscious of being afraid.

My body, and mind, were exhausted by the relentless punishment they had taken. The Naval Padre was going amongst the wounded offering what spiritual comfort he could. Kneeling beside me he said, "Would you like to say a prayer, son?" Dumbly, I shook my head. I had never been religious, what hypocrisy to start praying now death beckoned. The Arctic weather was rapidly freezing my thinly clad, tortured body, I felt no pain, even the spurting blood became bloody icicles. The vast ocean, the towering superstructure of the cruiser belching flames and smoke, the scream of escaping steam, the shouts and cries of crew about their various duties, all began to fade into a swirling, grey mist. I was dying and felt warm and contented.

The Gods, however, were not done with me. The Old Man with a scythe over his shoulder thought there were many more ways to make me suffer before he took that final swipe!

I came to in an officer's wardroom. It was packed shoulder to shoulder with wounded. I was wrapped in blankets and my wounds redressed. A seaman was trying to get me to take a hot drink. It seemed unnaturally quiet and the ship was almost on an even keel. "Come on, mate, try and get this hot drink down you - warm you up." I managed a few sips. "What's happening?" I asked weakly. "Well - - (he paused for a few seconds - no doubt weighing up how much to tell me) things are not too bad, old son. The Engineers have got the pumps working and Damage Control has patched up the holes, so we're near level now. (Another long pause) Problem is that last torpedo blew the bloody stern off and we have no rudder and only one undamaged propeller. At the moment the ship's going round in circles at 4 knots. You've got to laugh haven't you mate?" I knew he was not being funny! Even I, weak and help-less, flat on my back, could appreciate the terrible dilemma we were in. A disabled cruiser with little means of propulsion, crawling round at a snails pace in U-boat infested waters! Even worse, they did not have to find us; Kapitan Teicher who torpedoed us would have radioed our position to his comrades who would be rushing in for the kill like hungry wolves. It was too horrible to contem-plate. The wounded in my vicinity had been following this dialogue with horror. My sailor now rose and tried to reassure all. "Now, lads, don't you go worrying. We've got two fine destroyers, HMS Forester and Foresight racing to our assistance and they will be with us in a few hours. They are going to tow us back to Murmansk. Should take three or four days - so you see you've got nothing to worry about." Of course the rating was doing his best but we were not fooled. There was the matter of those few hours before the destroyers arrived, and again, how were two small destroyers going to tow a water logged, ten thousand-ton cruiser. Further more, it was out of the question that 'Jerry'would stand by while the Navy attempted this feat. No, the venture was doomed before it commenced.

Some time later, HMS Harrier and Gossamer joined us. These were Fleet Minesweepers and much smaller than destroyers being armed with a single 4 inch gun. For the next two days these small vessels endeavoured to tow this huge cruiser. The Herculean task was quite beyond them and towing wires constantly snapped as the Edinburgh, subject to wind and sea, took wild lunges. On the second day a Russian tug arrived on the scene but it quickly became apparent it was not powerful enough for the job. At this stage HMS Forester and Foresight appeared, it was decided Foresight would tow from ahead, while Foresight acted as a rudder astern, to keep the cruiser on a straight course. This manoeuvre appeared to be working and at last the ship was going ahead on a straight course at about four knots. We had 250 miles to go and at this speed it would take at least three days, assuming the seas remained moderate - which was most unlikely!

The ship's officers, when they could spare time from their arduous duties, were constantly assuring us things were going well and we would be back in Murmansk in a few days.

The mood of utter dejection had slightly lifted. Despite the galley being completely wrecked, the cooks - somehow - produced a constant supply of hot drinks, soup, sausage rolls and sandwiches. I had not touched food for two days and now realised I was hungry. We began to think that perhaps - just perhaps - we might make it.

This hope was cruelly dashed in the early hours of 2nd May, when the expected three heavy German destroyers, Z24, Z25 and the Herman Schoemann arrived and engaged the Edinburgh. The Forester and Foresight immediately cast off the tows and dashed ahead to give battle to the Germans. The Edinburgh fell off into a slow circling movement with her only undamaged gun turret blasting away at the enemy, hitting the Herman Schoemann and setting it on fire. The little Minesweepers also made straight for the enemy, their tiny guns spitting defiance. Such was their aggression the Germans mistook them for destroyers and retired behind a smoke screen. The Forester and Foresight had made contact with the Germans and, although they had done some damage, both had been hit by the superior weight of gunfire by the Germans and suffered severe damage. The Captain of the Foresight being one of many killed. It was a confused battle conducted in a series of dashes in, and out of snowstorms and smoke screens. Of course, we survivors witnessed none of this, we were confined below, but the thunder of guns, the screaming shells, and the detonation of penetrating shells, left nothing to our imagination.

At one stage of the battle the Germans fired a fan of torpedoes at the Edinburgh. They were clearly observed approaching by the bridge, several passing harmlessly by, one, however, was destined to strike the ship amidships on the starboard side directly opposite the previous torpedo strike. Captain Faulkner was helpless to take avoiding action, and with a violent explosion the torpedo tore a great hole in the ship's side. The Edinburgh heaved herself out of the water, and then rapidly listed over on her starboard beam.

We knew instinctively from the agonising sounds of tortured metal her back was broken, and she was done for. This was quickly confirmed by the order to abandon ship. The surviving passengers and wounded were brought out onto the open deck. It is near impossible to express the terrified horror we felt as we lay watching the sea climb up the ship's side. It seemed inevitable that at any moment this great ship would roll over, sweeping us to a watery death. The events leading up to this moment had clearly robbed me of my senses. My brain had stopped working - as though frozen - I looked around like a disinterested spectator. Clearly, this could not be happening to me!

With all hope of survival vanished, the cry went up that the Harrier was coming alongside to take off survivors. Hope eternal flared in our breasts, perhaps there was a chance we would yet escape? HMS Harrier, a Fleet Minesweeper of about 800 tons, looked like a toy ship as she skilfully came alongside the doomed cruiser. The task of getting several hundred men off the cruiser was horrendous. Obviously, the wounded were dealt with first, and were stretchered from one ship to the other. This was very difficult as the Harrier was rising and falling some ten feet in the seas, and timing was essential. Even so, several slipped off stretchers and crashed to the deck.

My stretcher had been placed some distance from the disembarking point, and watching the press of men trying to get off, I began to wonder if I would make it in time? At this stage a sailor settled down beside me and drawing a packet of cigarettes out lit two and gave me one. I thanked him through chattering teeth and inhaled deeply. We silently watched the desperate struggle to get the wounded onboard the Harrier, while several hundred seamen patiently waited their turn. Then, quietly, as though to himself, "Christ, mate, its going to take a bloody miracle to get that lot off before she goes down!" Taking a deep drag on his cigarette, "How you feeling, mate?" "Bloody cold." I replied through chattering teeth. He nodded. "Do you feel up to taking a chance?" He pointed to a projection overhanging the Edinburgh's side - it was either a piece of wreckage, or a torpedo tube - he had noticed that every time the Harrier rose on a swell it was level with her deck. "If I give you a bunk-up you could crawl across." The will to live flared through my body, and I nodded eagerly. Without hesitation, he picked me up and placed me on the projection. "Good luck, mate." I had no time to thank him as I started to inch my way across. The surface was rough and jagged and several times I struck my raw stump causing it to haemorrhage a fine spray of blood. There was no time to worry about that as I clung to the metal and looked down on the freezing sea. Willing hands grabbed me and I was rushed down to a small cabin and placed in a bunk. The ship's surgeon was called and he applied a tourniquet and gave me a shot of morphine before dashing off on another mission of mercy.

I had been placed in the Chief Petty Officer's cabin who, on his return, found his previously immaculate cabin reduced to a state of complete chaos, his bunk a blood stained mess with a miserable, shaking wretch occupying it. He could have been excused some sign of annoyance, or dismay, on the contrary, he was kindness, and consideration personified. I was shaking uncontrollably and he found extra blankets to wrap round me, saying, "You're in a bad way old chap, but you will be alright now. I know just the stuff to make you feel better." So saying he produced a bottle of neat Navy Rum, and poured out a generous glass full.

Raising myself, I was struggling to control my shaking hands while lifting the glass to my lips, when the ship's surgeon passed the open door. "What in God's name, Petty Officer, do you think you are doing? Don't you know this man as just had a serious haemorrhage - are you trying to kill him?" he roared, before racing off to the next emergency.

There followed what only can be described as a 'pregnant pause' neither of us saying anything and yet each reading the other's mind. Then, steadying my shaking hands he raised the glass to my lips saying gruffly, but kindly, "Well, lad, if we've got to die we may as well die happy." The golden liquid coursed through my body like rivers of fire, and burst into my lower regions in an explosion of luxurious warmth. The gut wrenching tension in my body oozed away, and the shaking subsided. I lay back and drifted off on a pink cloud. Who says ships' surgeons know more than Petty Officers?

In this happy state I became aware that Admiral Bonham-Carter and Captain Falkner were having a heated argument in the alleyway, immediately outside the cabin I was in, totally unaware of my presence. Captain Falkner, in a cold and angry voice was demanding an explanation of the Admiral's manoeuvres before the sinking. "Good God, Sir, I did advise against the action you took in leaving the convoy without an escort." And more in the same vein. The Admiral, trying to placate his Captain, said in a blurred voice, "Now, now, my dear fellow, I take full responsibility and it will be recorded in my official report to the Admiralty." "That's all very well, Sir, but I have lost a fine ship, and many men." Retorted the Captain. The drama of the argument drifted away down the alleyway. Perhaps I do the Admiral an injustice inferring he was tipsy. I certainly was!

The Harrier was still alongside the Edinburgh, bumping and grinding with the sea swell as she took off the remaining seafarers. Such was the weight of extra bodies that the Harrier took on a dangerous list, and officers were shouting to the men to spread themselves more equally. A Russian destroyer had arrived on the scene and was signalled to come along side and take off some of the survivors. This it did in a most unseamanship like fashion, colliding into the side of the Harrier. The resultant crash caused the Harrier to heel over and we, down below, thought another torpedo had struck. The officers quickly dispelled the panic. Fortunately, apart from a few buckled plates, no harm was done. The Russian Commander later wrote to Captain Hinton of the Harrier, a charming - if slightly amusing letter: -

Dear Sir,

Soviet's seamen was witness of heroic English Seamen with predominants powers of enemy. English seamen did observe their sacred duty before Fatherland. We are prouding to staunchness and courage of English seamen - our Allies. I am very sorry what injured your ship by approach to board for what I must beg your pardon.

Commander of Division.

Shortly after this incident our nerves were again set on edge by a series of explosions. Sadly, we were told our forces were giving

126

HMS Edinburgh the 'Coup de Grace'. Stubborn to the end, she resisted depth charges and gunfire, finally a destroyer was ordered to torpedo her. She sank with her Battle Ensigns flying and a trumpet sounding the Last Post thinly over the icy waste. Today, many, many years on, I still have difficulty controlling my emotions whenever I hear the Last Post.

HMS Harrier, laden with survivors, left the scene in a great rush. The hull vibrated under maximum engine pressure, and the halyards and stays shook and rattled in the wind. Stopping only briefly for a sea burial, the desolate sea gave way to the depressing shoreline of the Kola Inlet. The snow covered mountains, and low lying clouds, created a peculiar mist that rolled down over the water creating a surrealist picture of ships sailing through fluffy clouds.

First stop was Pollyanna, Russia's Northern Fleet Base. Here, also, was the Royal Navy HQ controlling convoy operations from Russia. It was a fact that the Russians had a very small and badly trained navy, and played a limited role in escorting convoys. All the Royal Navy ratings were disembarked at this station. Merchant Navy survivors were taken up river to Murmansk. where a fleet of ambulances waited to take us back to the hospital we had so recently left. Quite a number of nurses who had waved us goodbye were there to greet us. Many cried and were quite desolate to find some of the original party had been lost.

CHAPTER 11

RETURN TO MURMANSK

Our arrival at the hospital coincided with the inevitable air raid and we were rushed inside to the same large ward - or assembly hall of the school - it hardly seemed possible so few days had elapsed since we left. Somehow, the room seemed to have shrunk and grown ever grimmer. The faint yellow glow of the electric lights in the blacked out ward barely illuminated the nurses as they hastily put us into our narrow, iron beds. Ironically, I found myself almost in the same bed I had previously occupied. There was the large statue of Stalin, standing high up in a boarded window alcove, staring down grimly at me as if to say, "So, you thought you had escaped me - did you!"

When the air raid had passed over, those survivors who had thought themselves unlucky not to have been included in the Edinburgh party, anxiously questioned us as to what had happened. We were too physically and mentally exhausted by our experience to go into detail, but what little we related caused great concern as they realised the insurmountable dangers of a return to the UK. Here and there, someone would ask after a shipmate only to learn he had not made it. An oppressive air of doom hung over the ward.

The following day the Senior Naval Officer, North Russia, Admiral Miles paid us a visit. I always had great admiration for Senior Naval Officers; they personified the ultimate in breeding, humanity, discipline and kindness. When the 'chips' were down they have the natural ability to talk to seamen man to man. Admiral Miles was no exception but he needed all these qualities to convey the awful news he brought. "The Admiralty" he said, "had instructed him that no further attempts were to be made to repatriate survivors. It was too dangerous. We must prepare ourselves for a long stay" He hesitated over the next few words. "Possibly to the end of the war." The Admiral's quiet words stunned us into silence. An intense wave of anguish, fear and nausea gripped us so tight by the throat we could not speak. Some were physically sick. Even the nurses who understood nothing of what he said paused in their work, conscious of the electrical emotion gripping the ward.

We were well aware of the reality of the situation. The war was not going well with the Russians, they were being pushed back on every front. The Germans, who had lain siege to Leningrad, had pushed on and were now a mere thirty miles from Murmansk. If they broke through they would raze what was left of Murmansk to the ground. The fact there were several hundred Merchant Navy survivors in a hospital would not enter into their calculations. Likewise, the fanatical Russians would defend the port to the death. In the heat of battle they would have little time to worry over a few British Seamen while their own forces were being slaughtered.

Slowly, like drowning men when we came out of our stupor we began to bombard the Admiral with angry questions and demands. These were not directed at the poor man but at the authorities safe in London. Why could we not be taken back? It was our lives and if we were ready to take the risk then it was our own responsibility. Either way, we considered ourselves dead men if we stayed here. Far better to die at sea than be blasted out of a hospital, or over run by Germans!

The Admiral listened to our entreaties with great sympathy. Wearily shaking his head, "Listen, men, I tell you in all honesty, even if I emulated that great Admiral Nelson, and turned a blind eye to Admiralty orders, I simply do not have the facilities, or ships, to do what you ask." What the Admiral knew, but could not say, was that the last convoy PQ17 was one of the great disasters of the war. The 1st Sea Lord, Admiral Sir Dudley Pound, suffering from a brain tumour and under the impression the German Battleship Tirpitz had left its Norwegian lair to attack the convoy, ordered it to scatter. Up to this point the convoy with a large escort was faring well, and had high hopes of reaching Murmansk with minimum losses. The large and powerful escort was ordered to return to base, the rest is history. Undefended, the convoy was slaughtered by bombers and

U-boats. Royal Navy officers were filled with shame at this apparently cowardly act. Winston Churchill ordered the facts to be made secret, and not disclosed until the end of the war for fear public morale would suffer. He also closed down any further attempts to run a convoy until the darker, winter nights. We were therefore effectively isolated in Russia.

Although Admiral Miles was officially restrained from giving us the true facts, the calamity that befell this convoy quickly became common knowledge as the survivors daily poured into the hospital, with harrowing stories of finding themselves alone in the Arctic Ocean, fighting off bombers with antique WW1 guns. One ship that was sunk only had a rifle on board - and that belonged to the Captain!

We were to remain in this hospital for a further six weeks. There was nothing to distinguish one day from the next. Each was as terrifyingly awful as the next. Constant bombing coupled with the naked fear of being taken down to have our wounds dressed. The food was appalling, bordering on starvation level. The main meal consisted of watery soup with a hunk of rock hard black bread, which had to be well soaked in order to force it down our throats. I remember one day an orderly came in with a large basin of small fish, freshly caught and uncooked. I reckon that by the time they were distributed we each had half a dozen of these tiny silver fish. They looked revolting and we were undecided what to do with them. The orderly soon demonstrated by taking a handful and stuffing them in his mouth, saying, "Uchin Koroshor." (Very good) at the same time glancing around in case he had been observed by a Commissar.

Admiral Miles used to pay us regular visits, and there was an amusing side to these visits. The wily Admiral was well aware that amongst the Russians accompanying him would be a KGB Agent, ready to report his every word, and so he indulged in extravagant, fulsome praise of our great and glorious Ally, Russia. Admiral Miles felt sure we all appreciated the wonderful way the Russians were looking after us, and how honoured we were to be here witnessing their heroic fight against the Fascist Beast. Each of the Admiral's phrases was met with an ironic cheer, and he would smile broadly at us, as if to say - well done lads - we understand each other!

Naval personnel from the ships in the Kola Inlet, hearing of our plight took every opportunity to visit us bringing whatever food they could spare. Chocolate and cigarettes were especially welcomed. On one occasion a Navy Padre paid us a visit and held a church service. The Russians received this in a most hostile manner, it being against their political dogma. They filled the doorways shouting and laughing, and making derisory remarks. The Padre manfully ignored them and completed the service. In a sense, I was in sympathy with the Russians - what in the name of God had I to be thankful for!

Royal Navy surgeons also came and were appalled at what they saw. Any offers of assistance were rejected and they could only standby in helpless frustration and watch survivors being butchered on the operating table. It was a sickening experience for them. So strong were their protestations to the Admiralty that something must be done to alleviate our suffering, that a medical team, and equipment, sufficient to man a forty bed hospital was dispatched. Unbelievably, the Russians refused to allow them to land on the grounds they had no prior knowledge of their dispatch, and no Russian visas had been issued.

This led to a serious diplomatic crisis taken up at the highest level between Churchill and Stalin. Churchill was so incensed at this callous action he threatened to stop all further convoys. He was speaking the only language the Russians understood - force majeure. However, President Roosevelt over ruled him. Stalin would not give way, so the medical team was sent back to the UK.

This diabolical, inhumane act was hard to excuse, and yet the British did handle the affair badly. Knowing the Russian's paranoid suspicion of their Western Allies it is difficult to understand why they did not consult the Russians, or apply for visas. It was begging for trouble attempting to present them with a fait accompli. Despite this, it is my personal opinion that even if the British had gone about it in a proper manner the Russians would still have refused. Why? Well their National Honour was being impugned. We would be openly inferring their medical standards, and skills were medieval - which they were - but nobody likes being told the truth. In any case, their standards applied to their own servicemen who, obviously, never complained!

In small ways, and subject to their acute shortages, we did receive better treatment than their own forces. The battle front was only a few miles away and wounded streamed back for treatment. The hospital was crammed to capacity and badly wounded soldiers lay on stretchers in every conceivable space, eventually, many were housed in temporary shelters erected outside in sub zero temperature. We at least had beds.

The Russian soldier was an extraordinary fighting machine. Badly clothed, poorly fed, and commanded by Generals who had little regard for human life. Their main strategy being mass, suicidal attacks, regardless of horrific loss of lives. The fighting man carried out orders convinced it was his sacred duty to die for Mother Russia and Stalin. When wounded he rarely complained or showed any signs of distress.

The bombing of Murmansk had now reached a peak of ferocity not experienced by any other town in WW2. Eight or ten raids a day were not uncommon. The hospital shook and rocked almost continually. Nurses carried out their duties in a semi-crouched position, as though dodging bombs. The Germans seemed to have a set bombing pattern, first would come the Stuka dive bombers falling out of the sky with their special screaming device, to terrorise the citizens. Then the JU 88's and Heinkel's would over fly dropping 500 pound bombs. The air reverberated with engine noise, exploding bombs, and the roar of anti-aircraft guns, sending one's senses reeling to the brink of madness.

The effect on the patients was traumatic, we just had to lay there and take it! The few patients who were mobile would rush into a corner, or crouch against a wall in the futile hope it might save them. At least they had some release for their panic. Other patients dived under their beds re-opening their wounds, or sat in bed clutching their heads, rocking back and forth, as though to drive the nightmare away. Some lost their reason and screamed in sheer terror.

I was no braver than the next man was but fear took me in a different form. I literally froze like a block of ice. I could not move or speak until the all clear went.

To retain my sanity I dreamed long and hard on my early days, of my home, and more especially of the girl I loved, Alice. I relived every moment of our courtship until fantasy merged into reality. It was as though I physically conjured her presence into my life, blotting out the hell I was in.

We were just out of school when we met, it was an adolescent love that matured into a deeply consumating love that endured for five years. I was bewitched by this attractive, vivacious girl with deep brown laughing eyes set in a pretty rounded face, with a mass of shimmering auburn hair falling about her shoulders. It was a picture that I desperately clung to as the bombs rained death down from the skies. Step by step, I blotted out the appalling suffering and misery around me by reliving every precious moment with Alice.

How the memories flooded back. I would recall those shy - almost furtive - early meetings. The accidental touching of hands that sent waves of excitement racing through me. Soon we were meeting on a regular basis. In the early days Alice had to stay in and look after two younger children while her parents went to the local British Legion, her father being a disabled ex soldier. "Would you like to come home on those nights?" Alice asked. I hesitated; I did not know her parents, what would they think if they knew the boy friend was visiting in their absence "What will your father say?" "Oh, that's alright, I've already asked Dad." So, twice a week throughout that winter I joined Alice baby-sitting. Sounds dull? Not a bit! Once the children were in bed we settled comfortable on the sofa to practised the age old ritual of youthful courtship, a little wrestling, a little tickling, and then trying to steal a kiss, stoutly resisted until the last possible moment. Then, to my astonishment, I found it was not necessary to struggle for a kiss, Alice was passionately kissing me. My education in the wiles of the fair sex had begun!

Winter turned into a glorious summer, the last year of peace before World War 2. We wandered through a pastoral countryside that has long since vanished. Broad, open meadows ablaze with masses of fragrant wild flowers. Coppices of trees on the skyline inviting young lovers to investigate their inviting seclusion. Warm evenings spent on the river, punting and swimming. Weekly visits to the cinema where in the dark seclusion of the back row we would kiss and cuddle, my arm circling her waist, hand cupping her warm breast. "Stop it." She would say in a soft yielding voice, of course I never did.

Two blissful years slipped out of our grasp, but were not lost, being forever indelibly printed in my memory. Alice matured into a lovely, curvaceous young woman. I would marvel at the thought she was all mine and get insanely jealous if another chap so much as looked at her. I need not have worried, because Alice was infatuated with me, a fact that always amazed me, as I never regarded myself special. But then, if I am to be honest, I was not unattractive to the opposite sex. I was tall, well built, not bad looking, and had a certain cocky, assertive manner, and I guess cut a dashing figure in uniform. I was not a womaniser but it would have been so easy to have been 'Jack the Lad' in my travels abroad, but I remained faithful to Alice.

Shortly after my sixteenth birthday I joined the Merchant Navy. This did not come as a shock to Alice, she had always known I was going to sea, but when it happened she was terribly upset and cried a lot. I was upset too, I did not want to leave her realising I would be away for long periods. I didn't believe the old adage 'Absence makes the heart grow fonder' she was an attractive girl in a town full of servicemen, why should she forego the pleasures of being young and enjoying herself? Once again I was wrong, and failed to appreciate the depth of her love for me.

Alice wrote regularly every week, letters full of undying love and endearments, of the joy we would have when we were together. Letters delayed months somehow lost their urgency, then owing to pressure of docking and arranging leave; I barely had time to read them. On leave, I enjoyed meeting my mates and acting the big tough merchant seaman back from the war, spinning yarns and getting drunk, forgetting I had a date with Alice that night. My last leave was a disaster. I was home several days before I contacted Alice, and then, on my last night, I went drinking with the boys. When I did eventually call at her home to say goodbye she was in a fury, and screamed, "I never want to see you again - you can go to hell!" slamming the door in my face.

Well, I had certainly come to hell. Thinking of that last encounter I berated myself for being such an inconsiderate, stupid, bastard!

I had certainly lost her now. Wild, irrational thoughts raced through my brain. Who would be enjoying the warmth of her embrace now; who would be kissing those soft lips? These thoughts drove me mad, and I groaned inwardly. I was torturing myself, and yet, like an old familiar record, I kept replaying the memories. It was all I had to hold onto in these terrible days.

Then the inevitable happened, a bomb struck a wing of the hospital. The violence of the explosion rocked the building, plaster and dust rained down from the ceiling. Acrid, choking smoke billowed through the corridors; everywhere, cries and shouts from the Russians as they battled to contain the fires mingled with the screams of helpless patients. There must have been a Red Army Camp nearby for within minutes soldiers were swarming through the hospital, lifting patients out onto the open ground. Here we lay spectators to the air battle raging overhead. Shrapnel fell from the sky like metallic rain, nasty, vicious, red-hot shards of jagged metal that would tear a body to pieces. No, it was not a pleasant experience laying in the open during an air raid, but I do believe we had faced so many horrors, and looked death in the face so many times, that we were becoming traumatised into accepting our fate.

The raid over and damage to the hospital contained, there seemed no alternative but to take us back into our ward. However, for the British Naval Mission in North Russia this was the last straw and they demanded we be evacuated to a safer place as soon as possible.

Moving several hundred wounded merchant seamen presented the Russians with a huge logistical problem, but they could not fail to appreciate the catastrophic consequences of having a large number of British seamen killed in their care, and the effect it would have on future convoys. Churchill would undoubtedly have told Stalin, "If you cannot protect our wounded there can be no further convoys." At that stage of the war, Stalin was desperate for every tank and gun we could send.

The Russians acted with commendable speed, and within a day, or so, we were told we were being evacuated to Archangel. We were dispatched in a variety of ways; some were put on a Russian hospital ship, others taken by the minesweepers, Harrier and Gossamer, and the remainder sent overland by train. It was my misfortune to be included in this party.

135

Under normal circumstances a journey by train across North Russia could have been exciting. The vast forests, snow covered mountains, endless miles of tundra. Viewed from a warm carriage window could be considered romantic. Sadly, my experience bore no resemblance to this picture. I remember being put into what appeared to be cattle truck, rather like those Wild West wagons with a big sliding door. Around the sides were tiers of bunks - little more than shelves - and in the centre a small wood burning stove. An Army orderly was in charge of our wagon and his job to maintain the stove, cook the food, and generally attend to our needs. We called him 'Boris Good Enough', couldn't possibly have been his real name but he always answered to it with a smile. He was a comical character in his baggy trousers and blouse, with fur hat and flaps hanging over his ears. He was small, wizened, and looked much too old to be in the army. Fortunately he had a happy nature and appeared pleased with his position - much better than fighting at the front! Boris could not speak one word of English, yet we had long, unintelligible conversations sustained only by the little Russian we had picked up. Each party to the conversation pretending to understand the other. It would have made a hilarious music hall sketch - especially with Boris as the leading character! A classic example of this occurred when the train ground to a halt for several hours in the vast emptiness of the tundra. We asked Boris why had the train stopped? He immediately went into a grand pantomime performance, acting out a battle and taking up either side. Then, pointing to the rail tracks he held up two crossed fingers. It was all perfectly clear, the Germans had advanced and cut the rail line, the Russians counter attacked and repaired the line, soon we would be on our way - and we were.

Every army has its scroungers and Boris must have ranked with the best. Scrounging or pilfering call it what you will, was a dangerous business in Russia. One was liable to be shot on the spot if caught. This never deterred Boris, who was off the train like a shot whenever it stopped, returning with suspicious bulges about his person. Of course, the only thing worth scrounging was food, and I must say we fed far better than in hospital. Boris's speciality was a kind of Borscht that he prepared in a large pan over the stove. God only knows what the ingredients were, but it was very nourishing and tasty. He would also give us strips of dried meat which, while chewy, filled our bellies. We understood the natives in this frozen wilderness lived by trapping their food. After the animal had been skinned and cleaned, the carcass would be hung outside to preserve it - rather like putting it into a refrigerator. Many a trapper must have cursed the train when he found his carcass was missing!

Our first main stop was Belomorsk, a junction between Leningrad, Archangel and Moscow. Boris assured us we were going to Leningrad. Obviously, he was totally ignorant of the true state of the war, and unaware Leningrad was under siege. When we reached our next main town, Obozerskaya, the line branched off either to Moscow or Archangel.

Boris was now convinced we were going to Moscow, waving his arms expansively, saying, "Moscow, Uchin Bolshoi (Very big), many hospitals, make you koroshor mano (Good legs), plenty food." Such was his enthusiasm we almost believed him. We could have strangled him when the train pulled into Archangel. But there, he had been doing his best in typical carefree Russian manner, and he was a likeable character, so we parted with much cheek kissing.

CHAPTER 12
ARCHANGEL

When I say the train pulled into Archangel it was, in fact, a desolate spot several miles from the City. A line of ambulances met us and we trundled down a rutted, dusty road, to the broad banks of the river Divina over which we had to cross. The Russian summer had arrived and it was hot and sunny, everywhere the snow had melted and greenery sprouted from the ground. The river Divina, which was frozen solid during the winter had not yet thawed, but was covered with a sheen of water as the top layer melted in the sun. I don't know why the drivers decided to cross over the ice, perhaps the bridges were down, but cross over the ice they did. The drive was one of the most memorable and frightening experiences of my life. The vehicles slowly splashed through the surface water, the ice creaking and groaning under their weight. Crazy cracks began to open, and the drivers with their mad fatalistic attitude to life, whooped and yelled in wild excitement. Talk about playing Russian roulette - those idiots certainly enjoyed it!

Life started to improve when we arrived at the hospital, where we were put in a light airy ward one floor up. The windows were not boarded and fresh airs circulated. There were about twenty patients in my ward and reasonable spacing between beds. The food was also marginally better, and we not help noticing that the doctors and nurses were much cleaner in their personal appearances. Bed bugs and lice less affected us patients, and rarely did we wake in the mornings with lips and eyebrows swollen from bed bug bites as we had in Murmansk.

With the coming of summer the warm weather, and non-stop sunshine rapidly raised our spirits. Our wounds were healing and there was less pain to be born. The skin had grown over my stump and I no longer had to suffer the torture of dressings. For the first time we became a social group, not inanimate bodies lying in beds.

There was Bill Short, ship's engineer, minus two legs, Jimmy Campbell, cabin boy aged sixteen years, minus a leg and hand. Baxter, Carney and Pike, all seamen who had lost a leg. A Chief Steward whose name I forget missing a leg. Then there was a Portuguese seaman whose name we never knew because he could not speak English. We christened him Pedro. His was the most tragic case possible having lost both arms and legs. He was a most fantastic character, always laughing and waving his stumps about, but then I suspected he was totally mad. Then there was Frank Finn; a cheeky Welshman from one of the rescue ships sunk in the ill-fated PQ17 convoy. I forget what Frank was in the hospital for because he had all his extremities. He was a rarity! There was also an American, Jack Gamblin, a USN Ensign from Texas, he had received shrapnel wounds but was otherwise all right. My half dozen Arabs were still sticking to me like glue.

We were a diverse bunch of characters but got on well with each other. Our American from Texas tended to get on our nerves with his big talk and snide remarks about the British. He thought he was God's gift to women but he truly got his just deserts when he called over our attractive translator, Tanya. Beckoning her down, as though to say something confidential, he caught her in an embrace and gave her a long, lingering kiss. Tanya, recovering from the shock, delivered a perfect right hand to his jaw knocking him unconscious. The whole ward cheered and shouted, "Uchin koroshor." (Very Good)

The Russians were now genuinely doing their best for us and a charming lady, Madame Wright, had been sent from Moscow to look after our welfare. We understood she had been a University Professor. She was a cultured lady who spoke impeccable English, stylishly dressed for a Russian, and in her fifties. From the respect shown to her by the hospital authorities, and the Russian officers, she was undoubtedly a Senior Party Member.

Madame Wright spent much time talking to us on almost any subject - except politics. At one time she attempted to teach us

Russian, but as most of us were ignorant of basic grammar in our own language it was an impossible task. Nevertheless, some of us rapidly increased our spoken Russian, and that was most useful in the coming months.

By this time, most of us were recovering from our wounds, and I for one, was getting around on crutches. Boredom was the chief enemy and to relieve the situation Madame Wright organised a series of concerts, one such was a string quartet. The highly acclaimed artistes sat in the centre of the ward surrounded not only by patients, but medical staff and quite a number of army officers. Other Russians unable to get in crowded the doorways and corridors, eager to listen to these talented musicians. To our untutored ears it sounded the most awful cacophony of sound and I'm ashamed to say we failed to show appreciation. The Russians, however, were ecstatic and broke out into tumultuous applause. For a brief period in their miserable lives they had been transported to a higher plane.

We experienced a similar sensation when an RN rating brought in a battered, portable gramophone. This decrepit machine had obviously seen many years' service in seamen's messes, and should have been pensioned off. The spring, about to expire, barely had enough strength to turn the table for a record. The sailor also brought half a dozen Glen Miller records. Like the machine, these records had been played almost to extinction and produced a fine variety of hisses and crackles. Regardless, that gramophone became the centre of our universe, every night it was played until we knew the tunes and words off by heart. We would sit around allowing the music to waft us back home. Each, and every one of us, would have memories stirred as we recalled where we last heard a particular record - at home - in a pub - on a dance floor - with one's girl. All in another world now seemingly unobtainable.

I found the Russians an unfathomable race; subject to the harsh Bolshevik regime, worked until they dropped, starved near to death, devoid of life's meanest comforts, and yet they all had a deep love of their homeland and were prepared to die for it. Those who could read only read good literature; there was no such thing as comics or magazines. They were beautiful singers and their songs - even in Russian - could move one to tears. And yet - and yet, these same Russians had no mercy on any one who transgressed their laws, or Party politics. Exile to a Labour Camp, or shot, was a harsh fact of life in Russia.

I know it is a generalisation to say all Russians were dour, suspicious and brutish, but in 1942, at the height of a frightful war in the Arctic, they most certainly were.

However, given the opportunity they were capable of exhibiting their wild, exciting Slavonic nature, which I was to discover.

There was great excitement when a high ranking General visited the hospital. Though the purpose was to see his soldiers, Madame Wright informed him of our presence and a visit from the General would be considered a great honour. Madame Wright pre warned us saying the General had just won an important battle on the Murman Front, and as a mark of respect we should all clap when he entered. This we enthusiastically did. The General was an imposing figure with a glittering array of medals on his chest. He slowly passed down the ward having a word with every second or third patient, which Madame Wright translated. I was standing to attention on my crutches when he arrived at my bed. Pausing, he had a short conversation with Madame Wright, the gist of it was that to celebrate his victory he was holding a banquet at the Civic Hall, and he would like to invite a small number of our brave British Allies. Turning, he greeted me saying, " Would you like to come, Comrade?" Before Madame Wright had chance to translate, I accepted and thanked the General in Russian. This amused him, smiling; he patted my shoulder and continued down the ward.

It was pure luck on my part that the General chose to pause at my bed, and engage in conversation with Madame Wright, especially as only two or three others were selected for a 'once in a lifetime'experience.

A large army car conveyed us to the City Hall, we were met by various officials who, viewing our disreputable appearance, were not quite sure who we were and had to be assured by our escorting officer that we were invited guests of the General.

The mere mention of the General was enough, and we were shown into a large, handsomely decorated Hall. The walls, of course, were decorated with the usual portraits of Lenin and Stalin, and I believe the flags and banners belonged to the General's Army Group. At

141

the head of the hall was a raised dais on which the General and his party sat. His military bearing had impressed me when I last saw him in hospital, now he was positively magnificent in full dress uniform. Row upon row of medals smothered both breasts, glittering gold epaulettes on shoulders, and vivid broad red stripes down the uniform trousers.

Stalin, in the years leading up to the war had purged his army, slaughtering half his General Staff, abolishing all rank and insignia - every one was a comrade. Now that he desperately needed them to save his tottering State, he lavished medals and honours on them, and by God they earned them.

There were several rows of tables leading off the dais, and officers were seated according to rank. I think I was almost seated in the corridor! A military band played in an alcove, and the waitresses must have been specially selected, for they were all extremely attractive. The table groaned under every conceivable delicacy. Never in my life had I seen so much food. After months on watery soup, black bread and raw fish, I almost became delirious at the sight of it. The grandeur of the occasion faded into insignificance compared with the vast array of dishes. My mind, heart, body and soul had only one desire - eat - eat - eat! There were many toasts between courses to Stalin, Political Leaders, Generals, Admirals, Air Marshals, and to the General's credit he proposed a toast to our brave British Sailors. Raising my glass, I wondered why the General kept swinging round. Why can't the silly bugger stay still I muttered as I gracefully slid under the table.

My exit was not taken amiss, after all, the Russians take pride in drinking themselves under the table, and the true hero of Russia is the last man standing on his feet. I have no recollection of being taken back to the hospital, I only know it took several miserable days for my bloated stomach to again accept black bread and watery soup, as for raw fish - UGH!

It had been a wonderful party but I could not help reflecting that in this Communist State, where all were supposed to be equal, there was this staggering difference between the ruling class and the working class. When the General sat down to his banquet did he spare a thought for his starving countrymen? I doubt it. I also found it difficult to imagine a Western General throwing such a party every time he won a battle. But then, at that stage of the war our Generals hadn't won any battles - so who knows?

I found the Russians had a bizarre sense of humour, often at the injured party's expense. In my case I was descending the broad curving staircase leading to the ground floor, when my crutch slipped and I went tumbling down head over heels, crutches clattering around my ears. Subconsciously, I protected my stump but was quite bruised and winded when I arrived at the bottom. The Russians in the vicinity roared with laughter, and applauded as though I had just performed a circus act. Grinning from ear to ear they picked me up, patting my back in a congratulatory fashion to indicate I had made their day.

About this time the Russians obtained some vintage films, mostly old musicals of the Great Waltz variety. They were shown in a large room on the ground floor and projected onto a whitewashed wall. On this particular occasion, the Interpreter announced we were to see Charlie Chaplin's 'Great Dictator'. This he said was the only copy in Russia and was the personal property of Comrade Stalin who, hearing about the brave British Seamen in hospital had ordered it to be flown in for our entertainment.

The Interpreter, swelling with patriotic pride, pointed out that even in the midst of his titanic struggle with the evil Nazi swine, our great and glorious leader, Comrade Stalin could still find time for the wounded in Archangel, and so on - ad infinitum! What utter rubbish. That psychopath, Stalin, was already shooting his Generals who had been forced to retreat. Then there was the incident when Stalin refused to allow a medical team sent for our succour to come ashore. The Interpreter would have us believe this man in the Kremlin, specially arranged for a film to be flown from Moscow to Archangel, for our entertainment! Any idiot with a grain of intelligence would have known what farcical rubbish he was talking.

Having endured this political harangue for some thirty minutes, we sardonically applauded to signify our relief it was over, and the film started. Now, I have never been a fan of Charlie Chaplin, indeed I find his humour banal. However, I need not have worried over being bored as my whole attention was focussed on a huge Russian soldier sitting at my side. He had a childish sense of humour and roared with laughter at every silly joke. At times, especially when the two Dictators met at the rail station and the flunkies were trying to get the red carpet in correct position, he was convulsed with laughter. Rocking back and forward with tears of laughter running down his cheeks, at the same time giving me vicious pokes in the ribs to emphasise a joke. By this time I was enjoying myself and laughing almost as much as he - but not at the film! It was the only time I have been to see a picture and derived more pleasure from watching a man enjoying a film, than watching the film myself - if that makes sense!

Reading this one could imagine we were enjoying our sojourn in Russia; the odd banquet, film shows and mooning over sentimental music. Far from it, life was exceedingly harsh. The war was at a critical stage with huge battles being fought on the Eastern Front.

Casualties continued to pour in from the battlefields. Food became even shorter, and there were regular air raids. Not on the scale of Murmansk but sufficient to keep our nerves jagged and raw. Six months had elapsed since I left home and the prospect of getting back receded with each passing day. I later learnt my parents received, one telegram informing them my ship had been sunk, and that I was wounded - after that nothing. It must have been hell for them too. We could neither send, nor receive mail; we were totally isolated from all that was dear to us. No wonder depression was rife among the survivors.

The only redeeming feature being we were now well into the Russian summer, it was hot, sunny and almost daylight round the clock. Windows were thrown open letting in fresh air. We had discarded winter clothing and our bodies could breath, leading to greater cleanliness. No longer plagued by lice and bed bugs it was now the turn of mosquitoes. It seems hard to credit mosquitoes within the Arctic Circle, but this was a vicious breed that swarmed out of the forests and timber yards, and made our lives a misery. I was severely bitten at the start of the season then, as though they had had enough of me, they left me alone.

On the subject of cleanliness, most of us were now getting around on crutches and the urgent cry, "Sudna Paljalista." (Bed pan, please) was heard less frequently. When one required the toilet we simply made our way down to the communal toilet on the ground floor. Now, this is not a delicate subject but must be explained to show the deplorable conditions we lived in. The toilet was a long narrow room with a pole, approximately four feet off the ground, running the length of the room, beneath it an open sewer. The person relieving himself or herself would drop his trousers, or in the case of a woman, her pants - assuming she wore any, and it was surprising how many didn't - then locking arms around the pole would relieve themselves.

There was no flush and piles of excrement lay in the drain. The stench was indescribable and the air full of horrible black flies. Occasionally, an old woman with a bucket and brush would come in and sweep the revolting mess down a drain. Of course there was no such luxury as toilet paper, one had to hoard every scrap of paper and Russian paper had to be seen to be believed. It was thick, coarse, and resembled matted straw. There were no washing facilities and it's a wonder we did not go down with some dreadful plague.

Once a week we went down for a bath when we were given a change of rough underclothes. Our outer garments, such as they were, were never changed or washed. Incidentally, initially I had no clothes and was taken to a basement room to select articles from a pile of old clothes. I think I ended up with a pair of army trousers that came well above my ankle, a Russian type blouse, and a blue tunic that might have been airforce issue. Needless to say, I looked a most peculiar figure. Later I discovered that behind the closed door of the room I had been in was the mortuary. No prize for guessing where my clothes came from!

To return to our bathing session, the bath was a large tub set in the ground at floor level, and would take six, or more persons, and frequently did. Nurses would think nothing of joining in, and when we got over the shock we thought nothing of it. Pedro, our Portuguese seaman who had lost both arms and legs, delighted in his bath and would thrash away with his stumps. There was always a nurse in the water supporting his deformed body. To illustrate the peculiar Russian sense of humour, she would take away the supporting hand, and Pedro, having no limbs would immediately sink headfirst. Up she would bring him coughing and spluttering, and breaking into maniacal laughter when he regained his breath. He appeared to love it and thought it no end of a joke. But then, I did say I thought he was mad!

Although the nurses enjoyed this joke at his expense, I must say they were very fond of him and treated him with great tenderness, taking endless trouble with his feeding and bodily requirements. Poor devil if he ever got back to Portugal he would join an army of beggars, in all probability being propped up out side some church with a begging bowl.

It was now mid-July, weather very hot and the season of the midnight sun. Most of us were fairly fit and spent restless days going round the wards visiting the less fortunate patients. We felt confined, restricted and yearned to get away from the confines of the hospital. It was a crazy situation; we were occupying valuable bed space while their own troops were deprived of proper hospital facilities. I don't think this was due to any beneficence on the part of the Russians, they were simply paranoid about us spreading our Western culture among their own people. So the question of our being billeted with Russians was out of the question. I did once briefly experience being billeted with a Russian family, I think it was in Murmansk after I had been bombed out of hospital. I recall a large, solid, one story wooden building. There was a central room where the whole family lived, ate, and slept around a large stove, big enough to sleep a person on top. I was a stretcher case and far from well, never the less, I was aware my presence disturbed them, and no doubt they had been given a lecture by the Political Commissar to the effect I was a British survivor, and should be treated with caution. Fortunately, they were good people and treated me with compassion

To return to July, as I said, we were really 'brassed' off being restricted to hospital and we approached Madame Wright requesting we be allowed out for walks. She thought this reason-able and would clear it with the Chief Doctor, by which we assumed the Political Commissar. We were pleasantly surprised to learn we were free to go out as we pleased, and even more surprising, we did not require passes.

Initially, we kept our walks short, as if fearful of loosing sight of the place we had grown to hate - the hospital. But we grew bolder and ventured further; no one took any notice of us as we blended in with the ill dressed, ragged people. Everywhere there were wounded soldiers with arms and legs missing, had anyone bothered to look at us we could have been taken for your average Russian.

There was one occasion that might have had serious consequences. Frank Finn, a perky little Welshman, and I had gone out together. Instead of making for the town we decided to go into what might loosely be called the countryside. It was a hot day and the dust rose from the rough, un-made road. Rounding a corner we found ourselves in the midst of a group of Russian wounded service men. They were a villainous looking bunch, dressed in the tattered remains of their uniforms. Quite a few supported themselves on crutches; some had an arm or eye missing.

If we had pushed through we might just have been ignored but I made the fatal mistake of greeting them in Russian, "Dobri Din, Tovarisch." (Good day, friends) Instantly the atmosphere became hostile. "Angliske." Enquired one, in a menacing manner, another demanded, "Paporosi." (Cigarette). Patting my empty pockets, "Sorry, Comrade, I have no cigarettes." Another, glaring into my face, demanded chocolate. Again I patted empty pockets. "Christ, Morris, this looks bloody rough." Said Frank. The Russians looked at each other, uncertain what to do next. Then one said the only English all Russian knew, "When Second Front?" meaning when are the Allies going to invade Europe. In desperation I said the first thing that came into my head, "Second Front starts next week. The Great and Glorious Leader Joseph Stalin as said so." It was ludicrous, but I realised they were poor, ignorant peasants, conscripted into the army and now discarded as useless. At the mention of Stalin's name they became very wary, no one joked about Stalin or contradicted any remarks attributed to him. It was too dangerous - someone might be listening.

Sensing I had captured their attention I playfully poked the empty trouser leg of one of the soldiers with my crutch, and then my own. Pointing to each other I said, "You - me - Comrades" Slowly it dawned on them we were all in the same boat, we had nothing to give and nothing to take, so, what the hell, we were all comrades. Scowls gave way to smiles and in the fashion of service men the world over we discussed how we had received our wounds. I did not pretend to understand all they said but from their graphic body language, illustrated by drawings in the dusty road with crutches, we got a good idea of the tremendous battles they had been involved in. One of them drew out a small screw of brown paper containing tobacco and proceeded to roll a cigarette. After taking a few deep draws he passed it to me. Its taste was the nearest thing to horse shit - it was vile! Managing a smile I passed it to the next man. That cigarette went round half a dozen men before coming back to me, a wet soggy stub. Restraining an urge to be sick I took the last draw. I thanked the donor who, after all, had shared his last cigarette with his comrades; not to mention his dubious allies - the English - no man can do more.

After this alarming experience we played it safe and kept to the main streets, but even here I could not escape the drama of Russian life. Out walking, I was going down a main street that was little more than a dirt road, with wooden buildings on either side. Arriving at a junction my attention was drawn to a military convoy driving down the road in a cloud of dust. At the crossing a woman police officer was directing traffic from a raised dais, with a baton in each hand. She was dressed in a bottle green uniform, skirt just below the knees revealing plump but shapely legs. She had a good figure that her tight uniform emphasised, and curls escaped from under her peaked cap.

I stood watching her twirling round on her stand and thought, "Mm, your not a bad looking girl, I wouldn't mind taking you to bed if only you'd take off that bloody great gun." While these licentious thoughts were passing through my head, I noticed an old peasant woman on the other side begin to cross the road. Oblivious of the heavy traffic she tried to get through a gap and was struck by a truck, throwing her through the air to land in the dust at my feet. I was shocked as I looked down, eyes set in a face as old as Mother Russia, were flickering and she was mumbling. I had no doubt she was dying, I had seen too many deaths, but the sight of this old woman dying in the dust at my feet had a poignancy that roused me to rage. I shouted for assistance to no avail. Yet again I was struck at the brutal nature of the Russians. This was nothing to do with them; to get involved might be trouble. In desperation I hobbled over to the policewoman and tried to point out the injured woman lying in the road. Waving her batons she gesticulated to me to move on. Thinking she had not understood I took hold of her arm and pointed to the injured woman. This really made her angry,

I had dared to lay a hand on a Russian official and something no Russian would have dared to do. Transferring a baton she placed her free hand on the butt of her revolver. I got the message very quick and beat a hasty retreat. Feeling helpless, I went back to have another look at the woman. Sightless eyes stared into the sky; there was nothing anyone could now do for this poor soul.

It was now well into September and my daily walks extended into the City. While I had no religious beliefs I enjoyed visiting the churches with their splendid Byzantine architecture, all colour and gilt. Especially with their gold leafed onion domes. The Communist closed them down after the revolution, but Stalin allowed them to be opened to encourage the vast number of deeply religious Russians to fully participate in the war. It was also a sop to the Western Allies. Despite this, few Russian Christians dared to venture inside.

On one of my jaunts I came to a stop in front of the State operated GUM store. It seemed familiar, with a start I realised it was here, a year ago on my previous voyage to Archangel, I had bought a present for my Mother. Then a cocky 17-year-old smartly dressed in uniform, with money in my pocket. Now, I was a ragged skeleton on crutches with a foot missing and not a kopeck in my pocket - what a contrast!

For a moment I toyed with the idea of going inside and reviving old memories then thought what's the point, I had no money and my very appearance would arouse suspicion. With a sigh I turned away, "Ah, well, Mother dear, there will be no present this trip.

Late September, Dr. Stephens who was popular with the patients, had a talk with a group of us who had lost legs. He said he was trying to get us transferred to Moscow where we would be fitted with artificial limbs. We were greatly excited by this news and thought how wonderful it would be to walk normally again, plus the excitement of going to Moscow. It was while we were in this state of euphoria that we received a visit from a Senior Naval Officer with even more splendid news. The Admiralty had relented and was now determined to get us back to the UK. As a first step we were to be transferred by a minesweeper to Polyarnoe, the Russian Naval Base at the entrance of the Kola Inlet. Here we would await suitable transport.

Of course we were ecstatic at the thought of getting home, but we were realists, and felt a chill at the thought of returning to the Kola Inlet where the bombing had not diminished. Then there was the fearful prospect of sailing through the Arctic Sea where battles still raged, and ships were still being sunk. Many of us still remembered the earlier attempt to get us home on the Edinburgh and were, frankly, bloody scared. Not withstanding this, we were all prepared to gamble our lives if there was the remotest chance of getting home.

We had all grown fond of the doctors and nurses in Archangel and I think it was reciprocal. We had behaved ourselves, shown our appreciation for their efforts to get us well, and respected their customs. Our departure was therefore accompanied with genuine regret and much Russian style kissing. Many of the doctors and nurses gave us a small present such as party badges. Sadly, we had nothing to give them but our thanks. As we drove away they waved goodbye from the windows and it brought a lump into the throat.

CHAPTER.13
POLYARNOE

It was a short drive to the landing stage where we were taken onboard HMS Gossamer, a Fleet Minesweeper of about 800 tons, and I was accommodated in the for'ard seamen's mess. The mess-deck was about twenty feet at one end tapering to virtually nothing at the bow. Some twenty sailors lived in this confined space. A double row of hammocks hung from hooks down the centre, below was the mess table, padded lockers ran round the sides which were for sitting on, or sleeping. Port and starboard bulkheads sloped sharply in to the shape of the bow. "Here you are Mate." Said a sailor pointing to a space on a locker, "That's your bunk until we get to Polyarnoe."

The voyage took several days and was quite an experience for me - a big ship man. Fortunately, the weather was fine and sunny; even so, I found it disconcerting the way the bows kept thumping into the seas and the peculiar corkscrew motion of the ship. God knows what it must have been like in heavy seas! These guys certainly earned their hard-laying money. The food was good by Russian standards, if somewhat basic and monotonous. In these small ships there was a tiny, central galley, with a cook and assistant. The routine was that each mess appointed a cook of the day, and it was his duty to prepare the meal for the ship's cook i.e. peel the spuds, cut up the vegetables and meat, then take it to the galley to be cooked. When cooked to return it to his mess and serve his ship-mates. One of the favourites with the crew was stew with dumplings. The dumplings were prepared on the mess table and I was told, in all seriousness, that the secret of fluffy dumplings was the precise moment they were dropped into the stew - a secret

151

known to few. Such things assumed tremendous importance on these small ships.

There was no 'Navy Bull' on these ships and the crew worked in a happy, informal manner, while showing due respect to their Captain and officers. The crew couldn't do enough for their passengers and I never lacked for smokes, 'nutty bars' and chocolate. I was even included in the rum ration. These were some of the finest sailors I ever sailed with. During the short voyage I felt no fear. We had been assured the ship's draft was so shallow torpedoes simply passed underneath, as for being bombed - not possible - we were too small. Sadly, this was far from true, knowing the hell we had already been through they were only doing their best to reassure us. Many of these gallant small ships were lost, including HMS Gossamer, which was bombed and sunk with heavy loss of life.

We watched our arrival at Polyarnoe through a porthole and what we saw was not very encouraging. It appeared we were entering a large horseshoe bay surrounded by the usual hills and mountains. Large buildings, four or five stories high were spread along the foreshore, and a rough road wound up the hillside. This was the Soviet's Northern Naval Base, also the British HQ.

HMS Gossamer berthed alongside the main building where we were to spend the next three weeks. A large barrack type building about four stories high with a broad, imposing, stone stairway leading to the first floor. The frontage was in the grand Romanesque style with large pillars supporting an overhanging roof. The interior was a labyrinth of corridors where one could easily get lost, however, when you met up with a Russian sentry with a gun you knew you were in a no-go area and instantly retreated. We were housed in a large, elongated room, which apart from being Spartan was infinitely better than what we had been used to. There was an old Russian orderly to keep the place clean.

He could usually be found sitting on a stool near the door smoking. He could be bribed to carry out any odd jobs, or run any errand, for one English cigarette. Food was supplied and cooked by the RN lads and superior to our Russian diet, although the navy men stationed here for many months must have had a few moans over the monotonous rations.

The weather was pleasantly warm and stirred by sea breezes. Our main recreation was sitting outside on the steps smoking and yarning. We were in a completely military environment and there was always something interesting to see. Troops marching by, sailors going to and fro to their ships, Russian and British ships moving round the bay. Every now and then Senior Russian Naval officers would arrive and ascend the stairs. Their reaction to our presence always amused us. Some would stride past without a glance, others would wish us good day, others, not quite sure who we were would hesitantly touch their peak caps in a form of salute. One Captain stopped and glared at us, obviously we were a blot on his landscape, calling a sailor over we could tell by his gesticulations he was demanding to know what we were doing here, cluttering up the stairway. Not that we were in any way impeding any one's passage - you could have marched a troop of soldiers up those broad stairs.

Murmansk lay some twenty miles up the Inlet and was still being savagely bombed. Here, in Polyarnoe, we were only occasionally raided; these appeared to be half hearted attempts. No doubt the German pilots had little stomach for the fierce barrage put up by local anti-aircraft guns, and from the naval ships? Never the less, these raids kept us in a constant state of nerves, not helped when a Russian submarine returning from a patrol fired its gun. We rushed to the window and saw her coming in with flags flying and martial music blaring from the conning tower. We later learnt that her commander had claimed to have torpedoed and sunk the Battleship Tirpitz. There were celebrations in the base and the Captain was made a Hero of the Soviet Union. We British viewed the claim with the utmost scepticism. How, we questioned could a submarine sink a 42000-ton Battleship - the most powerful warship in the world - when it had taken four torpedoes to sink the 10000-ton cruiser HMS Edinburgh. Not possible - and so it proved. The Tirpitz had not even left its Norwegian lair. Such was the Russian mentality that they enjoyed their alleged victory and then conveniently forgot about it when it proved false. I wonder whether they took away the Captain's medal? Or did he end up in Siberia?

The high spot of our stay in Polyarnoe was being taken to the Russian Navy Club, referred to as the Hall of Culture. A large imposing building with a grand flight of stairs leading to the entrance, there was a veranda at the top and a plaza at the bottom. On a warm evening one could sit on the veranda sipping a drink while watching the dancing couples below. There were always too few servicewomen but this never worried the men who quite happily danced with each other. It was a peculiarity of the men that they would often be seen walking hand in hand, and of course kissing was socially acceptable. We Brit's found it very strange - to say the least!

We greatly enjoyed going to the club although getting there could be a frightening experience. The soldiers taking us would arrive in a cloud of dust - they always drove like maniacs. Whooping and shouting they would load us into the trucks, off we would go with screeching, crashing gears. The soldiers thoroughly enjoyed themselves, laughing, shouting, and singing at the top of their voices. We would join in this mad jollity as the truck lurched and jolted its torturous way up this narrow, dangerous, mountain road. A frail looking bridge spanned a steep ravine and the drivers would battle with any oncoming traffic for right of way. At times it seemed a certainty we were destined to plunge over into the abyss. Finally, we would arrive to a stomach churning halt that have us sprawled into ungainly heaps.

The Russians on the veranda would join in the fun and rush down to assist us up the stairs. Seats would be found and we would be offered ice cream, beer, and even vodka. We would sit relaxed, exercising our limited Russian, and watching the dancing couples, or we could go inside and have a meal, or watch a film. Admittedly, they were Russian films and mainly of a patriotic nature depicting a hero of Russia single handily wiping out half the German Army, but we joined in the cheers when the deed was done.

We had no money but this never seemed to be a problem, those Russians were extremely generous, kind, and fun loving. This was the only time I enjoyed myself in Russia. I guess it was appropriate I should have one good memory of Russia after so much pain and suffering, for I was shortly to leave Uncle Joe's land forever.

Following a visit to the Navy Club we were sitting on the steps discussing the previous evenings events when we noticed Admiral Miles, Senior Naval Officer, North Russia, approaching. We made to rise but he motioned us to remain seated and sat down beside us. This was the third Admiral I had met in Russia and despite their exalted rank they were all thorough gentlemen. After some general conversation he gave us the news we had all been dying to hear. We were to join a ship the following morning. The Admiral would not disclose the name of the ship, no doubt for security reasons.

CHAPTER 14
USS TUSCALOOSA

There was little sleep that night as we discussed our uncertain future. Once again we were to venture out into the Arctic Ocean, we were too well acquainted with the dangers that awaited us to sleep with an easy mind. Please God let us make it this time, was our silent prayer. The following morning found us on the quay ready to join a large cruiser. We were surprised to find her flying the Stars and Stripes, and learnt she was the USS Tuscaloosa. About the same size as the Edinburgh but not as pleasing to the eye in design. However, a cruiser is a cruiser, let's hope this one doesn't take to straying over the ocean on her own - like the Edinburgh! No sooner were we on board than the medics immediately pumped DDT down the front and rear of our clothing. "Charming" we thought. Having had many baths and changes of clothing during the past few weeks we were long free of lice. We were then directed to a row of tables and told to take off our jackets and roll up our sleeves. The Doctors then proceeded to inoculate us against every known disease under the sun. I had a very bad reaction and for days my arm ached intolerably and was very painful to the touch.

I had always found the Americans to be warm hearted and generous, but our welcome onboard was very austere and clinical. I have since read accounts of survivors enthusing over the warmth of their welcome on board. I wish I could agree with them. Most of the survivors were spread around the ship in small parties. I was taken down into the bowels of the ship and given a bunk in a sailor's dormitory. I would guess there were upwards of thirty sailors in this quarter, berthed in iron bunks fixed to stanchions running parallel and three deep. "Here's Ya bunk, buddy." Said a sailor showing me a bottom bunk, "Any thing you want just holler."

It would not be fair to say the Yanks were hostile to myself, distant would be a better description. There was an air of barely suppressed anger. The reason was all too obvious. The ghastly facts relating to convoy PQ17 were becoming generally known through out the fleet in North Russia. This was the convoy scattered by Admiral Pound, First Sea Lord, on the dubious information the Tirpitz was at sea, and about to attack the convoy. In fact, the Tirpitz had not left its Norwegian Lair. The escort were ordered to return to base leaving PQ17 totally defenceless resulting in the loss of 24 ships, mostly American. The Royal Navy, who had gallantly fought convoys through the Arctic seas against tremendous odds, was deeply angered and ashamed at having to desert a convoy to its inevitable fate. They had, however, no alternative but to carry out orders. The commander of the close escort signalled the commodore of merchant ships, "I am sorry we are leaving you. This is a bloody business."

None of us knew of the reasons behind this fateful decision, least of all the Americans who thought the Royal Navy had deserted their countrymen to a terrible death. So, the off duty sailors would sit around their mess table talking of the limey bastards who weren't worth a pile of horse shit. Now it would require the good old US Navy to sort it out totally overlooking the fact they had only recently entered the war and only had a small fleet in the Arctic compared to hundreds of British warships. Lying in my bunk, I just had to grit my teeth and bear it. After all, I told myself it wouldn't be long before you are off this bucket!

The difficulty of moving around with crutches on a rolling ship meant I spent much of my time below decks. There was an occasion when the sea was moderate and I took the opportunity to get some physical exercise. I wandered through various alleyways and inadvertently came upon a small officer's mess. A Navy Ensign was sitting with his back to me drinking coffee. Hearing my approach he turned, and it was none other than Jack Gamblin, the American in hospital that had been knocked out by the nurse from whom he stole a kiss. I don't know which of us was more surprised! From his

157

expression I sensed he was about to enquire what the hell I was doing there, but I beat him to the punch by wheeling round and leaving immediately. Point to me, I thought.

There was another occasion when we were invited on deck to see the transfer of German prisoners from British destroyers to the Tuscaloosa. The British ships had encountered the German Minelaying ship 'Ulm' and in the ensuing fight sunk her. Being small ships they could not accommodate all the prisoners - hence the transfer.

It was a strange experience watching the transfer of prisoners. This was the enemy, part of the so-called super race that had been trying to kill me with their bombs and torpedoes, and had damn near succeeded. Why not snatch the revolver from the sentry and shoot a few of the bastards. In reality, I watched them come aboard with mounting sympathy. They were shivering from cold and fear. Many had bloodstained bandages. All had that shocked expression of men who had just been in battle. Impossible to hate them, we were all sailors doing the same job for different masters.

The only other event of note was a concert by the Marine Band on the open ship's fantail. It was a pleasant afternoon and the sun shone as we approached Iceland. A large number of crew were on deck enjoying the music, which was excellent, and ranged from light music to classical. It could have been a combination of music; sunshine and relaxation that made me feel melancholy. I was over-whelmed by feelings of sadness, apprehension - even panic.

This was the end of my Russian adventure. I had suffered agonising pain which I would have thought was beyond the human body's capability to bear, I had been terrified almost out of my wits by bombs, torpedoes and shells, starved nearly to death, and at times so bored I could have climbed the walls. Notwithstanding this, it had been a wonderful experience. I had travelled over the vast expanse of Northern Russia, met innumerable interesting people and sailed on a number of naval vessels. It had been my way of life for nearly a year. I had grown accustomed to it - I had coped. How well would I cope with the bleak future that lay before me? I had never wished to be a land animal and knew some gigantic hurdles faced me in settling down to shore life.

My first emotional battle would be meeting my parents and friends. What would they think of this shuffling skeleton on crutches, with gaunt features, hollow eye sockets and hair cut to the scalp? Inwardly, I recoiled at the very thought. Suddenly, I realised that the joy and anticipation of returning home was evaporating fast.

CHAPTER 15
SCOTLAND HAIRMYRES HOSPITAL

Some days later the Tuscaloosa entered the Clyde and anchored off Greenock. Although a large number of us could walk we were nevertheless strapped in stretchers and laid on deck awaiting disembarkation into tenders. This was the first time I had been to Scotland. From my prone position I could only see a vast stretch of water surrounded by distant hills. A soft rain was falling and I was not impressed. How was I to know what a large part Scotland was to play in my future life?

It was at this point that I had a sudden re-occurrence of the savage toothache that had afflicted me some month's ago in Russia. I had been taken to a dentist who turned out to be an Army woman dentist operating in a small wooden shack. The dentist's chair was no more than a kitchen chair and the patients stood around the walls. It was quite apparent her dentistry skills were limited to yanking teeth out. There were no injections and 'please rinse'nonsense. The patient sat down, opened his mouth, the offending teeth were pulled and tossed onto the floor, the patient spat out the excess blood - again onto the floor - got up and left. That was enough for me, wild horses could not have dragged me into that chair. Such is the psychology of fear that the tooth never troubled me until we arrived off Greenock.

When we were brought ashore we were laid out on the Esplanade in long rows. Various organisations moved amongst us pressing mugs of tea, cigarettes and sandwiches into our hands. Everywhere cheery Scottish voices welcomed us. Newspaper reporters probing

160

for stories. I had read a lot about the First World War and a set of war books owned by father graphically illustrated with pictures of war wounded being landed at ports from the Western Front. Even in my childhood those pictures had raised a lump in my throat, and now my life had merged into those pictures - I was living them.

Despite it being a chilly, damp day, a large number of the town's people had turned out to see this pathetic display of wounded sailors laid out in long rows along the Esplanade. I don't think it was solely to morbidly gawp at these unfortunate men. There was a genuine and tangible wave of sympathy for them. They had been inundated by the press and radio with stories of the gigantic battles in far off Russia and here was the solid, tragic evidence of British participation in that struggle.

I found it all acutely embarrassing and was relieved when the ambulances finally took us off to hospital, on the outskirts of Glasgow. Most of us were admitted into an Annexe consisting of several large wooden huts converted to hospital use. The whole Unit was under the control of the Canadian Medical Corps, and fine fellows they were. I had barely settled in when a Canadian Doctor came up and asked, "How you're doing, Pal." "I'm fine Doc. Except for this raging toothache." He looked into my mouth, "Say, that looks pretty bad - how long have you had it?" He gave a low whistle when I told him the story. "We'll soon fix that." And before I realised it I was sitting in a dentist's chair and the offending tooth painlessly extracted. Bliss, at last.

A day or so later, we were sitting in a group chatting when looking up I was astonished to see my father striding down the ward. I could not believe my eyes. We had barely arrived in the hospital, Huntingdon was hundreds of miles away, and yet here he was! It transpired that Dad in his official capacity of Detective Inspector was also the Liaison Officer at the nearby American Airforce Station, Alconbury, and was friendly with the Colonel C.O. Learning from my father I had just arrived in Scotland he said, "Say, Tom, if your prepared to leave now I can get you on a plane to Glasgow. It will only give you about an hour there before you have to return." Of course my father jumped at the chance and so visited me courtesy of the American Airforce.

Dad was not in a position to explain how he got here, or why he could only stay a short time. Strange to relate I was to learn the facts a year later from the American Colonel himself. But I'm jumping my story.

Given the circumstances our greeting could have been considered odd. Advancing, he held out his hand saying, "Hello, boy, nice to see you - how are you keeping then?" "Oh, not so bad Dad, I've just had a tooth out and mouth's a bit sore." He looked suitably concerned, studiously avoiding looking at my empty trouser leg. "How did you get back from Russia?" Briefly I told him I had come back on an American cruiser. "Ah, that sounds interesting - was it a good trip?" I realised we were both groping for words. This was hardly an emotional meeting between father and son after many desperate months of not knowing whether I was alive or dead. Oh, I know he was delighted to see me and I'm sure that under that tough exterior flowed the warmth of love, but there just was no way he could show it.

To understand this one had to take into account his background. Born at the beginning of the century in Ramsay, deep in the heart of East Anglian Fenland, to a poor farm labourer. Life was hard made worse by large families; Dad was one of thirteen. Children had no education and were expected to work on the farm from a very early age to bring in a few pennies. And so it was with my father until he was old enough to leave home and join the Army. Here he received a basic education and was moulded into a strict disciplinarian. Following Army service he joined the police force and by sheer guts, determination and study, achieved the rank of Detective Inspector, and ultimately Chief Inspector.

My earliest memories of my father were when I was four or five years old. Like all children we used to kiss our parent's goodnight, on this occasion my father drew back saying, "No, no, you're a big boy now and boys don't kiss. You must shake hands." I'm sure my father was not being cruel but his words struck me like a blow, and scarred me for the rest of my life. I have always experienced difficulty in showing true emotion - even to my nearest and dearest. Reflecting back I'm sure my father's intention was to start building me into a man, on the basis the younger the better. I like to think he made a good job of it but the process was certainly harsh. If I transgressed he never hesitated to use the belt. Despite this, I always had the greatest affection and pride for him. But I had difficulty equating the word love into our relationship. I think I only felt this emotion when he died.

Why am I saying all this? Simply because our reunion revived a lot of memories. It also explains our stiff upper lip approach. I dare say we both ached to clasp each other and have a good cry - I know I did - but that sort of thing is just not done - old chap!

Anyway, we had a good laugh at his expense. I had noticed my Arab firemen looking over very intently while I was talking to Dad. Unable to contain themselves any longer they shouted over. "That your father?" "Yes, Ali, this my father." Frantically beckoning he said, "I speak - I speak." Dad looked at me enquiringly and I explained they were from my ship and had followed me round Russia. "Go and have a word with them Dad, they don't speak much English but you can say hello." I watched with pride his military figure as he strode over to Ali, bending down to speak to him, Ali immediately embraced him in a bear hug and in true Arabic fashion planted kisses on each cheek. As if this was not enough he had to go through the same ordeal with the other Arabs. It was hilarious and had every one in stitches; Pedro was laughing his head off and waving his stumps in the air. It was a warm, delicious moment and at last we could relax and smile at foolish things.

Dad returned to my bed with a red face muttering, "What in God's name was that all about." "Don't worry Dad, they were only saying thank you for what little I could do for them in Russia" The Canadian Doctor who had joined in the merriment came over and introduced himself. "I'm glad you're here Mr Mills, I have something to say to your son and you may be able to help. First, I've given him a thorough medical and apart from being under nourished he's in fairly good shape," then, pulling my pyjama leg up to reveal my stump, "This is a mess. It's the sort of amputation that is done on a battlefield to save a man's life - even then I think I could have done a better job. This will never stand up to wearing an artificial limb. It will have to be re amputated to five inches below the knee. I will leave a flat of skin to wrap round the bone and stitched to the calf." He paused, looking long and hard at me. "I know you have been through hell, son, but its got to be done. Do you understand?" I nodded; in fact I had anticipated it. "Right, now the next question is do you want to be transferred to Queen Mary hospital, London, where you will be near your parents or do you want it done here?"

Without a moments hesitation I said I would like it done here. After the Doctor had gone I felt guilty, "I hope you did not take that the wrong way Dad. I just felt I would like to get it over and done with before I come home. I know you are hellish busy and Mum can't travel to London to visit, any way its nice and quiet here" I trailed off into silence. I thought I noticed a flicker of relief as my father said, "Don't worry boy, you just get better and we'll see you when your fit. I'll explain to your Mother."

The following days were spent in pleasant recuperation. Lots of rest, good food and walks around the grounds. A certain walk took one down to a duck pond shaded by bushes and with seats. Many a budding romance developed here.

One patient, who shall be nameless, courted his nurse in the seclusion of the bushes, and later married her. A few years later on joining an organisation I found he was a fellow employee and we had a great time talking over our Hairmyres days - but I don't recall the topic of the duck pond coming up!

We had many visitors and received a lot of media attention. Perhaps the most intriguing was a visit from two Russian reporters from the Soviet War News Weekly who wished to write an article about our experiences in Russia. The Newspaper was published in Russia and the UK. Eight of us contributed to the article: William Short, Ships Engineer, Ali Nasser, Fireman, Mohamed Maberok, Greaser, James Campbell, Steward's Boy, Walter Baxter, Ordinary Seaman, W. Pike, Able Seaman, John Carny, Ordinary Seaman and myself. We sat around a table in the ward and related our personal experiences. It was a long article and is reproduced as Appendix A.

Another visitor was Lady Bonham-Carter and her son Philip, then ten years old. She was a charming lady and made us feel we were personal friends of her husband, Rear Admiral Sir Stuart Bonham-Carter. It was a gracious and kindly act on her part to spare the time to visit us, and let's be frank, we were pretty low down on her social scale. Came the morning when Auxiliary Nurse Agnes - commonly referred to as Aggy - a cheeky young Scots lassie, approached my

164

bed bearing a steaming bowl, soap and a razor. "Right, laddie, I'm going to get you ready for the operating theatre. Get your pyjama bottom off." Meekly I complied desperately trying to keep the top over my privates. "Ooch, Mon, don't be so bloodie daft, I'm going to shave round your willy, lay back and enjoy it."

For months I had endured the indifferent treatment of Russian nurses, bathed and used communal toilets, and now I really felt embarrassed. No doubt Aggy was right when she said I was Bloodie daft!

When I came to in the ward after the operation it was night time, and the ceiling lights were on. I remember thinking how beautiful the stars were before drifting off into a deep sleep. It took about two weeks to recover and the only discomfort I suffered was a plaster cast. I had to lie on my back and as any one knows who has worn a plaster cast that can be a form of torture. I'd spend ages struggling to get on my side only to have a nurse scold me as pulled me back. It was a blessing when the damn thing came off, but not so funny having 32 stitches taken out of the soft calf!

After the trauma of Russian hospitals my stay in Hairmyres was a pleasant interlude. Excellent medical care, good food, warmth, and no bombs or guns to disturb the peace. I really felt I could stay there forever. But it was becoming apparent that our numbers were decreasing as more and more survivors were either being discharged, or sent to hospitals nearer their homes. I knew that soon it would be my turn. Before this happened a Mercantile Marine Superintendent and various shipping officials turned up to pay wages to the seamen. Many men had large sums of money due having been away for nearly a year, and no chance to spend it. I was not included being bound to my company and still their responsibility. Later that day after they had counted their money and found themselves suddenly rich, someone suggested a game of cards. Soon a gambling school started at the top of the ward. It began with small sums being waged but all too soon large piles of money were being tossed into the pot, as the gambling fever gripped them. To those of us not addicted to gambling it was a grim spectacle watching these men who had gambled their lives, and lost limbs on the Russian Run, throwing away their only recompense - a year's salary - on the turn of a card. Utter madness!

My father managed my financial affairs. My salary, such as it was, plus war bonus continued to be paid into my bank. The Ministry of Transport advised I had been awarded a 100% War Pension effective from the date of bombing, which was paid directly into the bank. Dad did all the business merely sending me forms with instructions to sign here. I had no worries or need of money. My only vice was smoking cigarettes and these were showered on me by all kinds of wonderful people. Never at any time in my life had I been so totally free of material worries.

It therefore came as a shock when the Doctors told me I was being discharged home. Frankly, I did not want to go and asked if it were not possible for me to stay and be fitted with an artificial leg, before going home. "Sorry, son, it's going to take a few weeks for your stump to harden." I was devastated, I had dreamt of going home on two legs.

CHAPTER 16
HOME AT LAST

Arrangements were made for my return home. I had expected to make the journey unaided but was pleasantly surprised when Dad turned up. To shouts of good luck, we were driven to Glasgow Central Station in an army car. The porter, after checking our travel warrants escorted us to a reserved compartment. Considering the chaotic travel conditions then prevailing we considered ourselves highly honoured. The other occupants were all military officers who looked rather dubiously at us, as though to say 'Who are these civilians receiving VIP treatment.'However, it was wartime and secrecy was the watchword - best not to ask questions.

The journey home was long, tedious and cold. We slept fitfully through the black night until arriving at Peterborough at six in the morning. Here we had an hour's wait to connect with the local train to Huntingdon. It was pitch dark and a cold wind blew through the station. No point trying to get into the waiting room which was jammed with servicemen sleeping on benches, tabletops and the floor. Dad was all for moving some of them but I would not hear of it. I had had too many horrendous train journeys myself to wish to disturb them.

Out of the darkness crept the local train. We knew it would crawl through the twenty odd miles to Huntingdon, stopping at every station and halt, but we were thankful to get onboard and find it empty. Of course there was no heating but after the cold station it was marginally warmer. The train dragged its laggardly way through the empty countryside as though in empathy with my inner feelings, reluctant to reach its final destination. My father was fast asleep in the opposite corner, sunken deep into his overcoat with hat pulled over eyes. Two long journeys with only a minimal break had exhausted him, and I knew that as soon as we arrived home he would be off to the police station to resume his duties.

I stared intently into the countryside as night surrendered to day. A morning mist lay over the fields encompassing hedgerows as though reluctant to let them escape. Here and there, cattle moved in search of fresh pasture, disturbing the mist into swirls and eddies. Tall oaks, chestnuts and elms, bare and stark stood sentinel over the land. My mind in a turmoil, pierced the morning mists and, momentarily, I was back in the land of forest covered mountains with bears and wolves roaming their slopes. I shut my eyes to blank out the picture, that was the past - this the future. But why did I feel so miserable and depressed?

Soon familiar landmarks came into view as the train drew into Huntingdon Station. It was a brief walk home, in a daze I entered the living room where my Mother overwhelmed me as she sobbed her heart out. That was the first hurdle over. I was home.

The following weeks were a period of terrible, dark depression. My nights made hideous by nightmares. My dreams were a maelstrom of raging seas, explosions, roaring fires that threatened to engulf me. I would awake dripping with perspiration and shaking convulsively. Once, in the grip of a nightmare, I threw myself out of bed under the delusion I had been torpedoed and was escaping from a sinking ship. My poor, suffering parents raced into the room to see what damage I had done to myself. Much later they told me my wild shouts and cries had often disturbed their sleep in the night.

This blanket of depression was not helped when I developed an ulcer on my stump. No way could I have an artificial leg fitted until it cleared up. Neither my GP nor the outpatients Dept. in the County Hospital could heal it. My days were spent aimlessly wandering around the town and the evenings were spent in the pub seeking oblivion. Many times did a friendly policeman take me to a place of safety and sober me up and never to my knowledge told my father who was their Inspector. Things came to a head when on a cold rainy day I slipped in the street and fell in the gutter, as I lay there winded, I was overcome with a boiling rage at my helplessness, and the thought of what a pathetic sight I must be. The rage was so intense it threatened to burst my head. A dear old lady rushed over to help me up and to my dying shame I snarled, "Take your Fucking hands off me. Do you think I'm bloody useless? Go on - bugger off." And much more.

Later, when I had recovered my composure I realised how disgusting my conduct had been. I was ashamed of myself and realised I must pull myself together. I had been in the gutter and could get no lower. Now, for the sake of my parents and friends I must start thinking straight.

On one of my walks down the High Street I felt a tap on my shoulder. Turning, I recognised a girl who worked in the Hosiery Mill, "Hello, Morris, lovely to see you back." She gave me a peck on the cheek. "How are you coping?" "Oh, not so bad Jean, I'm getting by I guess." After a few minutes conversation she gave a shiver in the cold wind. "Brr, its cold Morris, you can buy me a cup of coffee." When we had settled in the warmth of the café we chatted about things in general, and she brought me up to date with local gossip. "Did I know John and Mary had got married - wasn't it sad that Bill Williams had been killed - had I heard that Mary Smith had run off with a Yank." We both knew we were dancing round the central subject. Jean, of course, knew Alice and I had been lovers. Unable to stand it any longer I asked, "How is Alice these days. Is she still working at the Mill?" "Yes, Morris, she is still there and I think she is fine." Slowly I sipped my coffee hardly daring to ask the next question. "I suppose she is going out with some one these days - bound to be with all these servicemen and Yanks around?" She laughed at my hangdog expression, "As far as I know I don't think so. Would you like to see her again?" I shifted uneasily in my chair. "Well yes, I would like that but does she know the condition I'm in?" I gestured to my crutches in the corner. "Of course she does you fool, everyone in Huntingdon knows. Good God, we do read the local paper you know. Seems you're a hero." "Some hero." I muttered bitterly. Jean placed her hand over mine. "If you ask me nicely I'll go out with you." We both laughed. "Thanks Jean, that's the best offer I've had in a long time. You have restored my confidence. Seriously though, if you see Alice would you tell her I'd like to see her again, if only for old times sake. I will be at the bottom of

Cowly Road at seven-tomorrow night. If she doesn't want to come I'll quite understand and no hard feelings."

Preparing to go out that evening I was unusually tense, so much so, Mother asked me if I was all right. "Yes Mum, I'm fine." "You're not going out drinking, are you?" I put an arm round her shoulders and gave her a hug. Don't worry Mum, no drinking - I promise." I was on the point of telling her the true reason for going out, then checked myself. No point in advertising I was about to make fool of myself!

Leaving the house I made my way across a deserted High Street into a lane, through an orchard and arrived at the back of the engineering works where I used to work. It was here I first met Alice, was it possible that was four years ago? Then a love struck boy waiting for his girl to come dancing down the street, hair blowing in the wind, laughing and chatting to her chums, cheeky face and protruding tongue in response to my wolf whistles. The banter followed by the first date. They say the course of true love never runs smooth but, apart from the odd inconsiderate action on my part, ours had remained constant for four years. We had been deeply in love but perhaps I had taken our relationship for granted, and never fully appreciated the depth of love Alice held for me. Time and again she had forgiven me when I failed to keep a date while on leave. Then there was my deplorable action in not turning up on the last night of my leave. Her last words, "You can go to hell - I never want to see you again!" were still ringing in my ears. I had totally messed up our lives, and the war had ruined mine. What right had I to dare to think she would want to see me again?

I eased myself against the railings to take the weight of my crutches, and prepared for a futile wait. The night was pitch black. It was darkness of tangible texture; it seemed to swirl oppressively around me. A cold wind blew down the deserted street and the only sounds were the gurgling brook running alongside the road, and the distant drone of bombers returning to local airfields after a raid. The houses across the road were dark humps and Cowly Road running diagonally between them was totally lost to view. I shivered in the cold and cursed myself for being such a fool as to think she would come to me.

Then, in the stillness of the night I heard the tap tap of footsteps, with a rush a blurred figure crossed the road and Alice flung herself into my arms. I had stoically suffered months of pain, fear and anguish and never once had I cried, now this slip of a girl crashed through my emotional barrier and we clung to each other crying like children. Words of love and regret poured out in a torrent. The tender softness of her body in my tight embrace, her perfume, her soft voice speaking words of love, overwhelmed my senses. In the darkness my fingers explored her face, lightly brushing her eyelids, cheeks and mouth. It was as though I had been deprived of the elixir of life and could not believe I had found it again. The black night became a velvet cocoon from which we never wanted to escape.

The following weeks we were inseparable, Alice's love and concern for me had the desired effect and gradually I came out of my depression. That's not to say I did not have bouts of irrational conduct - I did for years - but she knew how to humour me using her considerable feminine wiles, knowing full well how desperately I needed her. In a strange way, this for Alice was a period of love, happiness and contentment. She had what she always desired - me - totally and completely. There was no danger I would pack a bag and be off. The question of marriage and settling down constantly arose, and while I warmed to the idea of having a loving wife to tend to my needs, the spirit of adventure was not dead in me. Despite the impossible odds, I yearned to go back to seafaring. I never hid this from Alice, who would chide me like a child. "Yes, of course you do Morris, when you are better, when the war is over - when - when." She had no doubt that once we were married I would forget all this silly nonsense. I compromised, and we became engaged.

The winter of 1943 was very severe with frost, snow and ice. Definitely not the sort of weather where Alice, and I, could get out to our favourite, secluded spots, and consequently we were thrown on the mercy of our parents. I confess I spent nearly all my evenings with her parents. Pa Robson would be sitting in his old comfortable chair with his leg off, and me, with my one leg would be on the sofa with Alice. The womenfolk would be quite content, Mrs Robson with her husband and Alice with me. The fact that we were crippled seemed to enhance their love and devotion. Pa

Robson would be discoursing on the war, pointing out why General Montgomery was not making sufficient progress. Alice, and her Mum, were quietly talking and every now and then my attention would be diverted at the mention of marriage, home, and such like. Alice snuggled up to me and my hidden hand wandered up and down her spine. "Don't do that." She said sharply. "You know what that does to me." Indeed I did. Pulling my arm round she held it closely nestling under her breast. Pa Robson looked up; surprised his daughter appeared to be questioning his military wisdom. Ma Robson, looking at her husband was smiling broadly, as if to say, 'You silly man'

"What you'm planning to do in the future boy?" asked Mr Robson. "I don't know, Pa." He gave the fire a poke. "I expect the Boss will fix you up with something." He always referred to my father as the Boss, which I found rather irritating because it emphasised their difference in status. Pa Robson may have been a simple countryman but in my eyes he was a true gentleman. "Perhaps he will Pa, but what he wants, and what I want, may be two different things." Alice broke in, "Now Dad, don't you go worrying Morris, it will be a long time before he is fit, and when he is we will sort it out." The propriety 'we' worried me slightly. Why did a vision of a small council house and a mundane job enter my head?

In a fit of abstraction I found myself, yet again, comparing the different lifestyles of our respective families. A father driven by ambition had strictly brought me up. His aim in life was to gain promotion in his chosen profession. He expected no less of me and, without fully recognising it, I had inherited those qualities. I would never accept a mundane job, or be content to be the subordinate. Then there was my Mother, an attractive woman in her mid forties. Fastidious in her dress and appearance, almost fanatically house proud. Quietly spoken with a retiring nature. The contrast between Mrs Robson and my Mother could not have been more dramatic. Mrs Robson was a little older and overweight, possible due to having had four children too quickly. She dressed plainly and her unruly hair was tinged with grey streaks. By nature a jolly, boisterous woman who spoke in a broad East Anglia accent. She kept an untidy house for which she was forever apologising, but never making any attempt to rectify. "Oh Lord'y, Morris, What ever you'm be a thinking on me." She would exclaim moving some object to enable me sit down. Similarly, any comparison with this enchanting creature curled up at my side was bizarre. Alice was voluptuously soft, warm, and sweet smelling and perfumed. Her fingernails lacquered and hair brushed until it tumbled down around her shoulders in golden waves. It was difficult to take my eyes off her as she animatedly discussed our future with her Mother. Was it really possible, I asked myself, that only a few months ago I was in Russia facing endless deaths, starving, freezing, and despairing of ever seeing this girl again?

The winter of 1943 being extremely severe curtailed outdoor activities, especially as I was on crutches. However, we did make a point of going to the pictures once a week, which was rather amusing. The usherettes, of course, knew us and always kept two end seats at the back and woe betides any one who attempted to sit there. They would meet us in the foyer and after solicitously asking after my health, would escort us to the seats and take away my crutches. Should any patron wish to take a seat further up the row they would be severely admonished to go carefully past me. I used to smile to myself as they profusely apologised for disturbing me. Those usherettes looked after me like mother hens! Newsreels played a large part in cinema going and action shots of the war at sea, and of ships sinking in convoys, was frequently shown. I would feel Alice going tense as she tightly gripped my hand.

Another weekly excursion was to Harry's Pub. This was the small pub that backed onto Murkett's yard where I used to work. Harry, of course, knew me from those days and we were most welcome. We would go into the small 'snug' warmed by a coal fire. Here the customers would greet me in a ribald fashion, "Hello, here comes Long John Silver." Or, "Move up there and let Peg Leg and his Gall sit down." It was friendly banter and we happily spent an hour, or so, over a single drink

Alice, of course, had to work during weekdays and so I was thrown onto my own devices. I no longer went drinking during the day, occasionally I would play snooker in the Billiard Hall, or read in the Library, but generally I stayed at home. One day, Mother came home crying. I was very concerned and asked what was the matter. Between sobs she explained she had been to the butcher's for the weekly meat ration, and when she had queried the weight he had

173

been nasty. "What do you mean nasty, Mum?" "Well, he swore at me and said I didn't know what I was talking about." I was enraged. My mother was a timid person, and far from well. "Don't tell your father, Morris, he's got enough worries." "Don't you worry Mum, I won't tell Dad." I made her a cup of tea and calmed her down. "I'm just going out for a few minutes Mum, I won't be long." When I got to the butcher's shop it was full but I forcefully pushed my way to the front. The butcher was about to tell me to take my turn, when I shouted, "Are you the little fat bastard who swore at my Mother?" He stood with his mouth agape as I continued, "Listen you fucking shit head, I'm in the Merchant Navy, one of the guys bringing food to this country and you insult my mother over two pennyworth of meat." I had now totally lost control of myself, swinging my crutch I aimed a blow at his head which by the Grace of God, and my unsteadiness, missed by a fraction or it would surely have brained him. He fell back in a panic shouting get the police - get the police! "I wouldn't do that Pal." Came a voice from the back. "His Old Man's Detective Inspector Mills." The butcher was now an abject wreck, not only had he insulted the Police Chief's wife but also threatened to call the police to his son who was the local war hero. He was in a no win situation and could not make enough apologises, but I was not listening being surrounded by good ladies calming me down. "Well done, son, he deserved that. Now you've said your piece and I'd go home if I were you."

The following week Mum was getting ready to collect the meat ration. I could see she was nervous and casually said, "I feel like a walk Mum, I'll come with you." "No, I'll be alright Morris, I'm fine." I was on tenterhooks until she returned and was relieved to see her smiling. "Do you know Morris, that Mr Bradshaw the butcher was ever so nice to me today saying he was sorry if he upset me last week. He gave me a nice piece of meat and I really think it was too much - but he insisted." I chuckled to myself, amazing what a swinging crutch can achieve!

All this time I was being plagued by this abscess on my stump, preventing any possibility of have an artificial limb fitted. As the days passed I grew more despondent. Medical reports flowed from my GP and the local hospital to the Ministry of Pensions. Eventually things came to a head and I was ordered to report to

174

Queen Mary's Hospital, Roehampton, for admission. Alice was upset when I told her the news. "Oh, Morris, we have had such a short time together, and now you are going away again." I did my best to reassure her, "Don't worry love, it will only be for a week or so." However, parting did seem to be the pattern of our courtship.

I had thought I was being admitted to a General Hospital but it appeared the Military had taken over, certainly my ward entirely comprised of soldiers, I was even issued with regulation hospital blues thus making me indistinguishable from the other soldiers. As soon as I was admitted to the ward I felt uncomfortable and out of place. Not because of the soldiers who were a grand bunch of guys, indeed, when they learnt I was Merchant Navy and had lost my leg on the Russian Convoys I became quite a novelty. None of them had, as yet, seen enemy action being medical cases suffering from various complaints. The Medical Officer in charge was a small Belgian Army Captain who spoke peculiar fractured English. He would take a perfunctory look at my stump and say, "Change zee dressing." At this rate it never would heal.

I had two visitors whilst in hospital, my Aunt Eileen and a Mrs Smith, neither did much for my morale. My Aunt embarrassed me with a hysterical outburst over her husband's death. She knew Jim had visited me in Murmansk. Weeping and wailing she begged me to say her dear Jim was not really dead. "There's lots of islands up there, isn't there Morris? Jim was a good swimmer, he could have swum to one." Pointless my telling her one barely survived for a few minutes in those icy waters even if there were any islands - which there were not. Looking at her grief stricken face I could not fail to remember the callous way she had treated him when he was alive. But there, love takes many forms. I could not tell a lie, or circumvent the truth, and said she must accept that Jim was dead. After another outburst of tears she regained her composure and left me emotionally drained. Her visit evoked vivid pictures of Jim's smiling face advancing down the ward in Murmansk, bearing chocolate bars, and a heavy weight of sadness descended upon me.

My next visitor was a middle aged lady who I noticed talking to a nurse who indicated my bed. "Hello." I thought, "Who's this?" Approaching I could see she would be in her forties, plainly dressed and with sad features. I had a premonition I was about to hear some

175

more disturbing news. "Mr Mills?" "Yes." I replied warily. "My name is Mrs Smith, I believe you were with my husband, George, in Russia?" The name meant nothing to me. "Well, Mrs Smith, I can't honestly say I knew him, you see there were several hundred of us up there." "I know he was in the same ward as yourself in Murmansk and Hairmyres Hospital. He is a Londoner; a big man with a full head of wavy black hair." Then it struck me, of course I knew her husband, he was the big mouthy Cockney whose hair turned white overnight during the air raids. He was so terrified his iron bed would shake and rattle. Not that I held that against him, he was one of many. No, what I could not stand was his endless bragging about how brave he was during the intervals between raids. "Those bastards don't scare me!" he would shout down the ward. He really was pathetic. I also recalled how he was one of the principal players in the card school in Hairmyres hospital where, after losing his entire payoff, boasted, "Easy come - easy go!" What an idiot!

George's frostbitten feet had healed and he had been discharged from hospital some weeks before me. Having no money, I presumed he did what all merchant seamen do, reported to the MN Pool and shipped out. None of this could I tell this sad lady who was desperate to contact her errant husband. I felt very sorry for her as she wished me well and departed dejectedly.

I sincerely hoped I would have no more visitors, I had more than enough problems of my own. My stump was not healing and continued to ooze puss. My morale was beginning to plummet, not helped by being the only civilian in a ward of soldiers who, although hospitalised were still subjected to strict military regulations, Matron's rounds being a typical example of 'Colonel Blimpishness' at its worst! Prior to rounds, those soldiers confined to bed had virtually to lay to attention, bed immaculate and not a crease in sight. Walking cases either stood to attention by their beds or sat upright in a chair. Personal possessions laid out on locker tops as per King's Regulations

Matron would enter like Britannia in full sail towing our little Belgian Captain M.O., a sergeant and his soldier clerk. It was difficult to know whom the Doctor feared most, the Matron or the sergeant, certainly he adopted a fawning attitude to both. The sergeant was possibly one of the most objectionable men it was my misfortune to encounter. Turned out like a guardsman he was immaculate from his shinning boots to his twinkling cap badge. The only thing missing was a complete lack of campaign ribbons on his blouse. This man had obviously got himself a cushy number and was out to make these poor 'squadies' lives a misery.

Passing down the ward he would find fault with the most stupid things; a soldier's comb not laid out in line with the brush, an article of clothing not correctly folded in a locker - etc, etc. "Take that man's name and number." He would bark at his clerk. In military parlance this was tantamount to being put on a charge and could lead to loss of privileges and/or pay. Arriving at my bed he found me casually lying on top. "What the bloody hell do you think you are doing?" he snarled. Feeling my gorge rising I snarled back, "What the bloody hell does it look like - I'm lying on my bed." His anger, almost visible, crackled from his shinny boots to his cap badge. A malevolent look of pleasure crept into his eyes, "Take that man's name and number." The soldier's pen poised expectantly. Looking long and hard at the Sergeant, I said, "Mills.M.O. No. R 258050, Merchant Navy, and you can't touch me Mate!"

"Merchant Navy - Merchant Navy." He spluttered, "What the bloody hell are you doing here." My short fuse had now expired. "I wish to Christ I knew why I am here. I can only say I'd rather be back in Russia than lying here listening to you - you stupid bastard!" Matron wisely moved on up the ward. I lay for some time in a black rage. What was I doing here? It was obvious the Belgian Doctor was not remotely interested in clearing up my stump abscess, and I had no doubt the sergeant would find some way of paying me back. There was only one thing to do, and that was leave.

The Duty nurse was quite flustered when I demanded my clothes and called the Doctor, who tried to reason with me, "Vat ees zee trouble now." "Look Doctor, I've had enough. I'm going home." "But I cannot permit it. You are a war pensioner and if you do not obey me you will loose your pension." There was no reasoning with me, "Ach! Give heem his clothes and let him go." I signed myself out and stomped off into the cold night, crossed London and caught a train for Huntingdon. My parents were astonished when I arrived late in the evening. Dad as usual, remained calm and listened to my story sympathetically, I felt sure that as an ex soldier he understood the position I had been placed in. Mother busied herself making tea and afterwards Dad said, "Right, boy, lets have a look at that stump. Bringing a bowl of warm water and lint he carefully bathed the wound and then examined it intently through his magnifying glass. "Aha, now boy, stay perfectly still, this may hurt a little." Producing a pair of tweezers he carefully probed and withdrew a sliver of bone approximately 5mm-long and needle thickness, residue from when the bone was sawn through. Within days the wound had healed leaving me with a small scar which I have to this day. For me, it was a miracle; my faith in doctors totally shattered. It had taken my father, a detective with a magnifying glass and tweezers to solve the problem.

I had expected repercussions from the War Pensions at my high handed manner in leaving Queen Mary's hospital, however, when I sent them a medical certificate of fitness they replied with instructions to attend the Artificial Limb Centre at Cambridge to have a cast and measurements taken for the fitting of an artificial limb. That was a great day, but nothing compared with the day I reported for a fitting. In 1942 artificial limbs had hardly progressed from the Crimean War - possibly longer! Being a below knee amputation the socket was made of wood in the shape of a leg, this was joined to a full-length leather corset by two metal hinges. A leather thong laced the corset. Two canvas belts were connected to the corset, one round the waist and the other over the shoulder. It was hideous and weighed a ton.

When I first saw this monstrosity I was filled with joy. There it was in all its ugliness and yet to me it was a thing of beauty. It was my salvation, a return to the human race. Once I had got it on the fitters had me walking between the parallel bars. "That's great, you're doing fine. Would you like to try it with two sticks?" What a question! "How about walking up and down the room with one stick?" Finally the fitter said, "You've done very well, now take it off and we'll have you back next week for more exercise."

"You must be joking." I said, "No way am I taking this off - I'm going home with it." A look of sympathy and resignation passed over the fitter's face, no doubt he had heard this many times, he would soon make me see sense. After half an hour he gave up. It was almost a mile to the railway station and by the time I got there I was exhausted. I recovered somewhat on the train but the last short walk home was excruciatingly painful, and there was a warm squelching sensation in the socket which I was convinced was blood. As soon as I got home I took it off and was relieved to find at least half a cup of perspiration. Those early legs sweated like the very devil. Looking back on that episode I am amazed I made no effort to get a taxi - I guess there must have been taxis - or phone home for assistance. It was just symptomatic of the war spirit; one simply gritted one's teeth and got on with it whatever the adversity.

Since coming home from Queen Mary's hospital I had been seeing Alice daily, she knew I was going to the limb Centre and would be worried. My stump was too sore to meet her from work, or go to her home, so I sent word asking her to call on me. When she came in and saw me standing unaided she rushed into my arms and burst into tears. We kissed passionately, and then became conscious of my parents and we were all a little embarrassed. My folks hardly knew Alice, and perhaps had not taken our relationship too seriously. They knew better now, I had the feeling my father was not over enthusiastic. He no doubt foresaw that if we did marry it would not be a marriage of families.

It was difficult to know what my parents really thought about our engagement and plans to marry. In the five years of our courtship neither of our families had met, or expressed any desire to do so. Alice rarely visited my home. Dad, ever conscious of his position and authority would have found it impossible to socialise with Pa Robson, a genial, simple man with limited interests outside the British Legion. As for Mother, the comparison with Mrs Robson was so wide as to rule out any meeting of minds. Mother was shy and retiring while Mrs Robson was jolly, gregarious and outgoing. Her usual greeting was a big hug and kiss. Mother would have been mortified. I hope this doesn't sound snobbish because I was extremely fond of Pa and Ma Robson, indeed I spent more time in their home than my own - perhaps this was resented?

Shortly after being fitted with a limb I was instructed to attend a War Pension Tribunal at Cambridge. Following a thorough medical I was pronounced fit for employment and my 100% War Pension was reduced to 50% taking into account my permanent disability.

My Indentures with Sir William Reardon Smith & Co. were still open and they had continued to pay my salary, including war bonus, which strictly speaking I was not entitled to, not being on active service. I therefore wrote them advising I was now fit for employment. They replied stating they were pleased to learn I was now fit, and did I have any plans for my future. I most certainly did!

Even in my blackest moments I had never wavered in my desire to return to sea. Interviewed by Russian and local reporters I had emphatically stated I intended to return to sea had been widely reported in newspapers. I told every one, including my parents and Alice, but I'm sure no one really took me seriously.

I replied to the company expressing a strong desire to resume seafaring in order to obtain a Navigating Officer's Certificate. In reply they thought I had not made a wise decision, however, they were prepared to see me and discuss the matter, and I was given an appointment to be interviewed by the Board of Directors in Cardiff.

The severe winter had given way to a pleasant spring, and I took Alice for a walk down the leafy lanes to our own secluded spot amongst the trees, with the intention of breaking the news to her. For some time we lay in a tight embrace murmuring sweet nothings, then, "Alice, my love, I have to go away for a few days. I'm going to Cardiff for an interview with my company." I felt her body go taunt. Pulling herself upright she brushed her hair away from a serious face. "Why?" I tried to be light hearted, "Well, you know I am still bound to them by my Indentures, and they have been very good in paying my money. They have a perfect right to call me up for an interview." This did not satisfy her. Angrily tossing her head she said, " I don't see why you have to go to Cardiff, they can easily release you by letter." Which was true. Then slowly it dawned upon her the true import of the interview. "Oh, no - oh, no, not again!" she gasped. "Morris, I love you with all my heart, I could not bear it if you go away again. Say you won't do it - please!" and then the tears flowed. I felt wretched and tried to reassure her. "Listen, my love, the company have already said I'm as good as daft to think about going back to sea, and its most unlikely they would take a one legged man back in wartime. No, I think they may possible offer me a shore job - perhaps in their Head Office." This explanation made sense - even to me!

I dried her eyes, and kissed her salty lips. "There, my sweetheart, you feel better now?" a muffled "Yes" came from the depth of my shoulder. Looking up with glistening eyes, "What if they offer you a job in Cardiff." "Well, my love, you will have to pack a bag and come with me." "Only if you marry me first."

Although I did not appreciate it then, that evening with Alice was to change my life. My antennae failed to pick up the subtle, telepathic messages that charged the air. Emotionally, I was torn between my desire to return to seafaring and my love for this girl. Had she bluntly said if you go we are finished, I may well have stayed. I honestly never thought the company would take me back as a seaman and with that doubt in my mind I would not have gambled on loosing her love. For the want of those few words our destiny was sealed.

On the appointed day I presented myself before the Board of Directors. The last time I had appeared before this august body was three years ago, then a callow youth of sixteen years, nervous, shaking, but filled with burning desire to go to sea. Now, older, wiser, a seasoned seaman and a casualty of the war, I walked in confidently and without any indication of a disability. Sir William, and the Directors, received me kindly and for some time questioned me on my experiences in Russia. Sir William called the meeting to order and my interrogation commenced. Had I fully recovered from the enemy actions? Did I think I was physically able to carry out seagoing duties? Why was I so keen to continue my career? Questions - questions. One of the Directors stated the company had re-employed a Bosun who lost a leg in a train accident. Another pointed out that while that was correct the Bosun in question had left the sea at the outbreak of war. At that point I knew my fate was in the balance.

Sir William, picking up a report, "Well, Gentlemen, I think it is time to hear what Captain Harris has to say about this young man." Oh, God, I thought. Here we go! Frankly, I had always thought Captain Harris abominated me, everything I did always seemed to annoy him. I came to dread the summons - 'Captain wants to see you!' Sir William read from the report: - Captain Harris considers him an excellent seaman who applies himself conscientiously to his duties, and will in due time make a good Deck Officer. His bearing under enemy fire was exemplary. There was more but I was carried away on a cloud of euphoria. You cunning old dog I thought. There you were having me running around ragged, giving me the rough edge of your tongue, while writing up my report.

Smiling, Sir William said, "I think that is satisfactory, if we are all agreed we will give this young man the chance to complete his Indentures" There were nods all round and quite a few congratulatory remarks. My final hurdle was to pass the Shipping Federation Doctor in Cardiff. I think the company may have phoned the Doctor because my medical was a farce. "Which is your good leg." The right. "Ok, lift your left. Fine now the right. Excellent. Fit for sea." Returning to the office I handed in my certificate and took a seat while papers were prepared for issue of seaman's documents. A clerk issued a rail warrant and instruction to provide myself with seagoing gear and stand by for joining instructions. I returned home in a daze.

Never in my wildest dreams had I dreamt I would succeed in my attempt to return to sea. My reception at home was funereal. Mother kept asking, "Why." And I could see Dad was concerned. I tried to lighten the atmosphere by saying how lucky I was to be given a second chance. How wonderful it would be to get back to what I loved doing. To no avail. Mother kept repeating, "But why, Morris, why?" I could see it was hopeless, and I still had to tell Alice.

That evening as we walked into the country I put off telling her until the last possible moment, although I'm sure she had a premonition, for she was very quiet. At last I blurted it out, "Alice, the company have taken me back and I'll shortly be joining a ship." I expected an outburst, tears and anger, but there was no response as she stared fixedly ahead. I tried to explain but she cut me short, "Yes, yes, I heard Morris and I'm pleased for you." I was baffled. Alice had given me all her love, body and soul, and I was getting no response from her. "Listen, Alice, this will make no difference to us, we're still ......" Again she cut me short, "Oh, you are such a bloody, bloody fool." She angrily retorted, "Of course it will make a difference, you will go away for another year and I'll have seven days to look forward to - if I'm lucky - if you don't get yourself killed. I thought you loved me and wanted to marry and settle down. Instead all you think about are your silly ships!" I made to take her in my arms but she fended me off. "I'm tired, I'm going home." We walked back in miserable silence. "I'll call for you tomorrow night. "No, I need a few days to think things over." I took hold of her arm, "Look, Alice, I'm joining a ship on Monday, let's at least have the last weekend to talk it over calmly. "What in God's name is there to talk over!" she angrily retorted.

CHAPTER 17

RETURN TO SEA

It was a sombre train journey to Liverpool to join my ship. My mind so clouded with thoughts and emotions I hardly noticed my surroundings.

The previous evening I had called on Alice to say goodbye. Although it was a warm evening she refused to go out, insisting we stay in. She was not going to be entrapped in the sensuousness of sweet smelling meadows, or leafy woods, where she knew her resolve might be weakened. Her parents were out for the evening. We sat in separate chairs and the big, old sofa stood forlorn and empty in the corner. This was going to be a difficult evening. I tried to make light of my going away saying it might only be for a few weeks. "What if you go to Russia again?" she retorted. "What if you get yourself killed the next time?" There was no answer to that. Again she begged me not to go. I could only reply, "I must go." For some devil was driving me. It was my turn to beg, "Please, Alice, give me one more year to get my Officer's Certificate, and then I will pack it in and settle down - I promise." She made no reply, staring obstinately at the floor with tight features and compressed lips. It seemed we had reached an impasse. After a long silent pause, I could stand it no longer, "Does this mean Alice we are finished?" She neither answered nor looked at me. I had to go, and made to kiss her goodbye but she sharply turned her face. I looked down at her for a few moments, at a loss, then saying, "Alice, I do love you." I left.

Now I had to face my next ordeal, joining a strange ship. The Orient City was in many ways similar to my last ship, slightly

184

larger but much more modern having been built late 1940. I particularly noticed her raked bows and cruiser stern. The difference in the accommodation was even more marked. Gone were the oak panelling and brass fittings in the officers' cabins to be replaced by veneer and Formica. The crew's quarters, although still basic, were greatly improved. No iron bunks and coal bogie now steam radiators and decent messing facilities. Arriving at the top of the gangway I automatically turned right and made my way for the Apprentice's cabin in the bridge housing. "Where you're going Mate?" enquired a seaman noting my uniform. I told him, "No, no, Mate, Apprentice's quarters on the engineroom boat deck, abaft the funnel." That was my first shock, the second was when I entered the cabin. No longer a poky hole for four strapping young men, but two to a cabin with a small writing desk and wash-hand basin - hot and cold, no less! Here was luxury indeed, certainly I was impressed with the accommodation but could not help thinking it was directly over the engineroom and, as every merchant seaman knows, precisely the spot U-boats aim for. Not a morale raising thought to begin a voyage with! After stowing my gear away I sat down, lit a cigarette, and through the open door took in the after-end of the ship. Not a lot of difference from the old 'New Westminster City'apart from the newer machinery, winches, derricks, etc. Nothing to worry about there I thought. I was contemplating my next move when a sailor's head popped in the door, "You Mills?" I nodded. "Captain wants to see you." I gave a grim smile, how often had I heard that request; it was almost like being back home.

It was not difficult to find the Captain's cabin; the layout was the same as on my last ship. Standing in the passageway outside the door marked Captain I had a strange feeling of 'deja vu'. I almost expected to hear the gruff, Devonshire accent of Captain Harris bid me enter. Captain Doughty rose from behind his desk and greeted me with a warm handshake and ushered me into a chair. This reception had my senses reeling. I had many acrimonious interviews with Captain Harris and never once had we shaken hands, as for sitting in his presence - unthinkable! Things are definitely improving I thought.

Captain Doughty could not escape the trite description of tall, dark and handsome. Irish born, he was conspicuous in his social equipment, with a typical Irish sense of humour. He had served thoughout the First World War and had been involved in many hot spots during the present war. He had all the thrills without paying the heavy price.

Having put me at ease we chatted freely about my experiences in Russia, he mentioned he had himself been to Archangel the convoy prior to my own. In a social manner we talked about various officers we had come into contact with, for in those days a shipping company was very much a family affair. He then came to the crux of the interview by reading out a letter from Sir William outlining the circumstances of my appointment. With the benefit of hindsight I can well understand that Captain Doughty must have been very concerned, not to say apprehensive, at having a one legged apprentice appointed to his ship. He would be responsible for my well being and safety, and God knows, shipmasters have enough problems.

Captain Doughty pointed out that it was some time since I had served on a ship, and I was to break myself in slowly. I was not to do anything foolish such as working aloft, or go down into the engineroom, neither was I to get involved in stowing hatch boards over open hatches. As he reeled of the 'Do's and don'ts' I began to wonder just what it was I could do!

So began a steady, insidious programme to demoralise me. Oh, I know it was not malicious, it was done with the best intentions but slowly it destroyed my confidence. I had gone onboard ready and willing to prove I was as good as the next man. What I needed was the harsh regime of Captain Harris, who would undoubtedly have told me I was a silly bugger for coming back, and not to expect any sympathy or mollycoddling. I needed to be fired up, made angry, told to get on with the bloody job. I knew there was no room for passengers on a merchant ship. I quickly realised I was under close supervision while reeving wires on a derrick. The wire had jammed in a pulley block at the mast crosstrees, without thinking I did the natural thing, placing a marlin spike in my holster I started to ascend the mast to release it, only to be stopped in my tracks by a bellow from the bridge. "Belay that Mills - let the AB do it." I was mortified. Again, we were stowing hatch beams, which are lifted by a derrick and dropped into slots either sides. Sometimes they do not drop right and one walks on the opposite beam to kick or knock it into place. When this occurred I, being the nearest man automatically started to do the job only to be stopped by the Chief Officer rushing up. "For Christ's sake! Get off that beam." I felt a complete and utter fool, and rightly or wrongly, felt the crew was laughing at me behind my back. And this was in dock; we had yet to put to sea!

While that period lives in my memory I cannot - apart from Captain Doughty - recall a single name, or face, of any other crewmember. My fellow cabin mate rejoined from leave and although we lived in close proximity for some time I cannot, try as I might, remember him. I can't justify this by saying my memory as gone, for I can still remember all the crewmembers on the New Westminster City. I can conjure them out of thin air, hear their voices, and relive the past. I have a strange memory block with the Orient City. Perhaps I tried too hard, worried too much, felt the bitter dregs of humiliation too deeply. Since coming back from Russia I had dreamt of returning to sea and for this I had caused distress to my parents and possibly lost the girl I loved. All for this crazy urge to return to sea, and now it was slowly slipping out of my grasp. Little wonder my mind has blocked out most of this episode.

Things were definitely not working out as I had hoped. For a start, I had not fully appreciated the effect two sinkings, and many months of continuous bombing in Russia had on my nerves. Without doubt, I was 'Bomb Happy'and my nerves were shot to hell! This became apparent even in dock where the noise of working cargo is constant. A shore crane lowering a heavy lift into the hold with a dull 'Thud'making the ship tremble would turn my stomach to jelly. Winches would scream and whine as they lifted cargo, causing me to jump out of my skin. I was not sleeping properly, and worse, I was not taking my leg off for fear something happening. I kept telling myself I would be all right when we got to sea and things settled down.

Finally, the Orient City was loaded and hatches battened down. Hands were ordered to stations for leaving dock. I made my way to the stern for letting go, only to be stopped and ordered to the bridge where I was to take the wheel. It was so bloody obvious; the Old Man didn't want me on the stern handling heavy ropes and wires. I could have worked off a lot of tension with hard physical work. There was nothing for me to do while the ship was leaving dock as it was under control of tugs. Idly, I looked around the bridge, which was far superior to the New Westminster City. The most immediate being the wheel which was much smaller and electrically operated. No rods and chains clanking through the apprentice's cabin on this ship. I noticed a telephone to the engine-room, no more blowing down a brass pipe to give changes in engine revolutions. The wheelhouse windows were not cluttered with concrete slabs and gave a good panoramic view. It also seemed strange there were no gun nests on either side of bridge wings; this gave the deck a wide-open look.

Clear of the dock, we entered the River Mersey and the tugs cast off. The engines turned the propeller and a wave grew from our bow. I was now steering the ship.

I have previously described what the helmsman's job was like on the New Westminster City, with its large oak wheel, rods and chains. How one spun the wheel several turns and waited for the bow to swing then, before the manoeuvre was completed the helmsman would take off helm to counter the swing. It was all a question of experience, judgement, and feeling the ship through the soles of your feet. The Orient City was a different beast all together, with its smaller wheel and telemotor it was much more responsive. I was quickly in trouble putting on, and taking off, too much helm. This is just not bloody fair I thought. On the open ocean a degree or two either way would not have made a great deal of difference until I got the feel of the ship. But here, in the busy River Mersey with lanes of ships either side it was no joke. I felt the sweat trickle down my back as I struggled to keep on course. Several times the Officer on watch looked into the wheelhouse, finally I called him over, "Its no good, Sir, I just can't get the feel of her, she's totally different from my last ship. I think I should be relieved." "That's all right lad, I'll get an AB to relieve you. What was your last ship?" I told him. "Well, well, the old Westminster, I did part of my apprenticeship on her. Proper cow she was to steer!"

Out beyond the Mersey Bat the sea was quite choppy and the ship took on a steady rolling motion. One of the first jobs on leaving port was to swing out, and secure, the ship's lifeboats ready to abandon ship in an emergency. It was standard procedure and a routine job.

188

The lifeboat was raised from its chocks by heaving on ropes fore and aft, then first the bow would be pushed out followed by the stern, and finally it would be secured to a canvas bound pole between the two davits. During this manoeuvre the sailors would be working on a wet, heaving, slippery deck with no guard between them and the boiling sea racing down the ship's sides. To a landsman this might be considered highly dangerous, but seamen looked upon it as just another job, no different than when sailors went aloft to unfurl sails. I was engaged in this job with my shoulder to the boat prior to pushing it outboard when I heard a near hysterical shout from the 2nd Officer. "For Christ's sake Mills, get back here immediately!" No one looked at me, no one spoke, but there was a bad atmosphere. At that moment I was totally destroyed. Any lingering thoughts that I was going to make it vanished into thin air.

I have very little memory of that voyage. I know I avoided all jobs with an element of risk simply to avoid being told not to do so. I thought most of the crew was shunning me and so I kept to myself as much as possible. I barely slept and constantly expected a torpedo or bomb to strike the ship. In fact, at no time was the ship involved in enemy action. Perhaps it might have been better had I experienced some action. Psychologically, mentally and physically, I had always responded to emergencies, it was as though I had to be kick-started. Instead, I had to endure this dreary voyage with little to do except stare out over the sea, imagining every wave crest was a torpedo. Sleepless nights listening to the thump as the bows plunged into the seas. It was a nightmare and could not continue.

When the ship returned to Liverpool I immediately saw the Captain and asked to be paid off. He was very kind and sympathetic, and I'm sure, very relieved at my request - and who could blame him? No doubt in his mind he felt that he had preserved me from danger, and made me see sense. Little could he have known he had killed off all my dreams and ambitions with kindness.

For a long time I was tormented by my decision to give up the sea. Had I lacked moral fibre? Should I have tried harder? Done another voyage? I shall never know! I had seen, and endured, more continuous enemy action than many a serviceman, and while my wounds had healed the mind was a different matter. I tried comparing myself with that great war hero, Wing Commander Douglas Bader, who lost both legs in a pre-war air accident, and went on to fly Spitfires. Shocking though his accident was, he was immediately admitted to a first class hospital and with the best treatment soon recovered and was fitted with artificial legs. If the film version of his exploits is to be believed, he was soon dashing down to the local pub, driving his sports car, and romancing his nurse while recuperating. Obviously, his mind had not been damaged. Then again, during the war when he returned to the RAF he would have his personal batman to dress him, a staff car would rush him to his plane where aircraftmen would assist him into the cockpit. Then off he would roar to glory.

By comparison, I would have a struggle putting on an old fashioned limb that required lacing up the thigh and dressing in heavy seagoing gear, all on a pitching and rolling deck. Make my way over a sea swept deck and climb several ladders to reach my station. In no way am I comparing myself favourably with Douglas Bader, who was a real hero. It does, perhaps, illustrate that the problems I would encounter getting to action stations were possibly greater?

Did I give in too soon? That is a difficult one to answer. I was conscious from the first day I joined the Orient City there was a campaign - albeit, well intentioned - to make me see the error of my returning to seafaring. The Captain and his Officers were gravely concerned that any orders they issued would result in my injuring myself, and thereby reflect on them. I was not some emaciated youth recovering from a serious illness; I was a tough young man who just happened to have an artificial leg. I honestly believe that had the Captain told his Officers, "Look, this idiot wants to return to sea, if he kills himself - tough!" I would have made it.

So ended my career at sea. I was nineteen years old and thought my life had come to an end, of course it was only the beginning of another chapter but I didn't appreciate it at the time. My return to Huntingdon went unnoticed, events in wartime moved rapidly, and I was yesterday's story. Most of my mates had joined up, or been conscripted. The town was full of servicemen, mostly Americans from the nearby US Bomber Station, Alconbury. Surprisingly, there were a lot of Italian Prisoners of War from a nearby POW Camp wandering around the town. They were an amiable lot and freely fraternised with the locals. Indeed, with the shortage of labour the local housewives surreptitiously employed them on domestic chores. One had to wonder how some women with a husband away in the forces arrived at a payment?

With the town overflowing with Americans and romantic Italians, the local girls must have thought their wildest dreams had come true. Poor 'Tommy'never stood a chance.

There had been no contact with Alice since joining the Orient City some three months ago I now decided to see her as soon as possible, hopefully to get our relationship back together. I remembered how angry and bitter she had been at our last meeting, but she had stopped short at saying we were finished. This time she would know I was totally, and irrevocably, finished with the sea. I would beg her forgiveness and ask her to marry me. Mrs Robson opened the door, "Hello, Morris, lovely to see you again. Have you come to see Alice?" "Yes" I replied. "Well, I'm sorry to say she has gone." I stared at her blankly. "Yes, my dear, she has gone and joined the Army. (A.T.S.) Would you like to come in and have a cup of tea?" "No thanks Mrs Robson. I'll be in touch." I left in a daze and walked back through the lane, across the meadow, to the group of trees under which we spent so many loving moments. How empty and deserted it all seemed now. I took out my cigarettes and sat down to collect my thoughts. I was stunned, how could she do this to me. When I most needed her love and sympathy she had deserted me. I had come back full of remorse intending to ask her to marry me. What a blind chauvinist fool I was! How could I have forgotten the times that I had deserted her for the sea, the long months she had waited my return? Now, at last, I realised why she was so bitter at our last meeting. Now I knew what it felt like to be deserted. It was a bitter pill to swallow.

Some time after this I received a letter from Alice - well, it was more of a note - no doubt her Mother had told her I was back. "Dear Morris, my unit is having an end of training party before being posted. Would you like to come? Love Alice." The brevity of the note and lack of endearments made me angry and I thought, "To hell with you." Then I thought why not have one last fling. I was not yet officially discharged from the Merchant Navy and still had

191

my ID Card. The A.T.S. barracks was in a large building in Knightsbridge, and when I entered I found myself in a large hall dimly lit with coloured lights. A small band played in a corner and couples gyrated on the floor. It looked as though the United Nations were there. Americans with rows of medal ribbons proving they had passed for Private 2nd Class, shot on the target range, Good Conduct Medal, crossed the Atlantic etc. etc. but had yet to fire a gun in anger. Was it any wonder I was cynical! There were Poles and Czechs all dressed like Generals bowing and clicking their heels. Free French kissing hands and murmuring "Ma Cherie." In the girls ears.

The majority of these A.T.S. girls had no doubt previously led humdrum lives in factories, offices and domestic service, and now liberated, they were the honeypot round which all these glamorous and exciting servicemen buzzed. Was it any wonder they were having a ball!

By a strange coincidence, I was the only naval person present, and must have stood out in my blue uniform, brass buttons, and two rows of campaign ribbons, anyway, I was soon surrounded by a bevy of girls who either wanted to get me a drink, a sandwich, dance with me, or find a secluded seat in a dark corner. Boy! I thought. Have I got it made? I was really enjoying myself when this strange girl came up and linking arms with me said, "All right girls, this one is mine." With a shock I realised it was Alice. What a transformation. Gone was the shimmering auburn hair that used to cascade down her back, that I loved so much, in its place a tight roll to fit under those ghastly hats they wore. A tight khaki shirt and tie encompassed those delightful breasts I used to caress. Shapeless khaki skirt and stockings that hid the sensuality of her legs. Gone was the soft, tender girl I had known and loved. She positively sparkled with excitement, obviously enjoying her military life. This girl was really living. Almost aggressively she would pull me over to be introduced saying, "This is my man." Until I began to feel like an appendage. I was at a loss to understand her attitude. Was she sincere or merely showing off? I could not catch any loving undertones in her voice. Eventually we found a seat in a corner and I thought we were going to discuss our future, not a bit of it. Alice was being posted to a gun battery on the South Coast; she had been trained as a Radar operator. She enthused over the effectiveness of the 88mm gun, its range, elevation, trajectory and so on. Her flow of technicalities only interrupted by various soldiers coming over saying, "Hello, sweetheart, hear your being posted tomorrow. See you in the canteen before you go." Of course I knew this was typical service banter, but it left a sour taste in my mouth. I could see I was getting nowhere and decided to let the subject of our future drop. We got some fresh drinks and there was a pause in conversation. Looking at me, for what seemed the first time, she said, "When are you going back to your ship?" "I'm not." I said abruptly. "Oh, why?" There really wasn't any point in talking about it now, "I'm being Discharged Medically Unfit for Sea Service." She stared intently at me as she absorbed my reply. I don't know what passed through her mind, perhaps she thought why, oh why, did this not happen three months ago. I think if I had laid my cards on the table and said Alice, will you marry me and I'll wait for you until your discharge from the Army, she might have said yes. But of course that would have been ridiculous. She was no longer the same person I had loved, and the mere thought of having a wife serving in the Army socialising with the soldiers was unthinkable.

Reaching over she took my hand, in a soft tender voice she asked, "What are you going to do now, Morris?" I shrugged my shoulders in a resigned manner. "I don't know - something will turn up." She released my hand. It was not the right answer. Later at the end of the party, in the cool night air we embraced, "I do love you Morris." I looked down into those deep brown eyes remembering those past years of love and passion. Perhaps if I had not been driven by a mad desire to return to seafaring we might have settled down to a happy, fullfilling life, but how was I able to quell my unsettled, questing nature? Now I had lost any chance of returning to sea , and the girl I loved. "I love you too, Alice." We kissed and said a goodbye that we both knew was forever.

CHAPTER 18
ELECTRICAL TRAINING

So, there I was, nineteen years of age. I had been to sea, fought in a war, been severely wounded and lost the girl I loved. I was living in a town in which I no longer knew anyone and all my pals had long since been called up for the Forces. I had no job and, as far as I could tell, no future. What a cornucopia of woe! Where was I going from here? The answer came in a brown envelope instructing me to attend an interview with the National Service Officer.

I duly attended and the NSO, a small, busy looking man, invited me to take a seat. Surveying me with mock seriousness, betrayed by a smile, he said, "I suppose you know there is a war going on?" A fact I could not deny. "My job is to place unemployed in work of National importance, and I have legal power to direct them. I only tell you that so as we understand each other." I nodded in agreement. "Now, I see you have recently been discharged from the MN, let me say how sorry I am over the loss of your leg, however, I must direct you into suitable employment. Have you any thoughts yourself?" I shook my head. "Well," he continued, "I understand your father could get you a job with Hoover's at Peterborough. That sounds suitable." He noted my look of surprise. "Oh, yes, I know your father well. He has kept me informed of your progress since you were bombed." "Good Old Dad," I thought. "Always working away in the background." I explained that after my experience of sea life I did not fancy working on an assembly line. He took my point, rifling through some papers he said, "How would you like to take a Government Training Course as an Electrician?" That sounded interesting. "The Government are desperately seeking trainee electricians to be employed on RAF Airfields. It is a six-month training course; you would receive a training allowance, free accommodation and food. On completion of training you agree to be posted to RAF Station anywhere in the country." Leaning back in his chair he took out a packet of cigarettes and offered me one. We both lit up and drew deeply on the cigarettes exhaling a blue cloud that ascended to the high ceiling. "Well, lad, what do you say?" What was there to say? Training course, free accommodation and food, a training allowance supplemented by my war pension. "Yes, Sir, thank you very much."

In due course I received a letter instructing me to report to the Training Centre at Feltham, London. We were accommodated in a large suburban house and I shared a room with three other young men. It was fairly obvious that for some reason or other they had been rejected for Military Service. My being a war casualty meant we had little in common and merely tolerated each other.

The Training Centre consisted of several wooden buildings situated in Feltham and there were a considerable number of trainees of either sex. The instruction was divided between classrooms and workshops. I recall one impressive practical demonstration when a high voltage was passed between two conductors, with the resultant crack and flash of electricity. To our inexperienced eyes it could have killed an Ox, our Instructor then astounded us by stepping between the two conductors and grasping each. Of course there was no reaction, he was standing on heavy rubber matting. We were then invited to take our turn, which we did with the greatest trepidation. It was a valuable lesson on the dangers of electricity and how to deal with it.

For convenience, the trainees were split into small working teams of about six. Selection was random on a 'You - you - and you' basis. I considered myself fortunate in having two attractive girls in my group. They had 'chummed up'and appeared inseparable. They could not have been more dissimilar in appearance and character, Susan was medium height, dark, Latin looks, rather shy and inclined to be easily embarrassed. Anne, on the other hand, was completely her opposite. Tall, slender, with a mass of glorious red hair. An attractive round face with green eyes, and a slightly crooked smile. She had a delicious Scottish accent, a vivacious nature and was highly intelligent. What is more, when she made up her mind for something she got it - and she wanted me! I enjoyed their company and was mildly flirtatious - nothing serious

While my electrical knowledge was limited, I had two years motor engineering experience, plus my sea training. I was familiar with machinery and tools. The girls, on the other hand, hardly knew the difference between a spanner and a screwdriver. It followed, therefore, that I was constantly being asked for help and advice, and so a friendship developed. Initially, we would go out in the evenings as a threesome, but Anne soon put an end to that and Susan dropped out of the picture. Anne, and I, took every opportunity to enjoy each other's company in war torn London, and friendship quickly turned into love. Returning from a night out in the West End, we had almost reached our lodgings when the air raid sirens sounded. The raid was a considerable distance from Feltham but a bomber - apparently lost - dropped his bombs a mile or so away. We were in no danger, but seeing a nearby shelter we dived inside and found it totally deserted. It was pitch black and we clung to each other for warmth, kissing and cuddling and then, as though it was the most natural thing in the world, we were making love. How had this happened I asked myself? I had not set out to seduce her. I had only known her a few weeks. Was it a passing romance? Was I being caught on the rebound after Alice?

What I had not realised was that when it came to the wiles of women, I was an innocent. Destiny was no longer under my control - if it ever had been? The last few weeks of the course gave me no time to rationalise my position or emotions. We were in close contact during the day and spent every evening together, taking every opportunity to satisfy our physical desire for each other. I only knew I wanted to spend the rest of my life with her. Tragically, the time was all too short

The training course drew to its inevitable end and we both qualified as Electricians (Dilutes). When it came to our postings we were devastated to learn Anne was to go to an RAF Station in Fakenham, Norfolk, and I was being sent to an American Bomber Station at Alconbury, six miles from Huntingdon. No amount of protesting to the Posting Clerk could change his decision. I suppose from his point of view he required an Electrician at Alconbury, and he had a trainee who lived near that station - what could be simpler!

CHAPTER 19
USAAF ALCONBURY

We were now in the last year of the war and the Americans were launching fleets of Flying Fortresses against Germany in daylight raids, and life on the base was exciting. Although this was an American Bomber Station the airfield was British and my job was to maintain the electrical equipment attached to the buildings. Sounds important, but rarely extended beyond changing fuses, light bulbs, and tracing faults.

Occasionally, an interesting job would come along such as installing a piece of electrical equipment. I was once asked to install a water heater in one of the pilots' Nissen Huts. This involved taking a lead from an outside point, running it into the hut, fitting a contact board and making necessary connections. The job took several days and I got to know the pilots well.

They were a good bunch of guys who took great delight in taking the 'Mickey' out of me, which I accepted with good humour. During a break I was sitting down with them enjoying a cup of coffee when one said, "Say, Buddy, have you ever flown in a plane?" I shook my head. This aroused mock astonishment. "Say, you guys, this limey as never flown. Hell, we can't allow that, can we?" There was general assent. "What you say your name was, Bud?" "Morris." "OK, Mac, now here's the plan. Tomorrow we are doing a practice flight, be on the flight apron and when you see my plane the good old 'Betsy' you just hop on board." I couldn't help laughing. "You've got to be joking." "Listen, Brother, there are some things I never joke about, and flying is one of them. Do you want to come or not?" Clearly the implication was are you scared. Frankly, I was shit scared, but no way would I show it.

197

The following morning I cycled to the take off apron, which was a mile or so from the control tower. Carefully placing my bike in the hedge I stood on the apron watching the huge bombers. One by one they rolled up and stopped while the pilots went through their routine checks. A flashing light from the tower and off they roared into the sky. I was fascinated and almost forgot why I was there. Then, there she was, the good old 'Betsy.' Big, fat, and bristling with a staggering thirteen 0.5mm guns paired in nose, dorsal, ventral and tail turrets, and a single gun on either beam. My friend, the pilot, sitting high up in the cockpit was waving to me. The mid - waist gunner frantically beckoning me in from his open door. I felt sick to the pit of my stomach, every fibre in my body shrieked 'Don't do it' but I knew I could never show my face again on this base if I didn't. Ducking my head to avoid the wash from the propellers I made a mad dash for the door and was pulled aboard. Inside, the noise was horrendous with the roar of four engines making the aircraft shake and rattle. The gunners were checking their weapons and dragging ammunition containers close to their guns. Amidst this organised chaos, I grabbed a gunner's arm and shouted, "This is a practise flight, isn't?"

"Can't say Bud, they never tell us anything." Slamming a belt of ammo into his gun, he turned. "Could be Germany." I felt an icy trickle of sweat run down my back and wondered where was the best place to be sick! After an agonising period I heard the engines being throttled back, and a sort of calm settled in the plane. A crew member was talking to the pilot on the intercom, coming over to me he said, "Sorry, Bud, flights been aborted, engine trouble. Better jump out now before we get back to dispersal." I needed no second bidding and rode a very wobbly way back on my bike.

Next day I was completing my job in the pilots' hut when my friend came in. Placing a solicitous arm around my shoulder he said, "Say, Buddy, I'm mighty sorry we didn't get you airborne. Had a bit of engine trouble. Now don't you worry, I'll fix it as soon as I can." Over my dead body, I thought. Fortunately my job was almost finished and I was able to steer well clear of him.

It was not unknown for certain local influential people to take unauthorised flights. The Americans were very easy going in this respect as I had discovered. Why any one should want to take this

198

unnecessary risk was beyond me. I even heard that my father had been on a raid over Germany. When I asked him about this he neither admitted it nor denied it, which made me think it was true. But there, as the Liaison Officer to the Americans, perhaps he felt he should have this experience the better to understand and deal with the Americans.

Shortly after this nerve-racking experience I was summoned to the Control Tower where some High Tech equipment was being installed. Qualified American technicians were assembling the machinery and my job was to connect the circuitry to the British system. A relatively simple job but one which the lease agreement with the Americans stipulated must be done by a qualified (Ha - ha) British electrician.

I had nothing to do until the Americans completed their job and was able to gaze out over the airfield and watch all the activity. I was at the very nerve centre of this bomber station. From this eyrie I could see the bombers taking off and landing. The control tower a hive of activity with orders flowing out of radios to the pilots, communication machines clattering away, telephones ringing, and every now and then a officer would go out onto the veranda and fire a flare. I was so engrossed with all this activity I was not aware of the distinguished officer standing beside me until he spoke. "Enjoying the view, Son?" I turned with a start and came face to face with a tall, immaculate officer, wearing rows of medal ribbons, silver wings on his tunic, and glittering Eagle Insignias on the shoulders. I knew instantly this was a Colonel and Commander of the Base.

"Yes, Sir." I stammered feeling guilty being caught doing nothing. "Tell me, what are you doing here?" he enquired. "Well, Sir, I'm an electrician and I am going to make a connection, but.." I trailed off embarrassed. "Well?" he waited for an explanation. Feeling a complete fool, I tried to explain that I could only do my job when the technicians were finished. "I'm sorry, Sir." I said lamely. He smiled warmly, "That's alright Son, no sweat."

My embarrassment increased as he continued to stare at me. "Say, aren't you Tom Mills's boy?" He saw the astonishment on my face, and again laughed. "Oh, yes, I know your father very well, and you're his double. Your Dad comes up to see me quite often and gives me hell when my boys kick up in town." Of course I then realised that Dad, apart from being a Detective Inspector, was also the Liaison Officer to the USAAF Base, and would have direct contact with the Colonel. "Your father often spoke about the rough time you had in Russia. Damn fine job you did. I believe he flew up to Scotland to see you in hospital."

Then the penny dropped, so that was how he managed to see me so quick. Without putting it into so many words, I thanked the Colonel, and I could see he appreciated that.

With a smile and a friendly word he turned to his other duties. I could not help watching him out of the corner of my eye. He exuded total authority and yet his approach to his various officers was casual, as indeed they were to him. There was no stiffening to attention, no cracking salutes, as there would have been by a British officer - especially to a Commanding Officer. His orders received a casual drawled 'Yes, Sir'and the mere flick of a salute but one knew instinctively this man was made of steel and not to be disobeyed.

There was nothing remotely casual about the deadly game the American Flyers were involved in. Day after day, weather permitting, the bombers took off on daylight raids against Germany. Everyone who could crowded the perimeter of the airfield to see them off, and then there was the agonising wait to count them back. Many returned badly shot up with engines pouring smoke, staggering in to make the last few miles to the runway. Ambulances and fire wagons raced to meet them as they rolled to a stop. I particularly remember one shot up bomber missing the runway completely, skimming over a public road barely missing a bus, the passengers gazing in horror as the stricken monster roared over their heads only to crash in a field in a gigantic flaming fire ball. At moments like this a savage, sombre mood gripped the Base and we British civilians felt intimately involved, and grieved with our American Allies.

As a safety valve, The Americans arranged many shows with top line artistes entertaining. I well remember seeing Bob Hope, Francis Day and Gerry Collona. That was a great show. Then there was James Cagney with a troupe of singers and dancing girls. I was never a James Cagney fan and seeing him in the flesh, so to speak, was a big disappointment. He was so diminutive, how he got the reputation of being a tough guy is a mystery to me. As for his singing, I thought it appalling, admittedly it was an open-air show and the acoustics were bad. His comic patter may have appealed to the servicemen but it left me stone cold. Still, I guess when one is living on a freezing airfield facing death; the most puerile joke can seem hugely funny. Laughter is a release of tension and that was the name of the game.

I joined the show as a casual observer right at the back, and when it was over Cagney made his way through the airmen stopping here and there to sign autographs. It so happened he exited right in front of me so offered my notebook, "Would you please give me your autograph, Mr Cagney?" Which he kindly did saying, "What's a British guy doing on this Base?" Before I could think up a smart answer he was away. That was my one and only contact with a film star.

Apart from the show people, there were many other important personages who visited the Base. On one occasion there was a high state of preparation. Buildings were tarted up, white lines in the road and signs re-painted. Officers and men were immaculate in dress uniform, even the airmen working wore overalls that looked as though they had just come from the dry cleaners. My workshop was a small Nissen hut behind the main block of buildings and had odd bits of discarded equipment lying around outside. A Provost Marshall's jeep pulled up and a sergeant came over, "Say, Mac, I want that load of crap cleared up and put out of sight." "OK, Sarge, where do you want me to put it?" "I don't care where the hell you put it as long as it's out of sight. And another thing, don't go wandering round the Base tomorrow.

Keep out of sight - got me!" "Right O, Sarge. Have you got a General coming tomorrow?" "You'll find out soon enough, Bud."

The following day I invented a little job that required doing in a small room below the Control Tower, but sufficiently high enough to give me a panoramic view of the airfield. A Guard of Honour was drawn up in front of the Tower, and a Military Band stood ready to play. With a clear view of the main gate I saw a fleet of cars entering, the leading car flying the Royal Standard. The Guard of Honour crashed to attention and the Band broke out into the National Anthem. From the car stepped King George VI, Queen Elizabeth and Princess Elizabeth. I felt a patriotic surge of pride as I viewed this scene. I know from talking to the Americans afterwards that despite their Republican feelings, they were greatly impressed. A large retinue surrounded their Majesties, but I was proud to see my father hovering on the outskirts.

The winter of 1944 was particularly savage, with freezing temperatures, snow and ice. Conditions on the airfield were diabolical, situated as it was in the flat Fenlands. Personnel slept in their metal Nissen huts under piles of blankets; airmen went to the canteens in full dress - even flying gear. Snowploughs regularly cleared the runways for take off and landings. I could almost imagine myself back in the Arctic. This awful weather played havoc with landing lights and flare paths, which meant I was regularly employed replacing bulbs and tracing faults. I can assure you this was no joke crouching down with frozen hands while bombers roared down the runway beside you.

Conditions were no better at home for my parents. It was a cold, meagre existence living in wartime England for all. At this stage of the war rationing was severe and commodities were measured out in ounces. Because Dad was a Policeman there was never the chance of a bit extra on the side. On the Base I was regularly employed in the kitchens, with all their electrical equipment, and became friendly with the catering staff who would give me little luxuries to take home, such as sugar, butter, jam, and such like. Mum, and I, never spoke about it in front of Dad, who would have forbidden it. Nevertheless, I was surprised he never wondered where that bit of extra butter and jam came from! Coal was strictly rationed so we only had small fire in the living room; the rest of the rooms were like iceboxes.

The airfield was six miles from home and I had to bike it. I would start about seven in the morning; it would be pitch black with roads covered in snow and ice. Strapping my tool bag on the bike I cycled that distance with an artificial leg. Late at night I would repeat the journey back home. God alone knows how I managed it month after month!

Throughout these miserable months Anne, and I, missed each other terribly. Norfolk was a long distance away and leave was at a premium, in addition travel in East Anglia was chaotic with many unexplained stops and changes. I believe we only spent three weekends together that winter. At the first opportunity I travelled to Kings Lynn which was near to Anne's RAF Station. We took a little room in a pub. It was a warm, cosy, peaceful haven against the bitter weather. Not even the drone of bombers flying overhead disturbed our tranquillity, lost as we were in the joy of our brief reunion. The landlady was a pleasant woman who fussed over us at the breakfast table, all the while smiling at us as though she knew our guilty secret - I'm sure she did.

A month or so later we managed another weekend. This time we met each other half way in London, booking into a dingy Hotel just off Kings Cross railway station. The place was so dreary we only had one thought, to seek the privacy of our bedroom. We were so in love we barely noticed our surroundings, but even here we could not escape the war as the sirens commenced their banshee wail, and the bombs began to fall. As usual, my stomach churned over but I put a brave face on it and agreed with Anne we should stay where we were.

Then the bombs fell very close lighting our blacked out window with a rosy glow. "My God! They are aiming for the rail station." I exclaimed. "Quick, we must get to the Underground." Hastily throwing topcoats over our night attire, we raced down the stairs into the street, which seemed to be ablaze. In our mad rush one of my shoes came off and in a Chaplinesque situation I hesitated in the middle of a burning street, with bombs falling, debating whether to carry on or go back for it. Fortunately I thought my shoe was worth more than my life and I retrieved it. We dived down into Kings Cross Underground to safety. The platform was packed with humanity; there were the regular Londoners who nightly descended to their selected spot armed with bedding, sandwiches and Thermos flasks. A mass of people pressing down the stairs to escape the bombing and, in many cases, to catch tube trains as they continued to whoosh in and out of the station. We were propelled down the platform by the pressure of bodies, in doing so I bumped into the back of an ATS girl. I was on the point of apologising when she turned round, and it was Alice.

We had last met at the ATS party in Knightsbridge, not so many months ago. Neither of us had explicitly said our affair was over, perhaps we thought time would re-kindle the love we once had, and which, in some enigmatic way, I never lost. The shock of this unexpected encounter reduced the moment to a frozen tableau.

Anne clinging to my arm, her face flushed with excitement, unruly hair, and topcoat revealing her nightgown. Alice, in uniform with cap tightly on head, gasmask and haversack over shoulder, her face a play of emotions; surprise, hurt, anger and resignation. I stood between the two women I loved most and could not utter one word.

Alice's glance flew from our barely concealed night attire to my face, her expression said, "How could you!" It was as though she had received the final blow. Turning sharply, without a word, she was swallowed up into the heaving mass. Anne was not aware of the encounter, looking anxiously at me she asked, "Are you all right, Morris?" I nodded, "Why?" She gave my arm a squeeze. "Because you look as though someone has just walked over your grave." It was a surrealist moment and I wished it had never had happened.

The next time we managed a few days off, Anne came and stayed with my parents. It was a joy to be together again but rather frustrating because, according to the moral standards of those days, we had to occupy separate bedrooms. My parents instantly took to Anne, who they rightly thought was a superior girl, and worthy of their son. It was during this visit we realised we could not carry on in this fashion; brief reunions separated by long, lonely months, and we decided to get married and settle down. But how and when was the question? In reality, I had nothing to do with the decisions. Anne, apart from being a lovely girl, was very intelligent and strong willed, and had already mapped out our future for us. Anne came from a middle class Scottish family, her Mother, a widow, had been married to a Builder and she owned a large house on the Isle of Cumria and a superior tenement flat adjacent to Glasgow University.

There were two brothers both with University Degrees serving in the Army. There was also a younger sister working in a bank. When Mrs Thomasson heard her daughter was returning to Glasgow with the intention of marrying, she generously offered to return to her house on the Isle of Cumbria and let us have temporary occupancy of the flat in Glasgow, on condition her son Raymond would stay with us during leaves, and live with us after his demob. This was extremely kind of her, especially has she had not yet had the dubious pleasure of meeting me! I can only say she must have had a lot of faith in her daughter's judgement.

The die was cast, and we both saw our respective National Service Officers and resigned on the grounds we were to be married and live in Glasgow. My friendly NSO raised no objections; other than to say I must report to the NSO in Glasgow who would arrange further war work. "After all, Son, we can't have that Government Training going to waste - can we?" The following day I handed in my security pass at USAAF Alconbury and I was on my way to Glasgow.

CHAPTER 20

BACK IN UNIFORM

I had an extraordinary war. I had been a motor mechanic, seaman, electrician, and now I was about to become a war worker. An episode noted for personally bringing the factory out on strike! A fact I will briefly gloss over.

My interview with the National Service Officer in Glasgow was brief, and to the point. He barely looked at me has he completed some forms and directed me to a factory in the East End of Glasgow, manufacturing military armoured trucks. The area was one of the most desolate slums I had ever encountered. I felt depressed entering it - never mind the factory itself. My job was to install electrical equipment in the vehicles; this came ready supplied and only required clipping into position. The only technical bit was checking with an ampere meter that the connections were correct. I was given a blue print to follow, which I quickly dispensed with; the job was too easy. I also had a team of girls to supervise. They were a rough and ready lot, but far superior, conscientious, and hardworking than any man in the factory, who appeared to be the sweepings of the Glasgow slums. They were lazy, illiterate, foul-mouthed, work shy, 'Bolshi'; I really cannot find enough adjectives to describe them. I had heard of the evil reputation of the Red Clyde workers, but it would have been difficult to beat this lot!

The factory was a high roofed building operating on the assembly line principle. At the head of the assembly line was hung a large banner proudly proclaiming the target output for the week. I quickly realised what a farce this was as, week by week; the target got lower, and lower. At the end of the building were raised glass fronted offices for the Manager and staff. From here the Manager could clearly oversee the whole factory.

My team was required to wire up one truck per day, this was easily accomplished in half a day and then we were compelled to stand around doing nothing. This was most frustrating and I took to walking up the assembly line demanding to know what the bloody hold up was. Naturally, they did not take kindly to this and a lot of verbal abuse ensued, with quite a few threats of physical violence. The verbal abuse was water off a duck's back, and being big, pugnacious, and possessing a fiery temper, no one tried their luck, but it was a very unpleasant atmosphere.

Things came to an explosive head when I heard them praising Russia and Stalin. They were mouthing off about what a wonderful country this would be when the Communists took over, and the workers would be the bosses. I could take it no longer, with all the terrible memories of Russia so fresh in mind, I lost control of my temper. Shouting, I told them I had been in Russia for a year, I had seen workers beaten, starved, and shot. I had seen women prisoners in shackles being whipped to the docks to labour on ships. Nearly berserk, I told them that if they were in Russia, Stalin would have lined them up against a wall and shot them for the lazy bastards they were. This time I knew I had gone too far, and beat a hasty retreat before they could lay hands on me.

The following morning when I turned up for work I found the big gates shut, and the workers milling around outside. I also noticed two policemen guarding the gate. As I approached the gate the workers crowded round me shouting abuse and waving their fists. The policemen quickly moved in, each taking my arm and escorting me in. I still did not realise what the commotion was about; becoming alarmed that the police were arresting me on some trumped up charge. I was led to the Manager's office where I found the National Service Officer and local Union Secretary seated. I was standing in front of the Manager's desk like a defaulter. Such was my nature in those days I felt a rising anger. The Manager explained that because of my belligerent attitude to the work force they had downed tools, and what had I to say for myself. My first reaction was to laugh. "This is not a laughing matter," admonished the Manager. I quite agreed and explained I was laughing firstly because I thought I was being arrested, and secondly because he had called that shower of lazy sods workers. The Union man began to get nasty; "Who the hell do you think you are criticising the workers, you're not even a qualified electrician." I ignored him, turning towards the Manager. "I know you can see me and my team standing around most of the day doing nothing, and you know why. It's because those lazy bastards keep falling behind the target and spend most of their day in the toilets doing the football pools, or betting on the 'Gee Gees'. Christ Almighty! my team could easily cope with two trucks a day if only they would come down the line."

Again the Union man broke in, "I've heard enough of this trouble maker, he's not qualified and I want him sacked." The Manager, who I believed was a decent man, lent back in his chair and surveyed the ceiling for a moment. "I quite agree with you Mr Union man, kindly supply me with a qualified electrician tomorrow." He knew perfectly well the only reason I was employed was because there were no qualified electrician available. The Union man was now all bluster but had to admit this was not possible. "Ah, so what do you suggest I do Mr Union man, close the factory?" Check Mate, I think.

The NSO now joined in. "Now, Mr Mills, don't you think you could be a little more conciliatory towards you fellow workers." No, I snapped, again feeling my temper rising. He had not been very approachable to me in his office and I was damn well not going to pander to him now. "Those so called workers are supposed to be building armoured trucks for the fighting man." I glared at all three of them. "Do you know what they are? They are bloody saboteurs. At least I've fought for my country which is more than any of those bastards have." I'd had my say and thought, sod you all. To his credit the Manager looked suitably embarrassed. He knew he could not sack me for misconduct, or fault my work. It would look pretty silly if he sacked me for having arguments with other workers, which he knew were perfectly justified. An impasse had been reached and no one knew quite what to do. Finally the NSO spoke up, "Look young man, I think it would be in every one's interest if you voluntarily resigned. I'll do my best to get you another job." Without a moment's hesitation I happily agreed and within the hour my wages were made up and I was out of that hateful place.

That evening I recounted the day's events to Anne. We could see the funny side of it and had a good laugh. Then seriously, we questioned what was I now going to do. I was a young man with a wife to support. The pay at the factory and been very good - well above the average. I would have to find a job quick. Suddenly Anne said, "Remember telling me of the time you were in Hairmyres Hospital in 1942, and how a Mr Murray, a Director in a Shipping Company befriended you, and said if ever your in Glasgow and need help don't hesitate to come and see me. Well, why don't you go and see him?" Fiercely independent, I shook my head. "No, I couldn't do that, it's a bit like begging." In any case I thought after a period of two years he would have forgotten me. Anne was exasperated, "I think you're very silly."

The following day Anne dropped a bombshell! "I've been to see Mr Murray." She said defiantly. "He is a very nice man and was delighted to hear you are in Glasgow, and that we are married." I was aghast. "You told him everything?" "Yes, and he insists you go and see him tomorrow." I looked at Anne in astonishment, wonder and pride. To have gone to a big Shipping Company and asked to see a Director, outlined our precarious position, discussed our marriage and plans, and then obtained an interview for me, quite took my breath away. What a girl!

I was ushered into Mr Murray's imposing office and he was genuinely pleased to see me. We had a long chat and he wanted to know all that had happened to me since we last met. He said how pleased he was to have met my wife. "Lovely girl - and so determined." He said with a twinkle in his eye. I knew just what he meant.

"Now, let's get down to brass tacks. You need a job, right?" "Yes, please." How would you like a job in the Shipping Federation, or, to be more precise, The Merchant Navy Reserve Pool?" This quite took my breath away. "Fantastic!" "Now," said Mr Murray, "I cannot guarantee you will be offered a position, that will be up to the Chief Officer, but I can arrange an interview." So saying he picked up the phone. "Yes, yes, a Mr Mills, yes I can bring him down now." We were shown into the Chief Officer's room and a tall, distinguished man in Merchant Navy uniform with three gold bands on either arm, rose and greeted Mr Murray with deference, offering a chair and coffee which he declined saying, "I can't stay, very busy. I just wanted to bring this young man down and intro-duce him. As you know, I have already given you his background over the phone."

Mr Jackson was a Londoner so we got off to a good start. I had excellent references from all the jobs I had been in (I exclude the factory), particularly from Sir William Reardon Smith & Co. which was the one that counted most. I was asked a few perfunctory ques-tions but it was obvious a recommendation from a Shipping Company Director was sufficient. "Well, Mr Mills, I am prepared to offer you a position as an Official of the MN Reserve Pool, you will be issued with a uniform, be provided with meals in the canteen, and receive a commencing salary of £3.10.0 per week. I took a deep breath at the mention of salary. I couldn't possible manage on that pitiful money. I thanked Mr Jackson for his offer and asked if I could discuss it with my wife before accepting He was quite amenable and agreed to see me the following day.

When I told Anne, she instantly said, "You have got to accept it." But, I explained, "How are we going to live on £3.10.0 a week. Good Lord, I have been bringing in twelve pounds a week and could possibly earn the same money in another factory." As usual, Anne sized up the situation far quicker, "Listen, Morris, the war is going to end soon and all these war factories will close, and that will be the end of the big money, then you will be desperate for any old job. This is a job with a career structure, the money will get better, in the meantime we will manage and you have got your War Pension." In fact, the salary steadily increased and with compulsory overtime virtually doubled. Of course, I was not to know this when I accepted the job and I feared I was not going to support Anne in a proper manner. I know she was delighted at. my change in status, no longer a factory worker, now an officer in the Merchant Navy Reserve, smart uniform; gold braid on sleeves, and medal ribbons on chest. Now she could hold her head up with family and friends.

As we begin a new Millennium few people appreciate that the Merchant Navy was one of the greatest assets this country possessed, now sadly reduced to insignificance. Still less do they remember the colossal part it played in both World Wars. At memo-rial services round the country people stand with bowed heads in remembrance of the Royal Navy, Army and Royal Air Force dead.

I venture to think very few think of, or even know of, the 35,000 Merchant Seamen who voluntarily laid down their lives.

It is understandable therefore that few will understand the functions and responsibilities of the Shipping Federation and Merchant Navy Reserve Pool in World War 2. A brief explanation is perhaps necessary.

The Shipping Federation (Now known as the General Council of British Shipping) was the employer's organisation in Shipping. In 1940 it operated through 23 Districts each in charge of a District Secretary, Registrar (Chief Officer) and staff. Obviously, there were major and minor Districts. Glasgow was possibly the largest with seventy-five staff. The District also controlled a Cookery School, Lifeboat and Ship's Firemen Training Centre, and arranged gunnery courses.

On 30th April 1941 the Ministry of War Transport signed the Essential Works (Merchant Navy) Order and thus was born the "Merchant Navy Reserve Pool" It was a Legal Entity. It had to deal with a constant manpower shortage, with reporting arrangements, discipline, releases and medical examinations. Payment of benefits to seamen awaiting a ship, payment of shipwreck monies and replacement of gear, and much more. In this we had the full power of the Law and were empowered to have seamen arrested, and tried in court, for wilfully failing to carry out our instructions, or refusing to join a ship. We did, indeed, have draconian power over seamen but I like to think we exercised that power with compassion, after all, we were ex seamen ourselves and many of us had experienced being bombed or torpedoed.

It was quite a responsible job; and there was always a hint of physical violence lurking in the background. We used to say it was a dull day if there wasn't a 'punch-up'. It must be remembered we were dealing with some very tough characters, in a very rough City. I thoroughly enjoyed the work, with its variety of jobs and sense of adventure.

Although the war was rapidly drawing to a close, Convoys were still being assembled and sailed from the Clyde. When this occurred on weekends we were committed to a stand-by watch. This involved remaining on the premises the whole time to deal with any problems. We were provided with bunk beds and catering arrangements. On this particular occasion, I was awakened by the telephone in the early hours of Sunday morning, and advised that a ship was held off Greenock, requiring one seaman to complete the crew. A quick check through the files revealed there was only one likely man, a nasty, vicious character, who I shall call Mac. When I reached the slum where he lived I made my way up the dark stairway - all landing lights had long been smashed - and by the light of my torch found his door which was streaked with blood. I was not a nervous person, in fact I considered myself tough, but I confess to a feeling of trepidation when I banged on the door. After an interval a blurred voice snarled, "Who the bloody hell is that?" and much other profanity. "It's me, Mr Mills from the Pool. I've got a ship for you." There was a shuffling sound, a bolt drawn back, and a bleary, unshaven face peered out. Instinctively, I stepped back a pace anticipating a blow - or even a razor. "Och, Aye, it's yourself is it Mishter. Mills, waah ye waan't." "I've got a ship held at the Tail of the Bank Mac, and I need an AB now. I've got a taxi waiting. Pack a bag and let's be having you." "All right, Mishter Mills, give me five minutes." And the door slammed shut. Shortly after he came out clutching a brown paper parcel. "Where's your gear Mac?" "Aah bluidy hell Mishter Mills, this is it!" The journey by taxi to Greenock, and the boat trip out to the ship was extremely tense. He was so unpredictable and vicious, however, I got him onboard and he signed the ship's articles as quiet as a lamb. I heaved a sigh of relief and considered myself very lucky.

The following morning I was called up to the Boss's office and found two CID officers there, who asked me if I had shipped out a seaman named Mac, which I confirmed. They then took a long statement from me, finally I asked them what this was all about and was told they wanted him for murder. Apparently, he had stabbed a man to death in a pub brawl only hours before I picked him up. The thought of that long ride with a killer sent a shiver through me.

Another money-spinner was escorting seamen to various destinations in the UK. I once had the job of escorting twenty Guatemalan's from Glasgow to Liverpool, where they were to join a ship back to their country of origin. At Liverpool I ran into a brick wall in the shape of a fat, greasy woman, who was the Guatemalan Consul, demanding an exorbitant sum to issue visa's, which I was not authorised to pay. I reported my problem to our Liverpool office who said in so many words, "Sorry Chum, your problem. We'll accommodate the seamen and you will have to negotiate a price with the Consul."

This took several days before I knocked this scheming woman, who was obviously lining her own pocket, down to half her original price. In the meantime I had been dossing in the China Town District of Liverpool, without even a toothbrush, to say nothing of the anguish of a young wife who's husband had vanished with twenty Guatemalans. All for a basic three pounds ten shillings a week. I ask you!

On my return I presented my overtime and expenses to the Boss, who immediately started to haggle, and question various items. I was now very, very, angry and fed up. I had a belly full of living rough, haggling with the Consul over 'buckshee'and now he was trying to reduce mine. "Forget it." I said snatching back my expense list, "I'll send it to Head Office with my Notice." Later that day he sent for me. "Sit down Mr Mills, now you were getting hot under the collar a bit earlier, weren't you? Feel calmer now? I was only going through the list to see there were no obvious errors. You must not take things so seriously. See the cashier and he will pay you." I thanked him and left. I came that close to losing a career that would see me rising steadily by promotion, and retiring in comfort.

In May 1945 the war in Europe came to an end. The Chief Officer, Mr Jackson sent for me. There was to be a grand victory parade through London. Stands were to be erected along the route for distinguished guests, and other participants in the war. One stand would be allocated to a limited number of war wounded veterans. Head Office had been requested to submit one such from the Scottish District to represent the Merchant Navy Reserve Pool. I was the only one qualified. My Boss obviously thought I would be delighted to go to London, all expenses paid, and represent the Merchant Navy Pool. He was dismayed when I declined the offer. I could give no reasonable explanation, I just knew I did not want to go. My reaction to the end of the war was curious. While the country on the whole was wild with excitement, there were many of us who were left with a sad, haunting feeling of anticlimax. For five years the war had dominated my life. I had experienced every conceivable emotion, seen, and done unbelievable things. I began to recall the faces of those who had shared the war with me, and whose names would be commemorated on some lonely war memorial. Perhaps that was the reason I had no desire to attend a victory parade.

END

APPENDIX A

EXTRACT FROM SOVIET WAR NEWS 29TH OCT.1942

British Seamen write to Soviet Doctors. "We'll never forget you."

The following letter will appear in the weekly "THE BRITISH ALLY," published in Kuibyshev by the British Ministry of Information. It was written from a Scottish Hospital by eight British merchant seamen, torpedoed while carrying arms to the USSR, and is addressed to the surgeon who attended them in Murmansk.

Dear Doctor Kozikov,

We don't suppose you will remember us. But we will not forget you as long as we live. Because we owe you our lives. We are some of the British seamen on whom you operated for frostbite and wounds back in April. We were in your hospital for about two months. Then the raids got so bad we were sent to other places, and some of us got separated. Finally we all met up again in Archangelsk. Now we are all safely back in Britain and doing fine thanks to you. We often said how much we would like to write and thank you. When we were in the USSR we used to wish we spoke your language, so that we could tell you, and the other Doctors and nurses, how grateful we were for everything.

"EIGHT OF US WROTE IT."

Then a few days ago we heard that if we wrote a letter it would be translated and sent to you. So eight of us helped to write it. That's why all our names are at the end. Some of the chaps have left this hospital to get new feet and other have gone to their homes. But this is meant as thanks as well from them as us, because we all used to talk about writing to you.

Five of us had frostbite badly. William Short, Engineer, and Walter Pike, able seaman, both had their legs amputated, and Short's hands are a bit crippled, too. Jimmy Campbell, Steward's boy, who is fifteen, lost one foot and a hand. Then there are two ordinary seamen: Walter Baxter, who lost part of one foot, and John Carney, whose toes have gone and who has frostbite in both knees.

Morris Mills, an apprentice, had his foot blown off when his ship was hit by bombs while unloading cargo in Murmansk. He was in his bunk when the bombs fell. It went through his cabin and killed fifteen Russians working in the hold. He remembers trying to stand up and being surprised when he fell to the floor again. Of course, he had only one foot.

HOW WE GOT TO MURMANSK.

Then there is Ali Nasser, a fireman who comes from Aden, in Arabia. His ship was bombed too, and he was blown from the deck onto the ice and picked up with a badly smashed leg, and lots of other injuries. The eighth man here is Mohamed Maberok, (We call him "Joe") from Assam in India, who was a greaser on a merchant ship. His ship was bombed twice in Murmansk harbour and sunk, but it wasn't until he was going back to Britain in a cruiser to get another ship that he was wounded. Then he got it properly. The warship was in action with three German destroyers and he was hit by shrapnel. One leg was badly broken, and he got a lot of splinters in him. That's how we all got to Murmansk.

You said that Short, Baxter and Carney were amongst the worst frostbite cases you had ever seen. But they all say it was worth going through to help the Russians. They were all in a lifeboat for four days in a blizzard after their ship was sunk. The submarine surfaced as their boat got away from the ship. Then the cowardly Hitlerites must have fired another torpedo although there were still other men on board. There was another explosion and the ship went down. They could see her faintly through the snow. There were still some of the crew, and engineers, the wireless operators, two of the officers and captain on board. The wireless operator must have got an S.O.S. away because a minesweeper came out to look for them. It searched for thirty six hours. Then it returned. No one could believe anyone could be alive in such terrible weather. Nine men died the first night. The others had to keep bailing to prevent the boat sinking. All their food and water froze, so they had to lick blocks of ice to keep going. They were nearly dead when a soviet plane spotted them. The next thing they knew they were being carried aboard a soviet warship, and being given vodka to drink. They weren't used to it and Jimmy Campbell said it nearly knocked him flat. But it helped to keep life in them.

An air raid was going on when we got to Murmansk but the Soviet seamen looking after us didn't turn a hair, they say. They just calmly got on with the job, although the bombing was terrible. They were grand chaps and we would like to thank them. We all want to know if you remember the English for "How do you feel." Because we haven't forgotten "Very good." In Russian. We'd like to tell you too how much we admired the doctors and nurses when the air raids were going on. The Hitlerites seemed to be bombing all day and night. One bomb dropped about 15 yards from the hospital and glass from the windows covered the beds. But none of them turned a hair. Nurse Vera and Nurse Zhenya even made a joke. Of course we couldn't understand, but we could see what they meant by the way they laughed and made signs.

How is Dr. Stefans? Please tell him Morris Mills is now hopping around on a crutch. And is Dr. Doradreni still in the hospital? We'd like to be remembered to them both especially Carney and Baxter, to Dr. Doradreni, who was one of the finest women we've ever met. Does she remember the day some of our chaps came back to Murmansk after leaving on a British warship? They had been torpedoed again. The Drs. and nurses went from ambulance to ambulance calling out our names if they were safe. When they did find them they shook their hands and cried with joy over them.

"PLEASE TELL Dr. DORA....."

Our chaps said afterwards their welcome helped to make up for the bad time they had been through. When we finally left the hospital we were lying on stretchers in the corridor, and Dr. Dora came to say goodbye. Please tell her Carney got her letter and treasures it.

We never realised how hard-pressed the Russians were until we saw how hard your Drs and nurses worked. About 24 hrs a day it seemed to us. Yet you always had a moment to help us when we were in pain.

Then there was the day Dr. Petrov returned from the front. We were sorry to see how tired, and haggard he looked. But we didn't know enough Russian to tell him how we felt. We'd like him to know now that we shall never forget his kindness, and we hope he gets safely through.

Mills and Carney and Baxter are determined to join another ship as soon as they leave hospital. "We'll give Hitler hell, we promise you," they say. And "Joe" the greaser and Ali Nasser say the same. It won't be long now, they hope, before they are back on the job of fighting the Hitlerites.

Have you made any more plaster legs? You remember you made one for the Chief Steward of the Aloona. You had him walking around in no time. My word how that cheered us up to see him hopping about. Pike and Short and Jimmy Campbell will be getting theirs very soon now. Then it won't be long before they are fighting somehow or other. They want to go into a war factory. If they can't take cargoes to the USSR, they can make weapons for some of those soldiers we met in your hospital. They were grand chaps, full of fight. All they wanted was to go back to the front and kill more Fascists.

Do you know what was one of our happiest moments in Murmansk ? It was when we saw the first of three British films you borrowed from the British naval authorities for us. The white-washed walls of the hospital were used as a screen and we cheered when we heard the first English words.

We hope the hospital is still standing. It had been a school, hadn't it? Joe and Ali and another Indian had beds on a high platform where the teachers used to stand. They were always the centre of attraction we used to say.

You'll be interested to hear that by the time we reached Archangelsk some of us spoke a bit of Russian. Perhaps the doctors and nurses there will read this letter and know we often think of them.

We hope Dr. Onoprienko still sings 'Tipperary'and, 'Pack up your troubles'. He remembered them from the last war and one of our chaps wrote out the words for him. He used to sing them whenever he could, and we'd join in. All of us 'John Bulls'- that was his name for us - send him our regards.

" SHE WAS GRAND "

Natasha Mannonova, the interpreter, and Madame Wright, from Leningrad, are two other people we would like to thank, and whom we talk about still. Mme Wright used to help keep up our spirits by organising competitions, with cigarettes as prizes. Then she discovered some of us could sing and play instruments so she organised concerts and community singing and kept us all cheerful.

She was grand. Carney still has the sheet of brown paper on which she wrote down the Russian Alphabet. He says he will always keep it and try not to forget his Russian.

We send our best wishes to the nurses at Archangel, - Tani. Zhenya, and Vera who were so kind to us. They'll be glad to know we are all safely back home. We often tell the nurses here about them, and the wardmaids - Isa, Zhenya and Bolshoi Vera - who were so kind to us. We used to call her 'Bolshoi' because she was so big, and to distinguish her from nurse Vera.

Well, that's all Doctor. You can see we haven't forgot our friends in the USSR and we hope they won't forget us. They can be sure we will all be back in the fight as soon as possible. And, after the war, perhaps we will all meet again.

It was with tears in our eyes, and hearts full of sorrow, we left our Russian friends to whose kindness and love we owe our lives, and though we are far apart you are always in our hearts.

We are proud to have received our wounds for such wonderful people.

Signed - William Short, Engineer, Morris Mills, Apprentice, Ali Nasser, Fireman, Mohamed Maberok, Greaser, James Campbell, Stewards Boy, Walter Baxter, Ordinary Seaman, W. Pike Able Seaman, John Carney, Ordinary Seaman.

October 29th, 1942.

APPENDIX B

EXTRACT FROM NEWSPAPER HUNTS POST

THE BULLDOG BREED. HUNTINGDON SEA HERO PRAISED

A 19 year-old Merchant Navy Hero, Morris Oliver Mills, eldest son of Det-Sergt and Mrs T.O.Mills, of Police House, St Johns Str, Huntingdon, was praised by his employer Sir Willie Reardon-Smith on Friday. Sir Willie paid tribute to Mills, who, maimed by enemy bombs, said he would not allow U-boats to interfere with his career.

Sir Willie went on to say that although Mills's foot was amputated in a Russian hospital, he now had an artificial foot, and part leg, and wanted to get back to sea. After Mills was put in a ship as a cot case to come home from Russia, that ship was also torpedoed. His Doctor has pronounced him fit again.

Sir Willie paid this tribute in his presidential address to the annual meeting of the British Channel Shipowners' Association.

Readers may remember that Mills, an apprentice Cadet Navigation Officer, was bombed on board ship, causing his foot to be amputated; was rescued from HMS Edinburgh when that ship was torpedoed by a submarine and attacked by three German destroyers; and was subsequently taken to a Russian hospital, which was bombed by German aircraft, causing him to be transferred to another.

APPENDIX C

Extract from OCEAN ODYSSEY By Stanton Hope

A Record of the fighting Merchant Navy

Courage is not always the hallmark of valorous deeds. More often it is the normal attitude of mind of men and women toward hardship and peril such as those inseparable from a seafaring life in wartime. This is illustrated in its ultimate by the case of Apprentice Mills, a well-educated English lad, eighteen years of age, six feet two inches tall and broad in proportion. The Captain of the Orient City showed me a letter from the owners concerning him which reads:

"We are arranging for an apprentice named Mills to work by the vessel whilst in port. This apprentice made two trips the winter before last to North Russia, and on the second occasion his vessel was bombed, resulting in a foot being amputated. Later an amputation was made below the knee. He was also torpedoed whilst returning to this country in a cruiser, and returned to North Russia. Despite these experiences, Mills wants to go to sea, and we are proposing that he works by vessels in port for a few weeks in order to accustom himself to being aboard vessels."

According to the Nazis, Britain, by all the rules, should have capitulated after the fall of France, a mistake primarily due to ignorance that this sea-girt land still produces the likes of young apprentice Mills and old Bob Young, seventy five years old repatriated prison of war whose first concern from his return from Germany was how soon he could get back to sea in the Merchant Navy again.